NAVIGATING SOCIAL MEDIA LEGAL RISKS

SAFEGUARDING YOUR BUSINESS

Robert McHale, Esq. with Eric Garulay

800 East 96th Street
Indianapolis, Indiana 46240 USA

Navigating Social Media Legal Risks: Safeguarding Your Business

ISBN-13: 978-0-7897-4953-6
ISBN-10: 0-7897-4953-X

The Library of Congress Cataloging-in-Publication Data is on file.

Printed in the United States of America

First Printing: May 2012

Trademarks

Warning and Disclaimer

Bulk Sales

Que Publishing offers excellent discounts on this book when ordered in quantity for bulk purchases or special sales. For more information, please contact

U.S. Corporate and Government Sales
1-800-382-3419
corpsales@pearsontechgroup.com

For sales outside of the U.S., please contact

International Sales
international@pearsoned.com

CONTENTS AT A GLANCE

TABLE OF CONTENTS

About the Author

Robert McHale, Esq., is the founding member of R | McHale Law (rmchale.com), a full-service law firm whose corporate practice represents clients on a wide variety of IT and intellectual property law matters, including privacy and data security, trademark, copyright, trade secrets, technology licensing, and other proprietary protections. By leveraging his business instinct, technical insight, and legal experience, Robert helps companies develop legal strategies that best promote their business objectives. His areas of focus include general corporate law, business litigation, web/mobile applications, online marketing, new media, and Internet and e-commerce technology.

Robert is a member of the Massachusetts bar and is admitted to practice before the U.S. District Court, District of Massachusetts.

He is a graduate of St. John's College (BA) and Boston University School of Law (JD).

You can reach Robert at robert.mchale@rmchale.com and follow him on Twitter at @rmchalelaw.

About the Contributor

Eric Garulay is a digital marketing and social media strategist holding the position of Digital Marketing Manager with Pearson, the world's largest educational publisher. With fluency in both marketing and technology and a background in product marketing and media influence, Eric operates at the cutting-edge of modern publishing and media convergence. Eric is also the Founder and Executive Producer of the OnPodcast Network, a video learning series which reaches millions of viewers with free educational interviews and tutorials, on a wide variety of technology topics, featuring top technologists, authors, trainers, and inventors.

You may reach Eric at egarulay@gmail.com or follow him at @onpodcasts.

Dedication

This book is dedicated to all my "monkeys," big, small, and still growing—Justin, Theo, Noah, Finn, Elsie, Sebastian, Gavin, Olivia, Jack, Ethan, Natalie, Alexandra, Max, Maddie, Winter, Jenna, Tage, Davin, Alexa, and Matthew.

Acknowledgments

I want to thank Eric Garulay for his inspiration and tremendously thoughtful contributions to this book.

I also want to thank my editor Rick Kughen in moving mountains to get this book published, and for his helpful observations throughout the editing process. For all the folks at Pearson and Que Publishing who made this book possible—thank you.

We Want to Hear from You!

As the reader of this book, *you* are our most important critic and commentator. We value your opinion and want to know what we're doing right, what we could do better, what areas you'd like to see us publish in, and any other words of wisdom you're willing to pass our way.

As an editor-in-chief for Que Publishing, I welcome your comments. You can email or write me directly to let me know what you did or didn't like about this book—as well as what we can do to make our books better.

Please note that I cannot help you with technical problems related to the topic of this book. We do have a User Services group, however, where I will forward specific technical questions related to the book.

When you write, please be sure to include this book's title and author as well as your name, email address, and phone number. I will carefully review your comments and share them with the author and editors who worked on the book.

Email: feedback@quepublishing.com

Mail: Greg Wiegand
         Editor-in-Chief
         Que Publishing
         800 East 96th Street
         Indianapolis, IN 46240 USA

Reader Services

Visit our website and register this book at quepublishing.com/register for convenient access to any updates, downloads, or errata that might be available for this book.

Introduction

Social media for business has evolved from chic, to mainstream, to essential. It represents a monumental shift in marketing because it facilitates unprecedented opportunities for companies to connect with their customers, generate business exposure, attract leads, drive website traffic, improve search rankings, increase sales, and to facilitate enterprise alignment, innovation, collaboration, customer service, and more.

Social media for business has evolved from chic, to mainstream, to essential.

Recognizing the value of interactive communications with their customers, companies are increasingly incorporating social media into their overall communications strategies. Unlike traditional *static* marketing, social media is a *dynamic* promotional tool enabling real-time, organic conversations between companies and their customers and among customers themselves.

By directly engaging with their customers, businesses are able to build audiences and reach, establish trust and digital influence, and groom evangelists who wield the power of word-of-mouth endorsements over their social circles. These spheres of influence comprise a landscape where individuals transform themselves into company spokespersons interacting directly with customers on the ever-increasingly networked and social public stage.

Further, compared to advertising campaigns in traditional media (print, radio, and television), the costs associated with adopting and maintaining a social media presence are relatively low. For a modest investment, social media delivers an extraordinary return—allowing companies to engage their customers and prospects directly, track who is following them, monitor what is said about the company and their services and products, update their followers on new products, and obtain instant consumer feedback. It is little wonder that a majority of Fortune 500 companies have either a Twitter or Facebook account and that an ever-growing number of small and medium-sized companies are leveraging social media in a variety of novel and innovative ways.

Despite the transformative power of social media for businesses, it is not without its unique set of challenges. Sadly, human beings are inherently prone to mistakes, misconduct, and both purposeful and inadvertent acts of mischief. It is here where social media's Achilles' heel is exposed. Given the viral nature of social media, a single human mishap can damage a business's reputation, brand equity, and goodwill virtually in seconds. It should come as no surprise, therefore, that the explosion in the business adoption of social media carries with it increased legal risks.

Disclosure of sensitive company information, inadvertent transmittal of customer contacts and business leads, unfair and deceptive company and product endorsements, and unwitting employment and labor law violations are just a handful of the everyday risks arising from the use of social media in the workplace. As the popularity and business usage of social networks continue to grow, navigating the legal risks therein becomes increasingly more challenging.

Note

This book's discussion is "limited" to U.S. law. It is not the author's inten-
tion, nor would it be feasible, to address the laws and regulations in every
jurisdiction. However, given that the four largest social media networks
(Facebook, Twitter, YouTube, and LinkedIn) are U.S.-based, a familiarity
with the U.S. laws implicated in this space is indispensable for any company conducting business within our borders. Further, while the solutions
proposed in this book may be country specific, the legal questions raised
herein have worldwide applicability. At a minimum, readers (wherever
located) should be alerted to the categories of potential pitfalls, and the
types of questions they need to ask, to appreciate the unique legal challenges social media creates and to better arm their organizations with the
tools necessary to implement secure social and mobile marketing programs.

How This Book Is Organized

This book is comprised of 12 chapters, each focusing on an important legal aspect
of the business use of social media and the special measures companies can adopt
to minimize their potential liability. The book may be read from cover to cover to
gain a comprehensive overview of the legal landscape. The chapters also stand well
separately on their own, serving as a handy reference guide and offering readers
the flexibility to find just the information they need.

Chapter 1: Social Media Promotion Law: Contests and Sweepstakes

Chapter 1 covers the legal rules governing online prize promotions (in particular,
sweepstakes and contests). Promotions conducted via social media sites are a valuable means of generating consumer traffic and brand awareness while simultaneously fostering customer loyalty and increasing sales. Nevertheless, advertisers
should pay close attention to significant legal compliance concerns. Indeed, under
certain circumstances, even innocuous-looking "promotions," such as requiring
an applicant to encourage friends to "like" you on Facebook, may unwittingly
transform the promotion into an illegal lottery. Advertisers must also comply with
platform-specific promotion and contest guidelines. For example, if people enter
your contest by "liking" your business page or leaving a comment, or if your promotion is being run on your Facebook page, your promotion violates Facebook's
Promotions Guidelines and may result in your business page being suspended or
terminated. Although the world of social media might often seem like the Wild
West, online promotions are governed by strict rules and regulations, which businesses must take careful steps to observe.

Chapter 2: Online Endorsements and Testimonials: What Companies and Their Employees Can and Cannot Tweet, Blog, or Say

Chapter 2 examines the Federal Trade Commission's updated *Guides Concerning the Use of Endorsements and Testimonials in Advertising*. The FTC guides apply to consumer testimonials, such as reviews and recommendations, that endorse a product or service on any social media site. Employees who post reviews of their employers' products and services on social media sites (either directly or through third-party advertisers) without disclosing their corporate affiliations can expose their employer to an FTC enforcement action. Failure to comply with the guidelines may result in liability for not only the employee endorser, but also for the employer.

Chapter 3: The [Mis]Use of Social Media in Pre-Employment Screening

Chapter 3 examines the permissible use of social media in pre-employment screening and reminds employers to avoid obtaining information that is unlawful to consider in any employment decision, such as the applicant's race, religion, or nationality. Further, employers should refrain from circumventing an applicant's privacy settings on social media sites, because such circumvention could expose an employer to an invasion of privacy claim.

Chapter 3 also alerts employers to the (for most, surprising) fact that social media background checks are subject to the Fair Credit Reporting Act (FRCA), a federal law that protects the privacy and accuracy of the information in consumers' credit reports. For companies that assemble reports about applicants based on social media content and regularly disseminate such reports to third parties (including affiliates), both the reporting company and the user of the report must ensure compliance with the FCRA, including obtaining the applicant's permission before asking for a report about him/her from a consumer reporting agency or any other company that provides background information.

Chapter 4: Monitoring, Regulating, and Disciplining Employees Using Social Media

Chapter 4 examines employer monitoring of employee online postings, together with the National Labor Relations Act's impact on social media-related employee discipline for both union and nonunion employees. In the past two years, employers have faced a mounting wave of regulatory action taken against them for:

- Instituting policies restricting employee use of social media where such policies impermissibly discourage employees from exercising their rights under the NLRA (that is, "to engage in … concerted activities for the purpose of collective bargaining or other mutual aid or protection")

- Unlawfully discharging or disciplining employees for their online communications where the specific social media post constituted "protected concerted activity" (that is, group activity protected by the NLRA) and the subject matter of the post involved wages or other terms and conditions of employment

Importantly, even employees' general complaints (whether on company time or otherwise) about their employment or about their co-workers may fall within the NLRA's purview and be considered *protected concerted activity*. Employers therefore face potentially liability any time they terminate or discipline employees for engaging in social media activity.

In this chapter, you will learn how to avoid unlawfully discharging or disciplining employees for their online communications, and guidelines for properly observing employees' rights to privacy.

Chapter 5: Social Media in Litigation and E-Discovery: Risks and Rewards

Chapter 5 examines the role of social media in civil litigation. With the rapid proliferation of social media, information placed on social networking sites such as Facebook, YouTube, Twitter, and foursquare is increasingly becoming the subject of discovery requests in litigation. Users of these sites may tweet or post detailed status updates without considering the implications of their posts as it effects their (or their company's) litigation position. Courts are increasingly permitting such relevant evidence to be used at trial, despite a party's privacy settings. Further, under both federal and state rules of civil procedure, companies have an obligation to preserve all relevant communications, documents, and information—whether in the form of hard or digital copy, email, social media post, or otherwise—whenever litigation is pending or is reasonably anticipated. A company that fails to properly preserve relevant information can face hefty sanctions by the court, including monetary penalties, dismissal of its complaint, or an entry of default judgment in favor of its opponent. Companies should therefore take time to review and update document-retention policies and ensure that such policies particularly include social media activity.

Chapter 5 also details the impact of the Stored Communications Act (SCA) on social media discovery requests. In addition to limiting the government's right to compel online service providers to disclose information in their possession about their customers and subscribers, among the most significant privacy protections of the SCA is the ability to prevent a third party from using a subpoena in a civil case to get a user's stored communications or data directly from online providers.

Chapter 6: Managing the Legal Risks of User-Generated Content

Chapter 6 discusses the legal risks for companies in allowing user-generated content (UGC) to be posted on their sites, and the associated legal protections. Two federal statutes in particular—the Digital Millennium Copyright Act (DMCA) and the Communications Decency Act (CDA)—are examined. Because social media sites are not exempt from traditional copyright laws, hosting infringing copyrighted content can create liability for contributory infringement. The DMCA shields online service providers (including website owners) from liability for copyright infringement by their users, provided that certain steps set forth in the DMCA are strictly followed. Importantly, however, DMCA immunity is not available for sites that receive a *direct financial benefit* and *draw* new customers from UGC. For social media sites hosting UGC, it is unclear under what circumstances courts will hold that the site is drawing in new customers to receive a direct financial benefit. Further, the DMCA protects from liability the owners of Internet services, not the users (including marketers) who access them. Marketers utilizing UGC are not shielded under the DMCA with respect to uploading onto a third-party's website copyright-infringing content.

Similarly, the CDA immunizes website operators and other interactive computer service providers from liability for third-party content, including content that may constitute defamation, invasion of privacy, and intentional infliction of emotional distress. The provider, so long as not participating in the creation or development of the content, or otherwise exercising editorial control over the content such that the edits materially alter the meaning of the content, will be immune from state law claims (except intellectual property claims) arising from third-party content. For companies that operate their own blogs, bulletin boards, YouTube channels, or other social media platforms, therefore, it is imperative that they avoid contributing to the *creation or development* of the offensive content so that their immunity is not revoked. In this regard, CDA immunity may be further forfeited if the site owner invites the posting of illegal materials or makes actionable postings itself.

Chapter 7: The Law of Social Advertising

Chapter 7 alerts social media business practitioners that they, like traditional advertisers, are subject to the FTC Act (regarding false advertising vis-à-vis consumers); section 43 of the Lanham Act (regarding false comparative advertisement claims); the Controlling the Assault of Non-Solicited Pornography and Marketing (CAN-SPAM) Act; and the Children's Online Privacy Protection Act (COPPA).

The CAN-SPAM Act of 2003 establishes the United States' first national standards for the sending of commercial email, provides recipients the right to opt out of future emails, and imposes tough penalties for violations. Despite its name, the CAN-SPAM Act does not apply only to bulk email; it also covers all commercial electronic messages, including business-to-business and business-to-consumer emails, as well as commercial solicitations transmitted through social media sites. If the primary purpose of a solicitation transmitted through Facebook or other social media site is commercial, care must be made to clearly and conspicuously identify the communication as such and to observe other requirements imposed by the CAN-SPAM Act. This is true whether the electronic communication was submitted by an advertiser or by a consumer who has been induced by the advertiser to send the message.

Further, COPPA, which was enacted in 1998, proscribes unfair or deceptive acts relating to the collection, use, and disclosure of information from children under 13 on the Internet. COPPA requires website operators or other online services that are either directed to children under 13 or that have actual knowledge that they are collecting personal information from children under 13 to obtain verifiable parental consent before such information is collected, used, or disclosed. In 2010, to account for the rapid developments in technology and marketing practices, and the proliferation of social networking and interactive gaming with children, the FTC proposed amending the federal regulations implementing COPPA (COPPA Rule). The proposed changes were finally made public on September 15, 2011.

The proposed changes, if adopted by the FTC, will profoundly impact websites and other online services (including mobile applications that allow children to play network-connected games, participate in social networking activities, purchase goods or services online, or receive behaviorally targeted advertisements) who collect information from children under 13 years old. Under the proposed Rule, operators who merely prompt or encourage (versus require) a child to provide personal information will be subject to COPPA.

Of special note, the proposed revisions to the Rule, among other changes, expand the definition of *personal information* to include not only names, addresses, email addresses, phone numbers, and other identifiers included in the current Rule, but also geolocation information, screen names or usernames, and additional types of persistent identifiers, such as IP addresses, unique device identifiers, and tracking cookies used for behavioral advertising. Similarly, photographs, videos, and audio files that contain a child's image or voice may also be added to the definition of personal information, as would all identifiers that permit direct contact with a person online, including instant messaging user identifiers, Voice over Internet Protocol (VoIP) identifiers, and video chat user identifiers.

The proposed change would also revise parental consent requirements. Currently, in order for operators to collect, use, or disclose personal information of children, they must first obtain verifiable parental consent.

The proposed changes add new parental consent mechanisms, including submitting electronically scanned signed parental consent forms, consent through video conferencing, and verifying a parent's government-issued identification against databases of such information. Further, the FTC's proposed Rule change would eliminate the less reliable "email plus" method of obtaining parental consent, which currently allows operators to obtain consent through an email to the parent, provided an additional verification step is taken, such as sending a delayed email confirmation to the parent after receiving the initial consent.

Chapter 8: Trademark Protections from Brandjacking and Cybersquatting in Social Networks

Chapter 8 discusses the importance of trademark and brand management in the Web 2.0 universe. In light of the high organic search ranking social media sites achieve on search engine results pages, social network usernames have increasingly become highly valuable commodities. A Google search of your brand can easily produce results from a social media page that appears to be an official brand page, but is in fact a page of a disgruntled customer or parodying competitor. Controlling your business's social network usernames—and securing your ability to protect your brand in each social platform—is therefore critical; after all, you do not want your company's image (or message) to be hijacked by spammers, cybersquatters, impersonators, or competitors. In addition to platform-specific brand-protection enforcement mechanisms, this chapter details the legal remedies available under the trademark infringement and anticybersquatting rules of the Lanham (Trademark) Act.

Chapter 9: Balancing Gamification Legal Risks and Business Opportunities

Chapter 9 explores the unique issues surrounding gamification and social media and the legal considerations that apply when companies employ the mechanics and dynamics of gaming to social media interactions on web and mobile platforms. For example, leader boards, badges, and expert labels (gamification staples) all implicate truth-in-advertisement issues (and FTC enforcement actions) to the extent that such labels imply an expert status that the user does not actually possess with respect to the endorsed product. Further, virtual currencies in the form of points, coins, redeemable coupons, and so on are subject to federal regulations prohibiting expiration dates less than 5 years after the virtual currency is sold or issued. Likewise, behavioral and hypertargeting—leveraging of social history data (where you are and what you are doing at any given time)—gives rise to a host of federal and state privacy rules regarding recording, storing, handling, and transferring geolocation and other consumer data.

Chapter 10: Social Media's Effect on Privacy and Security Compliance

Chapter 10 discusses the security and privacy compliance obligations of companies that gather personal information of its customers online. In particular, the recent FTC settlements with Twitter, Facebook, and Google highlight the risk of using social media without properly structured and implemented privacy and security compliance guidelines. Companies that collect or otherwise obtain consumer data (via online promotions, business apps, site registration, or otherwise) should conduct an annual review of their privacy and security policies, statements, and practices, and ensure that they are truthful, nondeceptive, factually supportable, and consistent with evolving legal standards and industry best practices.

Chapter 11: Legal Guidelines for Developing Social Media Policies and Governance Models

Chapter 11 provides detailed guidelines on how to write an effective corporate social media policy and how to establish the necessary governance models used to monitor employee and corporate usage of social media. This chapter provides a detailed list of vital social media policy provisions to aid you in drafting a policy designed to help your company get the most out of its social media programs while simultaneously minimizing its legal exposure. A well-drafted and consistently enforced social media policy should enable companies to mitigate liability issues and security risks; ensure compliance with federal and state legislation; protect a company's brand; increase productivity; better monitor and respond to their customers' performance evaluations, feedback, and complaints; and reduce the company's exposure to burdensome, costly, and PR-unfriendly litigation.

Chapter 12: Looking Ahead at Social Media Business Opportunities, Expectations, and Challenges

Evolving technologies, together with emerging platforms and channels of communication, inevitably raise new legal issues that employers must address and manage in the modern digital workplace. Because social media law is still in its infancy,

businesses are advised to keep abreast of the fast-pacing growth of laws giving definition to this space.

Who Should Use This Book?

The book serves as an indispensable and comprehensive guide to the legal risks
associated with the business use of social media. It was especially written for business professionals, and can be used as a valuable educational and reference tool to
assist companies of all sizes seeking to train their employees on the safe and legal
use of social media.

The intended audiences for this book include:

- Chief Executive Officers
- Chief Marketing Officers
- Chief Information Officers
- Chief Compliance Officers
- Business Owners
- VPs, Directors, and Managers of
  - Marketing/Branding
  - Social Media
  - Communications
  - Business Strategy
  - Public Relations
  - Information Technology
  - Customer Service
  - Human Resources
- Community Managers
- Social Media Strategists
- Word of Mouth Marketers
- Brand Evangelists
- Agency Account Managers

Features of This Book

Throughout this book, readers are provided with practical pointers to help ensure that their social media programs comply with the law. Each chapter ends with a Social Media Do's and Don'ts chart that summarizes in easy-to-understand language the principal legal issues addressed in the corresponding chapter.

Further, the appendixes contain the text of the laws referenced throughout this book so that readers might have a handy reference to these original source materials.

A Quick Note about U.S. Legal System

There is no single definitive body of law governing social media. Rather, an amalgamation of both U.S. federal and state law controls activity conducted in this space.

In the United States, courts are set up in a hierarchy:

- United States Supreme Court

- Lower federal courts

- State supreme courts

- Lower state courts

Generally speaking, lower federal/state courts must follow precedent established by a higher federal/state court as to the meaning of the law, even if the lower court disagrees with the higher court's interpretation. On questions of federal law, the U.S. Supreme Court has the final authority.

Further, lower federal courts are bound by the precedent set by higher courts within their "district." There are 94 judicial districts, including at least one in each state. These federal "district courts" (trial courts) must follow legal precedent established by the federal "circuit courts" (appellate courts) with the appropriate geographic-based jurisdiction. By way of illustration, a district court that falls within the First Circuit Court of Appeals (which includes the District of Massachusetts, for example) is not bound by rulings from the 9th Circuit (which includes the District of California, for example), or any of the other remaining eleven circuits.

Because many of the cases cited in this book are from the federal district court level, note that the holdings of these cases are not binding on courts that fall outside of these judicial districts.

Fortunately, courts may rely upon cases from other geographic jurisdictions dealing with similar issues as persuasive (but not binding) authority. This is particularly true for cases of first impression—an apt description for the growing number of social media legal challenges covered in this book.

Legal Disclaimer

The materials in this book, "*Navigating Social Media Legal Risks: Safeguarding Your Business*," are for informational purposes only. While we believe that the materials will be helpful, we do not warrant their accuracy or completeness. These materials are general in nature, and may not apply to specific individual circumstances. The information is not intended as, nor is it offered as legal advice and should not be relied on as such. Readers should seek specific legal advice with their own attorney before taking any action with respect to the matters discussed herein. We make no representations or warranties, express or implied, with respect to any information in this book. We are not responsible for any third-party websites or materials that are referred to in, or can be accessed through this book, and we do not make any representations whatsoever regarding them.

1

Social Media Promotion Law: Contests and Sweepstakes

Social media promotions, including contests, sweep-stakes, raffles, drawings, giveaways, and freebies, are an effective means to achieve the most highly sought-after social media business and marketing objectives, including:

- Growing your company's social influence and reach (for instance, increasing the number of friends, fans, followers, subscribers, group members, and the like within branded social properties)

- Growing brand awareness, demand, and loyalty

- Fostering brand engagement

- Submission of user-generated content (UGC) and the placement of valuable backlinks (for example, getting users to discuss your products and services, post their comments, reviews, endorsements, and so on)

- Promoting and evangelizing the value of your products and services on your behalf (that is, capitalizing on word-of-mouth buzz and referrals from friends)

- Increasing web traffic

- Improving your site's findability and search rank (through search engine optimization [SEO] practices)

- Increasing sales

In short, social media promotions provide companies with an opportunity to forge real-world connections and lasting impressions with their audiences by way of immersive branded experiences and thereby (it is hoped) sell more products.

Unfortunately, the laws governing the sponsorship and hosting of social media promotions are widely overlooked or misunderstood. This chapter provides a brief overview of the laws you need to know to avoid placing your business at legal risk. The advice here applies regardless of whether you're an independent blogger, a sole proprietor, small to mid-sized business, or a large multinational conglomerate. This chapter also identifies the steps you can take to minimize legal exposure while reaping the benefits of social media promotions.

Online Promotions

Generally speaking, there are three types of online promotions:

- **Sweepstakes**—Sweepstakes are prize giveaways where the winners are chosen predominately by chance. A sweepstakes prize can include anything from a free downloadable music video to an all-expense-paid trip to Paris.

- **Contests**—Contests are promotions in which prizes are awarded primarily on the basis of skill or merit (for example, the best poem or the winner of a trivia game). Entrants in a contest must be evaluated under objective, predetermined criteria by one or more judges who are qualified to apply such criteria.

- **Lotteries**—Lotteries are random drawings for prizes wherein participants have to *pay to play*. A lottery has three elements: prize, chance, and *consideration* (as defined here). Unlike sweepstakes and contests, lotteries are highly regulated and (with the exception of state-run lotteries and authorized raffles) illegal. Further, each state has its own definition regarding what constitutes consideration. Usually, it is money, but it generally also includes anything of value given in exchange for the opportunity to enter and win, including the entrant's expenditure of considerable time or effort.

Note

People often use the words *sweepstakes* and *contest* interchangeably, but the words have different meanings. Generally speaking, a sweepstakes refers to a promotion in which prizes are awarded based on chance, whereas a contest awards prizes based primarily on skill. A sweepstakes can avoid being considered an illegal lottery (prize + chance + consideration) by eliminating the element of consideration. In a contest, however, it is the element of chance that is removed (or predominated over by skill).

Legal Insight

You might be asking yourself what legal risk could there possibly be in offering the chance to win a free prize in exchange for *liking* your Facebook page, *following you* on Twitter, *joining* your LinkedIn group, *uploading* a photo to your Flickr group, *signing up for* a newsletter, or *downloading* an article. Making these actions a requirement to participate in your online promotion could be construed as consideration, transforming your "simple" sweepstakes or contest into an illegal lottery, although (in the absence of any case law to date stating otherwise) this is not a likely outcome. Whereas requiring a simple thumb's up would likely not constitute consideration, some commonly seen requirements perhaps could (for example, requiring the entrant to post a Facebook comment, send multiple re-tweets, complete a lengthy survey, or refer a friend to the sponsor's dedicated social media site). Bottom line: Make sure your sweepstakes really are *free* to enter—even if participants also have the option to "like" you.

Sweepstakes Laws

All sweepstakes must have official rules, which cannot change during the lifetime of the sweepstakes. To comply with all 50 states' statutes (and corresponding case law), the official rules should typically include the following information:

- Clear and conspicuous statements that "no purchase is necessary" and "a purchase will not improve one's chances of winning"

> Make sure your sweepstakes really are *free* to enter— even if participants also have the option to "like" you.

- The method of entry, including a consideration-free method of entry that has an equal chance with the purchase method of entry (so that all entrants have an equal chance of winning the same prizes)

- Start and end dates of the sweepstakes (stated in terms of dates and precise times in a specific time zone for online promotions)

- Eligibility requirements (age, residency, and such)

- Any limits on eligibility

- Sponsor's complete name and address

- Description and approximate retail value of each prize, and the odds of winning each prize

- Manner of selection of winners and how/when winners will be notified

- Where and when a list of winners can be obtained

- "Void where prohibited" statement

 Note

Eligibility might be further limited to particular states within the United States that have relatively more stringent legal requirements, including Florida, New York, and Rhode Island, where sponsors are required to register with the appropriate state authorities all sweepstakes and contests where the aggregate prize value exceeds $5,000. In Florida and New York, a bond in an amount equal to—or approximately equal to, in the case of New York—the total value of all prizes must also be submitted with the registration.

 Note

To avoid Federal Trade Commission (FTC) and state Attorney General scrutiny (and potential liability), the official rules for online sweepstakes and contests should be clearly and conspicuously displayed, and not hidden in tiny print or accessible through a secret link. At a minimum, the promoter should also include an abbreviated version of the official rules on the same page as the entry form, with the abbreviated version containing the following provisions: no purchase necessary, void where prohibited, deadlines, special eligibility, statement of odds, and where the Official Rules can be found. The sweepstakes or contest promoter may also consider using a click-wrap license that requires entrants to review the official rules and click "I accept" to be permitted to enter the promotion. Care should be taken to avoid pre-checked buttons, however, as these are increasingly becoming the subject of regulatory disfavor.

Whenever consideration is involved in a sweepstakes, a free alternate means of entry (AMOE)—for example, an online entry form, entry by mail, or entry by email—must be offered to maintain the legality of the promotion. This requirement, which would appear simple enough to satisfy in theory, has proven quite tricky in practice, as the concept of "consideration" is deliberately amorphous and subject to different interpretations from state to state.

 Note

Although completing and submitting an entry form online is now a commonly used and widely accepted AMOE, Florida once took the position that entering a game via the Internet constituted consideration because of the cost associated with subscribing to an Internet service provider. Recognizing that the Internet is widely available and (in public libraries, for example) accessible for free, and that a consumer would most likely not subscribe to an Internet service solely for the purpose of entering a sweepstakes, Congress expressly excluded Internet access from the definition of consideration when it adopted the Unlawful Internet Gambling Enforcement Act[1] in 2006.

To complicate matters further, some states require the free AMOE be in the same form that is used for the pay method of entry. In 2004, for example, the New York Attorney General challenged the retail-drug store chain CVS for offering an in-store sweepstakes—a "Trip of a Lifetime" sweepstakes with the grand prize trip to Oahu, Hawaii—in which customers using a store loyalty card were automatically entered into the sweepstakes, while non-purchasers were required to enter online. Because not everyone has access to the Internet, the NY AG reasoned, an off-line (that is, in-store) AMOE needed to be offered as well, regardless of whether the consumer has made a purchase.[2]

To preserve the legality of sweepstakes, AMOEs need to be carefully structured to ensure that they are known and made available, with equal prominence, to the same potential population as the paid entries.

Contest Laws

Like sweepstakes, contests are also subject to specific state laws. Generally speaking, for a national contest, the official rules must contain at least the following disclosures (which, absent extreme circumstances or circumstances identified in the rules, cannot be changed during the course of the contest):

- The name and business address of the sponsor of the contest

- The number of rounds or levels of the contest, the cost (if any) to enter each level, and the maximum cost (if any) to enter all rounds

Note

Some states prohibit purchase requirements altogether (for example, Colorado, Maryland, Nebraska, North Dakota and Vermont), even if the contest winners are selected based on skill. You should exclude entries from these states from online contests that have a purchase requirement.

- Whether subsequent rounds will be more difficult to solve, and how to participate

- The identity or description of the judges and the method used in judging (for example, what objective criteria is being used to judge the entrants and what weight is being assigned to each criteria)

- How and when winners will be determined

 Note

To avoid being classified as a sweepstakes, contests should remove—or at least significantly reduce—the element of chance from the process affecting either the selection of the winner (for example, "first 100 to respond"), the amount of the prize, or how the prize is won. For example, many so-called contests provide that, in the event of a tie, the winner will be selected by drawing lots. Such a provision transforms the promotion into a game of chance (that is, a sweepstakes) and therefore no consideration can then be required for entry. Accordingly, to minimize the degree of chance present in a skill contest, the choice of a winner should be based on pre-established skill criteria, even in the event of a tie. For example, if two participants receive the same top score in a trivia contest, ties should be resolved through a further test of skill. Alternatively, prizes should be awarded to both top winners.

- The number of prizes, an accurate description of each prize, and the approximate retail value of each prize

- The geographic area of the contest

- The start and end dates for entry (stated in terms of dates and precise times in a specific time zone for online promotions)

- Where and when a list of winners can be obtained

Lottery Laws

When a promotion combines the elements of prize, chance and consideration, it's a lottery—and it's illegal! By eliminating any one of these elements, companies may avoid the illegal lottery designation. In the case of sweepstakes, the element of consideration is generally omitted; in the case of contests, it is the element of chance that is removed—or at least, significantly reduced—to make the promotion legal. Promotions would have little appeal if the prize were removed, so this element usually is left intact.

So what is consideration? In the context of sweepstakes, contests, and lotteries, consideration is generally defined as anything of value given in exchange for the opportunity to participate in the promotion. Consideration generally takes one of two forms: monetary, in which the consumer must pay the sponsor to play (purchasing a product or the payment of an entry fee, for example), or non-monetary, in which the consumer must expend substantial time or effort (completing a lengthy questionnaire or making multiple trips to a store location, for example) to participate.

The majority of states have adopted the monetary approach, providing (by statute or judicial opinion) that non-monetary consideration is not deemed to be consideration for purposes of lottery laws. Further, virtually every U.S. state will authorize a promotion to include a "pay-to-play" component, provided a free AMOE is also made available by the sponsor.

As noted, eliminating the element of chance from a promotion removes it from the ambit of lottery prohibitions. However, depending upon the degree of chance present, a promotion intended to be game of skill (contest) could be unwittingly transformed into a game of chance (lottery).

The determination of whether a contest constitutes a lottery can oftentimes be rather tricky, as there are several factors that must be considered and states generally employ different tests, namely:

- **Dominant Factor Test**—Under this test, followed by a majority of U.S. states,[3] a promotion is deemed a game of chance (lottery) when chance "dominates" the distribution of prizes, even though the distribution may be affected to some degree by the exercise of skill or judgment. In other words, in these states, a promotion is legal if it is based on at least 50% skill, and illegal if based on more than 50% chance.

- **Material Element Test**—Under this test, followed by a minority of states,[4] a contest will be considered a game of chance (lottery) if the element of chance is present to a "material" degree.

- **Any Chance Test**—Under this test, a contest will be categorized as a game of chance (lottery) if there is any degree of chance involved, however small. As virtually every game has some element of chance, most skill games will be categorized as illegal lotteries in those states that apply the *Any Chance Test*.

- **Pure Chance Test**—Under this test, which is rarely followed, a promotion must be entirely based on chance to be an illegal lottery. The exercise of any skill by a participant in the selection or award of the prize removes the promotion from the definition of a lottery.

DOMINANT FACTOR TEST DEFINITION

The *Dominant Factor Test* was defined in 1973 by the Supreme Court of Alaska in *Morrow v State*,[5] which set forth the following four-part test to determine whether skill dominates over chance:

- "Participants must have a distinct possibility of exercising skill and must have sufficient data upon which to calculate an informed judgment. The test is that without skill it would be absolutely impossible to win the game."

- "Participants must have the opportunity to exercise the skill, and the general class of participants must possess the skill. Where the contest is aimed at the capacity of the general public, the average person must have the skill, but not every person need have the skill. It is irrelevant that participants may exercise varying degrees of skill. The scheme cannot be limited or aimed at a specific skill which only a few possess."

- "Skill or the competitors' efforts must sufficiently govern the result. Skill must control the final result, not just one part of the larger scheme.... Where 'chance enters into the solution of another lesser part of the problems and thereby proximately influences the final result,' the scheme is a lottery.... Where skill does not destroy the dominant effect of chance, the scheme is a lottery."

- "The standard of skill must be known to the participants, and this standard must govern the result. The language used in promoting the scheme must sufficiently inform the participants of the criteria to be used in determining the results of the winners. The winners must be determined objectively."

Potential Legal Issues Associated With Public Voting

Companies are increasingly structuring their online promotions to encourage the submission of user-generated content (UGC) and public voting. Such interactive campaigns not only create more views for the contest, but they also increase a company's web and social media page views, number of followers, and brand awareness.

A typical UGC-based promotion allows consumers to upload a photo or video incorporating the sponsor's product for a chance to win a prize. The public is then invited to view the submitted content and vote for the "best" (the funniest or cutest, for example). Usually, the video that is watched the most or the photo that receives the highest number of "likes" is the winner.

The Doritos "Crash the Super Bowl" contest launched in 2006 is a perfect example of the power of social media promotions to generate brand loyalty, good will, and consumer engagement. The "Crash the Super Bowl" contest allows entrants to create and submit home-made Doritos commercials where each year the winning and second placed ads—as voted online by the general public—are aired during the Super Bowl. The success of the Doritos contest has led to an explosion in promotions involving UGC.

Despite the obvious advantages of interactive UGC contests, such promotions are not without legal risk. First, because promotions contain elements of both skill (creating the "best" video) and chance (video popularity with voting public), they may unwittingly convert a contest into a sweepstakes, and thereby effect not just the need for registration and bonding, but the promotion structure and entry requirements (including the need for an AMOE) as well.

As noted earlier, if the promotion is open to residents of Florida or New York and the total value of the prize offered exceeds $5,000, then the promotion must be registered and bonded in those states if the promotion is deemed a game of chance (sweepstakes), and not a game of skill (contest). In both Florida and New York, the failure to register and bond a sweepstakes with a prize value exceeding $5,000 exposes the sponsor to both civil and criminal penalties.[6]

Additionally, if public voting is used to determine an online contest winner, it could render the promotion illegal if consideration was required as a condition of entry. While most states permit the requirement of consideration for entry into a contest, it is unlawful to require consideration to enter a sweepstakes. Without exception, a promotion based on chance that requires consideration or a purchase to enter for a chance to win a prize is an illegal lottery.

Further, as members of the public may try to manipulate the voting process (for example, voting for their friends and encouraging others to do the same), some states may find that public voting injects too much chance into the contest, thereby transforming it into a sweepstakes or (worse) an illegal lottery. Companies running interactive promotions must also be prepared to stave off complaints of fraud or unfairness.

Finally, if public voting is used to determine an online contest winner, it could compromise the promotion's legality. Indeed, in states applying the *Any Chance Test*, any contest which includes public voting as a judging element would most likely be construed as an illegal lottery.

The analysis is much more nuanced (read: complex) in states applying the *Dominant Factor Test* or *Material Element Test*. In assessing the degree of chance versus skill, the following factors are generally considered:

- The degree of skill required to make the submission

- Whether eligible participants are likely to have the degree of skill necessary to win

- Whether the promotion is limited or aimed at a specific skill which only a few possess

- Whether there are distinct voting criteria

- Whether the public is qualified to apply the defined criteria

- The number of rounds of voting and whether public voting is considered in each round

- Whether a qualified judge's vote is considered (and, if so, the amount of weight it is given)

- Whether there is a limit on the number of votes a person can make

A promotion is more likely to be considered a game of chance if voting is unrestricted.

To reduce the legal risks associated with public voting, the promotion rules should limit votes to one vote per person (tracked by IP address), clearly explain the judging criteria applicable for public judging, and require that the selection with the highest public vote count as only a percentage of the overall criteria by which a winner is ultimately selected, with professional judges having the final say.

Note

> UGC contests raise additional legal concerns, including compliance with third-party copyright and trademark rights; rights of privacy/publicity (for example, using the name and/or picture of the entrant without his/her express permission); the Children's Online Privacy Protection Act (regarding collection of information from children); the Lanham Act (regarding false advertisement); the Digital Millennium Copyright Act (regarding copyright infringement); the Communications Decency Act (regarding UGC host liability); and the FTC Act (regarding false or deceptive business practices in the collection or use of consumer information). These matters are discussed later in this book.

Keeping Social Media Promotional Campaigns Legal

The settlements of the long-running class-action lawsuits over the legality of allowing consumers to enter sweepstakes offered by popular television shows such as *The Apprentice, American Idol, America's Got Talent*, and *Deal or No Deal* underscore the importance of having legally compliant social media promotional campaigns and demonstrate how even innocuous-looking sweepstakes entry mechanisms can backfire.

In "Get Rich With Trump" sweepstakes, viewers watching the NBC show, *The Apprentice,* voted for the contestant whom they believed would be the target of Donald Trump's "You're Fired!" by either sending a premium SMS text-message costing 99 cents, plus any applicable standard text messaging charges, or by entering for free online. Correct answers earned the participant a chance to win a prize.

Likewise, viewers of *American Idol* and *America's Got Talent*, for example, were allowed to send their predictions on the outcome of the show via a premium text message, costing 99 cents. Viewers who guessed correctly earned sweepstakes entries.

Prior to the class-actions lawsuits, such network program sweepstakes were rapidly rising in popularity and the promoters of these sweepstakes were amassing fortunes from the entry fees (collected as premium text message charges paid by viewers), without giving the entrants anything of value in return.

However, unlike promotions where a consumer is asked to purchase a product as a condition of entry (a soft drink, for example), consumers participating in these network program promotions received nothing in exchange for their .99 cents, other than a chance to win.

This method of entry quickly came under attack as constituting an illegal lottery, in violation of various states' anti-gambling laws, even though a free AMOE was also available to the participants.

In the lead case of *Karen Herbert v. Endemol USA, Inc.*,[7] the plaintiff challenged the play-at-home sweepstakes promoted by various game/reality shows in which viewers were allowed to register and be given the opportunity to be awarded both cash prizes and merchandise, either via an SMS text message sent from a wireless device or online via the program's website. No fees were charged to persons entering via the Internet, but entrants who registered via text message had to pay a $.99 premium text message surcharge in addition to the standard text messaging fees charged by the viewers' wireless carriers.

In denying the defendants' motions to dismiss, the U.S. District Court for the Central District of California held that the plaintiffs had sufficiently alleged that the defendants' actions constitute illegal gambling as a matter of law, despite the fact that the defendants offered a free AMOE:

> *The critical factual distinction between cases in which a lottery was not found ... and those in which a lottery was found ... is that the former "involved promotional schemes by using prize tickets to increase the purchases of legitimate goods and services in the free market place" whereas in the latter "the game itself is the product being merchandized." ... The presence of a free alternative method of entry in the leading cases made it clear that the money customers paid was for the products purchased (gasoline or movie tickets), and not for the chance of winning a prize.*
>
> *The relevant question here, therefore, is whether the Games were nothing more than "organized scheme[s] of chance," in which payment was induced by the chance of winning a prize. The relevant question is not, as Defendants contend, whether some people could enter for free. In [cases where a lottery was not found], the courts concluded that those who made payment purchased something of equivalent value. The indiscriminate distribution of tickets to purchasers and non-purchasers alike was evidence thereof. Here, however, Defendants' offers of free alternative methods of entry do not alter the basic fact that viewers who sent in text messages paid only for the privilege of entering the Games. They received nothing of equivalent economic value in return.*[8]

—U.S. District Court for the Central District of California (11/30/07)

Pursuant to the terms of the settlement, the defendants agreed to:

- Refund any premium text message surcharges paid by consumers if the consumers did not win a prize.

- Reimburse the plaintiffs more than $5.2 million in legal fees.

- Submit to a 5-year injunction enjoining them from "creating, sponsoring, or operating any contest or sweepstakes, for which entrants are offered the possibility of winning a prize, where people who enter via premium text message do not receive something of comparable value to the premium text message charge in addition to entry."[9]

Although the settlements are not binding on companies that are not parties to the lawsuit, the settlements are nonetheless instructive. As a general rule, it may be best to avoid premium-SMS-entry promotions altogether. For companies that decide to conduct premium text promotions, it is critical that a free AMOE (for example, entry by mail or 1-800 number) is made available *and* that paid entrants are given something of verifiable equivalent retail value in return for what they paid to enter.

Online Promotions Outside the United States

Online promotions are potentially subject not only to the laws of all 50 states but also to the laws of every country in which the promoter's website appears. Notably, certain countries (for example, Belgium, Malaysia, and Norway) prohibit sweepstakes altogether, whereas other countries (for example, France and Spain) require registration and payment of fees. Therefore, it is critical that sweepstakes and contest eligibility be carefully limited, such as, for example, limiting eligibility to U.S. residents.

Sweepstakes Versus Illegal Online Gambling

Internet sweepstakes must also avoid being classified as illegal online gambling; otherwise, the sponsors risk severe criminal and civil penalties under the Unlawful Internet Gambling Enforcement Act of 2006 (UIGEA).[10] Since the enactment of UIGEA, it has been illegal for any person "engaged in the business of betting or wagering" to "knowingly accept" most forms of payment "in connection with the participation of another person in unlawful Internet gambling."[11] In other words,

Internet sweepstakes sponsors must avoid promoting campaigns that could force the sponsor to be classified as a "business of betting or wagering," such as conducting ongoing online sweepstakes advertising that participants will receive something of value based on an outcome predominantly subject to pure chance. In such circumstances, sponsors are also legally precluded from accepting credit card payments, checks, or electronic fund transfers as part of their offerings.

> Internet sweepstakes sponsors must avoid promoting campaigns that could force the sponsor to be classified as a business of betting or wagering.

Platform-Specific Guidelines

In addition to structuring sweepstakes and contests so as to comply with federal and state law, companies must take care that their promotions also comply with the terms and conditions of social media networking sites, particularly site rules regulating consumer sweepstakes and contests.

LinkedIn

LinkedIn prohibits its users from uploading, posting, emailing, or making available any unsolicited or unauthorized advertising or promotional materials.[12]

Google+

Google+ prohibits online promotions directly from a Google+ page, but allows users to "display a link on your Google+ Page to a separate site where your Promotion is hosted so long as you (and not Google) are solely responsible for your Promotion and for compliance with all applicable federal, state and local laws, rules and regulations in the jurisdiction(s) where your Promotion is offered or promoted."[13]

Twitter

In contrast to the prohibitive policies of Google+ and LinkedIn, Twitter specifically authorizes users to conduct promotions on its platform. In fact, Twitter's Guidelines for Contests on Twitter (which, despite its name, applies to both contests and sweepstakes) appears to encourage promotions provided that the Twitter user experience is not compromised. For example, Twitter requires contest promoters to disqualify any user who enters a contest from multiple accounts; encourages entrants to include an "@reply to you" in their update so that all the entries are seen; and discourages multiple entries from the same participant on the same day, presumably to discourage posting of the same Tweet repeatedly (à la "whoever re-Tweets the most wins" variety).[14]

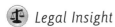 *Legal Insight*

The sheer reach of social media promotions can work both great magic and harm for a company. In November, 2011, for example, Australian airline Qantas launched its "Qantas Luxury" competition on Twitter, asking users to describe their "dream luxury inflight experience" in exchange for a pair of Qantas first-class pajamas and a toiletries kit. Reportedly that same day, more than 22,000 tweets were sent using the designated "#QantasLuxury" hashtag, many critical of the airline for having canceled its flights a month earlier due to a union strike, and many ridiculing the airline's service (and its pajamas!).

Companies should always be prepared with a coordinated legal, PR, and social media marketing crisis response plan in the event their social media contests or sweepstakes backfire.

Facebook

On November 4, 2009, Facebook issued new Promotions Guidelines that contain specific rules for administering sweepstakes and contests on its website. These guidelines were again most recently revised on May 11, 2011. Under this revision of the guidelines, *administering* a promotion on Facebook means "the operation of any element of the promotion, such as collecting entries, conducting a drawing, judging entries, or notifying winners."[15]

As of the date of publication, promotions are subject to the following guidelines:

- **Must use the Facebook platform app**—Facebook requires that all promotions on its site be administered via a third-party Facebook platform application, within Apps on Facebook.com, either on a canvas page (that is, a blank page within Facebook on which to load and run an app) or an app on a page tab. If you do not want to use an app to run your promotion, you should consider running it on your own website or blog, and simply have contest participants like your Facebook page as a part of that contest.

- **Use the allowed functions**—Facebook now allows only three site functions to be used as a condition of contest registration or entry:

    - Liking a page

    - Checking into a place

    - Connecting to your app

 Note

With the exception of the three functions noted above, entry into a promotion can never be conditioned upon a user providing content on the site, including liking a Wall post or commenting or uploading a photo on a Wall. In 2011, Scandinavian Airline's Facebook page was temporarily suspended for violating this rule. To promote a million seat fare sale, SAS ran a competition on Facebook where SAS fans could "grab" a free trip (see Figure 1.1). Fans were asked to change their profile picture into the custom made "Up For Grabs" image and post a matching image on the company's Facebook Wall. Although the clever promotion garnered a lot of social media buzz, it used prohibited Facebook functionalities (posting a photo, for example) as a condition of contest registration, in violation of Facebook's rules.

Figure 1.1 *SAS's "Up For Grabs" Promotion.*

- **May not be used for a promotion's registration or voting methods—**
  Facebook features and functionalities cannot be used as a promotion's
  registration or entry mechanism, nor as a promotion's voting mechanism. For example, the act of liking a page or checking in to a place
  cannot automatically register or enter a promotion participant. So, no
  more "Just like our page, and you'll be automatically entered to win!"
  If you want to do a promotion for people who liked your page, you
  need the app you use to offer a way to enter, such as through providing an email address. Accordingly, although companies can condition
  competition entry on liking a page, the like functionality cannot be
  used as the actual method of entry itself. The action of becoming a fan
  can never alone equal an automatic entry into the contest or sweepstakes. Rather, after having liked your page, entrants must be directed
  toward a separate registration process administered through a third-
  party app on a separate canvas page (now a link, formerly a tab).

 Note

Contiki Vacations' "Get on the Bus" Promotion offered the travel firm's
Facebook fans aged 18 to 35 a chance to win a free trip worth up to
$25,000 (see Figure 1.2). The "Get on the Bus" promo challenged fans
to choose from one of eight travel destinations, gather a crew with four
friends together to fill a virtual "bus" (which incorporated music, movies,
Likes and other interests that users had in common), and then collect as
many votes as possible in order to win. To gather votes, participants were
encouraged to ask people to Stumble, Digg, Blog, Buzz, Tweet and Share
their bus page, create YouTube videos explaining why their bus should get
the most votes, ask celebrities to tweet on their bus' behalf, and create
handouts with their bus link to give to friends. Interestingly, just as the
"Get on the Bus" promo was launching, Facebook changed its policy about
the use of Likes—that is, no Facebook features or functionality, such as
the Like button, could be used as a voting mechanism for a promotion.
Contiki's response? It created a "Vote" button that was displayed above
each bus instead!

Figure 1.2   *Contiki Vacations' "Get on the Bus" Promotion.*

- **Facebook features may not be used to notify winners**—Companies are not allowed to use any Facebook features to notify winners, such as through Facebook messages, chats, or posts. Companies should establish alternate means of communication with all participants (such as email) to notify winners.

- **Must make proper disclosures**—The guidelines also require that the official rules for a promotion administered on Facebook include specific disclosures, including an acknowledgment that the promotion is not associated with or sponsored, endorsed or administered by Facebook, a provision releasing the social networking site from liability from each participant; and notice that information submitted by participants is being disclosed to the contest promoter, and not Facebook.

- **Do *not* use Facebook's intellectual property**—Companies are not permitted to use Facebook's name, logos, and so on in their promotions, other than to fulfill the required nonaffiliation disclosure.

It is only a matter of time before more and more Facebook accounts of both small businesses and major brands are suspended (or disabled) due to noncompliance.

Many companies appear to be ignoring Facebook's Promotions Guidelines, but it is only a matter of time before more and more Facebook accounts of both small businesses and major brands are suspended (or disabled) due to noncompliance.

 *Legal Insight*

In the first case of its kind,[16] the National Advertising Division (NAD), the advertising industry's self-regulatory forum, determined that Coastal Contacts, Inc. must provide, at the outset of any "like-gated" promotional offer, a clear and conspicuous statement for all material terms and conditions included in its Facebook promotion requiring consumers to like a product page. (*Like-gated promotions* are those in which a company requires a consumer to like its Facebook page to gain access to a benefit, such as a deal, a coupon code, or other savings.)

In this case, Coastal Contacts told consumers on its Facebook page to "Like this Page! So you too can get your free pair of glasses!" Competitor 1-800-Contacts challenged the promotion, however, claiming that Coastal failed to disclose that additional terms and conditions applied (for example, that consumers were responsible for the cost of shipping and handling) until after the consumer entered the promotion by liking Coastal's Facebook page. While restricting a coupon, deal, or discount to users who like a company's Facebook page is a popular promotion technique used by brands and businesses, companies should never use fraudulent or misleading offers to increase the number of likes on their Facebook page (for example, by claiming something is free when it is not). Consistent with FTC advertising guidelines (discussed in detail in Chapter 2), the NAD specifically observed that requiring employees to "like" a company's Facebook page without informing consumers that they work for the company is a fraudulent or misleading means of obtaining "likes." Furthermore, although not addressed by the NAD, to comply with Facebook's Promotions Guidelines, Facebook-based "like-gated" promotions need to ensure that entry is not conditioned solely on liking a page.

This chapter provides only a preliminary overview of the potential legal pitfalls facing companies which operate promotions through social media channels. Further, there are a variety of other statutes covering special types of promotions which were not addressed in this chapter, including: in-pack/on-pack promotions; bottle cap sweeps; preselected winners; everybody wins; retail promotions; promotions aimed at children; Internet and mobile promotions; direct mail promotions; and telemarketing promotions. Social media campaigns conducted in conjunction with these promotional techniques should be exercised with an extra degree of caution.

As the popularity of social media sweepstakes and contests continues to grow, the laws regulating this space will surely follow. It will probably be a few more years before we have a comprehensive statement of the law governing these issues—but even then, the rapid pace of technological advance makes obtaining a definitive set of laws almost impossible. Careful promotional planning, structuring, and oversight are the best means of running successful and legally compliant social media promotions. To that end, companies should heed best practices for social media promotions as summarized in Figure 1.3.

Social Media Legal Tips for Contests and Sweepstakes

DOs	DON'Ts
■ Brush up on your understanding of the basic legal differences between contests, sweepstakes and lotteries. Establish a promotional compliance checklist for each type of promotion to ensure your promotions comply with the laws which govern them.	■ Never structure a promotion based primarily on chance (a sweepstakes) to require any form of payment—otherwise, you may have created an illegal lottery.
■ If the primary method of entry in a sweepstakes involves payment or any other form of "consideration," be sure to provide—and clearly disclose—a free alternate method of entry (AMOE), such as mail-in entry.	■ Do not hide the free AMOE, make it less prominent than the paid method of entry, or make it available to only a few participants or on an unequal basis. The chances of winning must not increase (or decrease) for those who pay versus those that enter via the free AMOE.
■ As a general rule, avoid premium text messaging promotions wherever possible. If using such promotions, make sure you offer something of equivalent retail value (a free ring-tone, wallpaper, or t-shirt, for example) in exchange for the entry charge. This item should be a real product or service, otherwise widely available and marketed for purchase for at least as much as the premium text charge.	■ Do not charge entrants simply for the chance of winning. Establish promotions such that any money customers pay to enter are for the products purchased (for example, a soda, movie ticket, and so on), and not solely for the chance of winning a prize.
■ Companies using Facebook "like-gated" promotions should clearly and conspicuously disclose material terms and conditions of the promotion—such as any additional fees for shipping, handling, and product upgrades, for example—at the outset of any promotional offer, and on a page that is not "like-gated."	■ Do not use fraudulent or misleading offers or other inducements to increase the number of "likes" on a Facebook page (by paying a service to artificially inflate the number of "likes" or requiring employees to "like" their employer's page without disclosing the employment connection for example).
■ Remember that you may require someone to "like" your Facebook page or "check-in" to your place before entering a promotion, but these acts alone can never register or enter the participant.	■ Do not condition registration or entry into a contest or sweepstakes upon liking a Wall post, posting a newsfeed, inviting friends, updating status, uploading a Wall photo, or using any Facebook functionality other than "liking" a page or "checking into" a place.

Figure 1.3 *Social Media Legal Tips for Contests and Sweepstakes.*

CHAPTER 1 ENDNOTES

1   *See* 31 U.S.C.A. § 5362(1)(E)(viii)(I), which provides, "The term 'bet or wager' does not include … participation in any game or contest in which participants do not stake or risk anything of value other than— (I) personal efforts of the participants in playing the game or contest or obtaining access to the Internet …"

2   *See* NY Office of the Attorney General Press Release, *CVS TO AMEND SWEEPSTAKES PROMOTIONS: Spitzer Obtains Agreement To Ensure Non-Purchasing Consumers Can Easily Enter Contest* (Jul. 8, 2004), available at http://www.ag.ny.gov/media_center/2004/jul/jul08a_04.html

3   States that appear to apply the *Dominant Factor Test* include: California, Connecticut, Georgia, Idaho, Indiana, Kansas, Kentucky, Maine, Massachusetts, Michigan, Minnesota, Nebraska, Nevada, New Hampshire, New Mexico, North Carolina, North Dakota, Ohio, Pennsylvania, Rhode Island, South Carolina, and South Dakota.

4   States that appear to apply the *Material Element Test* include: Alabama, Hawaii, Missouri, New Jersey, Oklahoma, and Oregon.

5   *Morrow v. State*, 511 P.2d 127 (Alaska 1973)

6   *See N.Y. Gen. Bus. Law § 369-e; Fl. Stat. § 849.094*

7   *Herbert et al. v. Endemol USA, Inc. et al.*, Case No. 2:07-CV-03537-JHN-VBK (C.D. Cal. May 31, 2007))

8   *See Order Denying Defendants' Motions and Joint Motions to Dismiss* (Florence-Marie Cooper, J.) (Document 38) (Nov. 20, 2007) in *Herbert et al. v. Endemol USA, Inc. et al.*, Case No. 2:07-CV-03537-JHN-VBK (C.D. Cal. May 31, 2007)

9   *See Plaintiffs' Memorandum of Points and Authorities in Support of Combined Motion for Final Approval of Settlements* (Document 120) (Nov. 11, 2011) in *Herbert et al. v. Endemol USA, Inc. et al.*, Case No. 2:07-CV-03537-JHN-VBK (C.D. Cal. May 31, 2007)

10 31 U.S.C. §§ 5361-5366

11 *Id.* at § 5363

12 *See* LinkedIn's User Agreement, available at http://www.linkedin.com/static?key=user_agreement

13 *See* Google+ Pages Contest and Promotion Policies, available at http://www.google.com/intl/en/+/policy/pagescontestpolicy.html

14 *See* Guidelines for Contests on Twitter, available at http://support.twitter.com/entries/68877-guidelines-for-contests-on-twitter

15 *See* Facebook's Promotions Guidelines (last revised May 11, 2011), available at http://www.facebook.com/promotions_guidelines.php

16 *See* National Advertising Division's November 8, 2011 Press Release, available at http://www.narcpartners.org/DocView.aspx?DocumentID=8811&DocType=1

2

Online Endorsements and Testimonials: What Companies and Their Employees Can and Cannot Tweet, Blog, or Say

Businesses spend considerable time and money building and executing marketing campaigns to promote their brands when, in fact, one of the most effective advertising tools costs almost nothing: word-of-mouth advertising.

Happy customers and their endorsements can steer business in your direction quite effectively, and with little cost. Studies, such as the one recently published by the e-tailing group PowerReviews,[1] consistently show that customer reviews have a significant affect on purchasing behavior. This study indicates "shoppers today are spending more time reading reviews before making purchasing decisions, 64 percent take ten minutes or more (as compared to 50 percent in 2007) and 33 percent take one half hour or more (as compared to 18 percent in 2007)."

Further, "consumers today are also reading more customer reviews in order to be confident in judging a product, 39 percent read eight or more reviews (as compared with 22 percent in 2007) and 12 percent read 16 or more reviews (as compared with 5 percent in 2007)."

Online reviews and endorsements can also improve rankings in organic search results, leading to improved discoverability, an increase in web traffic, and greater brand awareness. For these reasons, capturing and leveraging positive customer reviews to drive consumer demand and increase sales is a critical component of today's marketing landscape. Nonetheless, online reviews and endorsements are not risk-free, and there are strict legal requirements with which businesses must comply to avoid liability.

Online endorsements and testimonials are subject to guidelines established in 2009 by the Federal Trade Commission (FTC) that impose liability on companies for the false claims of their endorsers (even if such claims were never previously authorized, approved, or used by the company) and for the failure to make required disclosures that exist between online posters and the companies about which they are commenting.

> Online reviews and endorsements are not risk-free, and there are strict legal requirements with which businesses must comply to avoid liability.

 Note

In 2009, the New York State Attorney General's office charged Lifestyle Lift, a cosmetic surgery company, with *astroturfing*—that is, the illegal marketing practice of posting fake consumer reviews on the Internet, hiring third parties to post positive reviews, and/or creating online communities for "customers" that are actually under the company's control.[2] According to the AG's office, Lifestyle Lift employees were instructed to create accounts with Internet message boards and pose as satisfied customers. The employees even created a website (MyFaceliftStory.com) designed to disseminate positive reviews appearing as if they were created by independent and satisfied customers. The AG's investigation discovered emails specifically instructing employees to post on the Web. One such message directed an employee to "devote the day to doing more postings on the Web as a satisfied client." Another email directed an employee to "Put your wig and skirt on and tell them about the great experience you had." As part of its settlement, Lifestyle Lift was required to pay $300,000 in penalties and costs to New York State.

Fundamental Principles of Endorsements and Testimonials

The *Guides Concerning the Use of Endorsements and Testimonials in Advertising* (Endorsement Guides)[3] incorporate three fundamental truth-in-advertising principles as they relate to social media posts:

- Endorsements must be truthful and not misleading;

- If the advertiser doesn't have proof that the endorser's experience represents what consumers will achieve by using the product, the ad must clearly and conspicuously disclose the generally expected results in the depicted circumstances; and

- If there's a connection between the endorser and the marketer of the product that would reasonably affect how much weight a consumer places on the endorsement, such a connection must be clearly and conspicuously disclosed.

Obvious relationships that must be disclosed include the employment relationship between the endorser and the company and whether the endorser is being paid or receiving some *quid pro quo* for the product being endorsed. Failure to make the required disclosure may render not only the endorser liable, but the company as well, regardless of whether the communication was known.

 Note

The Endorsement Guides are not limited to bloggers. In fact, these guides cover any advertising message on any social media site, including consumer testimonials or reviews, that *other* consumers are likely to believe reflects the opinions or beliefs of the endorser. According to the FTC, unlike with traditional reviews in newspapers, television or websites with similar content, "on a personal blog, a social networking page, or in similar media, the reader may not expect the reviewer to have a relationship with the company whose products are mentioned."[4] The FTC recommends including disclosure of the company you work for, and the products it sells, when discussing such products on social media sites, including an employee's personal Facebook page.

Endorsement or Not?

Given the wide variety of consumer-generated media (CGM), distinguishing between communications that are considered endorsements and those that are not may sometimes be more of an art than a science. Under the Endorsement Guides, an *endorsement* is defined as any advertising message (for example, verbal statements, demonstrations, or depictions of the name, signature, likeness or other identifying personal characteristics of an individual or the name or seal of an organization) that consumers are likely to believe reflects the opinions, beliefs, findings, or experiences of a party other than the sponsoring advertiser, even if the views expressed by that party are identical to those of the sponsoring advertiser. Therefore, a film critic's review of a movie excerpted into an advertisement would be considered an endorsement, as would an advertisement for golf balls depicting a famous golfer, even if the golfer made no verbal statement in the advertisement.

When a connection exists between the endorser and the seller of the advertised product that might materially affect the weight or credibility of the endorsement, such a connection must be fully disclosed. The dividing line between a material connection (requiring disclosure) and a connection that is not material is often difficult to gauge. The following examples illustrate how fine the line may be:

- An advertiser sends a video-game blogger its products for the blogger to use free of charge. The blogger then posts a review of the products on his personal blog. Disclosure is required.[5]

- A customer receives a coupon from her local store for a free bag of dog food for a brand which is more expensive than what she typically buys. She writes in her personal blog that the change in diet has made her dog's fur softer and shinier, and that in her opinion, the new food is definitely worth the extra money. Disclosure is not required. [6]

- An online message board designated for discussions of new music download technology is frequented by MP3 player enthusiasts, who exchange information about new products. Unbeknownst to the message board community, an employee of a leading playback device manufacturer has been posting messages on the discussion board promoting the manufacturer's product. Disclosure is required. [7]

- An advertiser sends a blogger a free sample of new body lotion and requests that she write a review of the product on her personal blog. Disclosure is required.[8]

- While attending an industry trade show, bloggers are given SWAG ("stuff we all get") from an advertiser. A blogger who attended the event writes about the free SWAG product he received. Disclosure is (most likely) not required.[9]

⚖ *Legal Insight*

Are Facebook or YouTube likes or Twitter re-tweets endorsements subject to the FTC Act? When a Facebook user likes a company's page, for example, his or her name and profile picture are displayed on the page for others to see, as well as on news feeds of the user's friends. In other words, users can express their affinity for or make a connection with particular content (be it a company or a company's product) by clicking the Like button. Although no court has yet decided the issue (at least at the time of this writing), prudence dictates that a party should disclose his/her relationship to the product or company being liked to avoid violating the FTC Act.

As can be seen from the above examples, there is no bright-line test as to which uses of CGM constitutes an endorsement. Rather, the fundamental question is whether the relationship between the advertiser and the speaker is such that the speaker's statement can be considered *sponsored* by the advertiser and therefore an *advertising message.*

Critically, an advertiser's lack of control over the specific CGM statement made would ***not*** automatically disqualify that statement from being deemed an endorsement within the meaning of the Endorsement Guides. Again, the issue is whether the consumer-generated statement can be considered sponsored. Relevant factors to consider in determining whether a statement constitutes an endorsement include the following:

- Whether the speaker is compensated by the advertiser

- Whether the product was provided for free by the advertiser

- The terms of any agreement, and the length of the relationship between the speaker and the advertiser

- Whether the speaker previously received (or is likely to receive in the future) products from the advertiser

- The value of the products received

Even remote affiliate marketers, bloggers, and other social media users might be deemed sponsored by an advertiser. The advertiser's lack of control over these remote social media users does not absolve the advertiser of responsibility for an endorser's failure to make the requisite disclosures.

For the FTC, if the advertiser initiated the process that led to these endorsements being made—for example, by providing products to well-known bloggers or to endorsers enrolled in word-of-mouth marketing programs—the advertiser is potentially liable for misleading statements made by those parties.[10]

Determining Liability

Whether an advertiser will be held responsible for a third party's social media communications hinges on whether the advertiser chose to sponsor the consumer-generated content and, therefore, established an endorser-sponsor relationship. In making this determination, the FTC considers the following factors:

- The advertiser's efforts to advise endorsers of their responsibilities (for example, by adoption of a blogger endorsements policy)

- The advertiser's efforts to monitor endorsers' online behavior

- The advertisers efforts to take corrective action against rogue endorsers (for example, ceasing to provide free products to noncompliant bloggers)

To avoid liability, advertisers who sponsor endorsers (either by providing free products or otherwise) to generate positive word of mouth buzz and spur sales should establish procedures to advise endorsers of their disclosure obligations. Advertisers should also monitor the conduct of those endorsers to ensure that they comply with their disclosure obligations. An advertiser's ability to avoid liability due to an endorser's failure to disclose will primarily depend upon the quality of the advertiser's policies and policing efforts. A written policy addressing these issues signed by the endorser is the best protection.

 Legal Insight

In general, a company that provides products to a blogger for purposes of a product review should never tell the blogger what to say in the review or ask to edit (save for minor grammatical errors) the review prior to posting. In the event of a negative review, the company may choose not to provide products to the blogger for future reviews.

Because FTC Endorsement Guides state that a company may be liable for claims made by a blogger, the company should carefully monitor product reviews made by bloggers to ensure that the claims are truthful and can be substantiated. A number of social media monitoring vendors provide solutions for tracking and monitoring mentions of your business or brand on the Web and in social media channels. (A list of free and paid social media monitoring vendors is provided on the following wiki: http://wiki.kenburbary. com/social-meda-monitoring-wiki.) These services simplify the critical task of keeping tabs on the reputation of your company's name and products.

Finally, on a separate (yet related) note, companies should also prohibit their employees from engaging in inflammatory disputes with bloggers (flaming) on any blogs, which may be considered illegal harassment.

Because the FTC knows businesses cannot realistically oversee all the social media posts by its employees to ensure compliance with the Endorsement Guides, it has stated that the employer should not be held liable in this situation under the following scenario:

- The employer has a social media policy concerning the *social media participation* of its employees.

- The established company policy adequately covered the employee conduct at issue.

- The employer has established procedures to monitor compliance with its social media policy.[11] Thus, the company can show that, despite its best efforts, the employee violated the Endorsement Guides and that the company should not be held liable for the employee's unauthorized acts.

> One rogue blogger will not likely trigger law enforcement action if your company has a reasonable training and monitoring program in place.

 Note

Although it is unrealistic to require employers to be aware of every single statement made by their employees or agents, they are still required to make reasonable efforts to know what is being said by their people about their products. That said, one rogue blogger will not likely trigger law enforcement action if your company has a reasonable training and monitoring program in place. As noted by the FTC's Bureau of Consumer Protection, "The scope of the program depends on the risk that deceptive practices by network participants could cause consumer harm—either physical injury or financial loss. For example, a network devoted to the sale of health products may require more supervision than a network promoting, say, a new line of handbags."[12]

Making Necessary Disclosures

Given the ever-evolving nature of social media platforms, not all disclosures are created equal. In 2000, the FTC adopted a *clear and conspicuous* standard to online advertising disclosures and set forth four key factors to determine whether the advertising is deceptive or misleading:

- Prominence

- Presentation

- Placement

- Proximity

That is, disclosures must be large enough for consumers to notice and read, in easy-to-understand wording and format, in a location where consumers are likely to look, and in close proximity to the claims they qualify. Whether a disclosure is sufficiently clear and conspicuous is measured by its performance; *i.e.*, how consumers actually perceive and understand the disclosure within the context of the entire ad. The dispositive factor is the overall net impression of the ad—that is, whether the claims consumers take from the ad are truthful and substantiated.

To make a disclosure clear and conspicuous, the FTC, in its 2000 "Dot Com Disclosures" guide,[13] recommends that advertisers:

- Place disclosures near, and whenever possible, on the same screen as the ad containing the claim (the "triggering claim").

- Use text or visual cues to encourage consumers to scroll down a Web page when it is necessary to view a disclosure.

In Figure 2.1, for example, the presence of the blue line helps alert consumers to the fact that there is additional information (here, a paid advertisement disclaimer) below the screen.

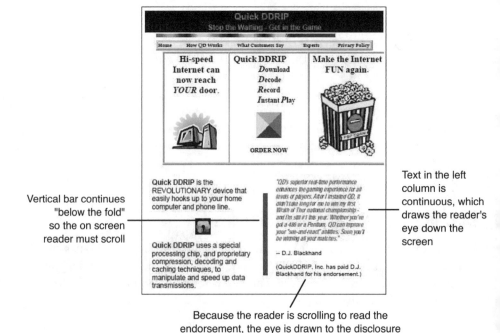

Figure 2.1   *Visual clues alert consumer to disclaimer.*

However, in Figure 2.2, there are insufficient visual clues prompting the consumer to continue scrolling. The consumer may altogether miss the disclaimer on the bottom of the page.

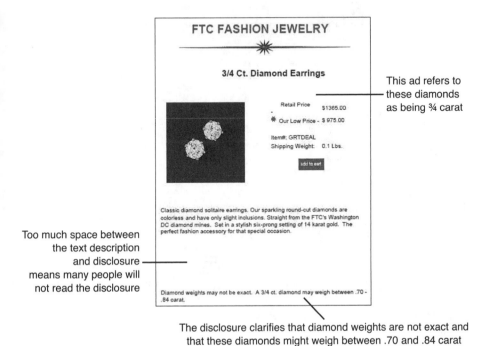

Figure 2.2   *Here, the important disclaimer regarding the diamond's weight would likely be missed by the consumer.*

Hyperlinked Disclosures

When hyperlinking a disclosure:

- Make the link obvious.

- Label the hyperlink appropriately to convey the importance, nature and relevance of the information it leads to.

- Use hyperlink styles consistently so that consumers know when a link is available.

- Place the hyperlink near relevant information and make it noticeable.

- Take consumers directly to the disclosure on the click-through page.

- Assess the effectiveness of the hyperlink by monitoring click-through rates and the amount of time visitors spend on a certain page.

In Figure 2.3, for example, simple creating a hyperlink to the disclaimer is inadequate. The ad must do more to disclose the fact that this is a paid endorsement.

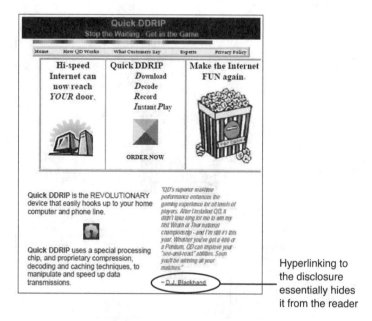

Hyperlinking to the disclosure essentially hides it from the reader

Figure 2.3 *The hyperlink fails to adequately alert the consumer that this is a paid-for endorsement.*

General Rules for Disclosures

Following are some general rules to follow when making disclosures:

- Recognize and respond to any technological limitations of making disclosures, such as frames or pop-up windows, to ensure that disclosures are visible and read. For example, requiring the consumer to take some affirmative step to proceed past the pop-up by clicking on a "continue" button is recommended.

- Display disclosures prior to purchase—that is, before clicking an "order now" button or a link that says "add to shopping cart." Recognize, however, that placements limited only to the order page may not always work as disclosures might be required in close proximity to the particular claim or product.

- Incorporate disclosures in banner ads themselves or disclose them clearly and conspicuously on the web page to which the banner ad links.

- Display disclosures prominently so they are noticeable to consumers, and evaluate the size, color and graphic treatment of the disclosure in relation to other parts of the Web page. The disclosure should not be buried in a long paragraph of unrelated text. In Figure 2.4, for example, a consumer would likely miss the fact that the endorser was paid for his endorsement.

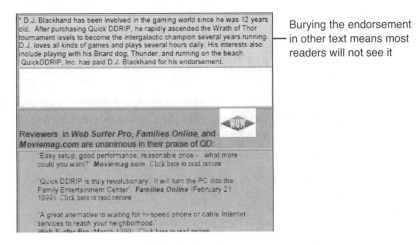

Burying the endorsement in other text means most readers will not see it

Figure 2.4 *This disclosure is too hidden to be effective.*

- Ensure that other elements of the ad—such as text, graphics, hyperlinks, or sound—do not distract consumers' attention from the disclosure.

- Repeat disclosures on lengthy web sites and in connection with repeated claims, both as needed.

- Use audio disclosures when making audio claims, and present them in a volume and cadence so that consumers can hear and understand them.

- Display visual disclosures for a duration sufficient for consumers to notice, read and understand them.

- Use clear language and syntax so that consumers understand the disclosures.

Disclosures in Social Media

These disclosure guidelines work well enough for traditional online marketing and advertising, but what about social media platforms, such as Twitter, where strict compliance with these disclosure requirements is practically impossible? To address these concerns, the FTC requested, in May 2011, formal public comments about how its guidance and regulations should be modified to reflect the realities of social media platforms. Public comments were accepted until August 10, 2011. The FTC identified the following areas of particular concern:

- What issues have been raised by new online technologies (for example, smartphones and tablets) and new Internet activities (for example, social networking and user-generated content)?

- What issues have been raised by new laws or regulations since 2000 (for example laws regarding privacy)?

- What research or other information regarding the online marketplace, online advertising techniques, consumer online behavior, or the effectiveness of online disclosures should be considered in a revised guidance document?

- What guidance in the original Dot Com Disclosures is outdated or unnecessary?

- What issues relating to disclosures have arisen from multi-party selling arrangements in Internet commerce, such as:

  - Established online sellers providing a platform for other firms to market and sell their products online

  - Website operators being compensated for referring consumers to other Internet sites that offer products and services

  - Other online affiliate marketing arrangements?

Although no revisions have yet been made to the Dot Com Disclosures (as of the date of publication), it is anticipated that any changes will keep intact the FTC's fundamental values of transparency and accuracy (to allow consumers to make intelligent decisions), while relaxing the rules and making them more flexible in light of the practical constraints of social media platforms.

Note

The FTC recognizes that it is difficult to make the required disclosures in a 140-character tweet, so it recommends using hashtags such as #paid-ad. For blogs, microblogs, online comments, social networks, video/photo sharing websites and podcasts, some recommend posting a link on the profile page directing people to a full "Disclosure and Relationships Statement." This statement should disclose how you work with companies in accepting and reviewing products and list any conflicts of interest that might affect the credibility of your sponsored or paid reviews.[14] The FTC's initiative to update its guidance or regulations concerning online advertising should clarify the appropriateness of such practices.

 Note

Note that the Endorsement Guides are administrative interpretations of the law designed to help advertisers and endorsers comply with the Federal Trade Commission Act (FTC Act).[15] These guidelines are not binding law themselves. In any law enforcement action challenging the allegedly deceptive use of testimonials or endorsements, the FTC has the burden of proving that the challenged conduct violates the FTC Act, which prohibits, among other things, "unfair methods of competition" and "unfair or deceptive acts or practices in or affecting commerce."[16] Whether a specific practice falls within the scope of conduct declared unlawful by the FTC Act must be decided on a case-by-case basis.

Lessons Learned from FTC Investigative and Enforcement Actions

The FTC's first "blogger-advertiser disclosure" investigation took place in April 2010, and targeted women's retailer Ann Taylor. According to the FTC, Ann Taylor violated the FTC's disclosure rules, by promising "special gifts" and entry into a "mystery gift-card drawing" to bloggers who the company expected would write positive reviews about its LOFT brand. The FTC expressed concern that bloggers who attended previews of LOFT's Summer 2010 collection failed to disclose that they had received gifts for posting blogs about the event.

Although an advertiser's provision of a gift to a blogger for posting blog content about an event would generally constitute a "material connection" (and hence trigger the need for disclosure), the FTC elected not to take action against Ann Taylor in part because:

- The event where bloggers were provided with gifts was a one-time occurrence; and

- The company subsequently adopted a written policy stating that it will not issue any gift to any blogger without first requiring bloggers to disclose receipt of any incentives.[17]

Similarly, later that year, the FTC brought charges against Reverb Communications, Inc., and its owner, for violating the FTC's disclosure rules.[18] In this case, the public relations agency, which was hired by video game developers, was accused of engaging in deceptive advertising by having employees pose as ordinary consumers posting game reviews at the online iTunes store, and not disclosing that the reviews came from paid employees working on behalf of the developers. (A sampling of the fraudulent reviews: "Amazing new game," "One of the best apps just got better," and "ONE of the BEST.")

Under the terms of the settlement, Reverb and its owner agreed to remove all endorsements that misrepresented the reviewer as an independent consumer, and agreed not to post any similar items without proper disclosures in the future. Notably, the company did not have to pay a fine nor admit any wrongdoing.

In November, 2011, the FTC also decided not to pursue enforcement action against Hyundai Motor America in connection with a campaign launched by a PR firm hired on its behalf to spark interest in Hyundai's Super Bowl XLV ads.[19] According to the FTC, bloggers were given gift certificates in exchange for linking to the car manufacturer's Web site in their blogs and/or commenting about the ads. The FTC further alleged that there was no disclosure that the bloggers received something in exchange for the promotion, as is required.

Following its initial investigation, the FTC eventually chose not to pursue enforcement action against Hyundai, citing several reasons:

- First, the car manufacturer did not appear to initially know about these incentives, only a small number of bloggers received the gift certificates, and some of them did, in fact, disclose this information.

- Second, the challenged actions were taken not by Hyundai employees, but by an employee of the media firm hired to conduct the blogging campaign. Notably, this individual's actions were in direct violation of

Hyundai's established social media policy, which called for bloggers to disclose their receipt of compensation, and the policies of the media firm.

• Third, the media firm promptly took action to halt the alleged misconduct upon learning of it.

 Note

It should be emphasized that the *Hyundai* decision is an apparent departure from the FTC's long-standing position of holding advertisers responsible for the conduct of their ad agencies and media firms. Companies should not expect to be automatically shielded from liability simply because it is the employees of the ad agencies they hire—and not employees of the companies themselves—that fail to make the proper disclosures required by the FTC Guidelines. Penalties for noncompliance can result in a $11,000 civil fine—per incident!

Other companies have not gotten off as easy. In March 2011, for example, a Tennessee company called Legacy Learning Systems, Inc.—and its owner, individually—were fined $250,000 for hiring affiliate marketers to pose as ordinary consumers and sing the praises of the company's guitar-lesson DVD series by writing glowing online reviews.[20] According to the FTC, such endorsements generated more than $5 million in sales of Legacy's courses. Because those affiliates failed to disclose they were getting paid substantial commissions for these endorsements, the FTC said the ads were deceptive and illegal.

The FTC's actions underscore the importance of companies establishing effective policies and compliance programs for their employees, and for the agencies and media firms they retain. At a minimum, companies should require—and vigilantly monitor and enforce—that all endorsers honor their obligation to properly disclose any incentives they receive to promote the company's products or services. This requirement should govern not just the conduct of the company's internal personnel, but that of outside agencies hired by the company as well.

Bottom line: Don't ignore the legal and ethical complexities of social media endorsements and testimonials; familiarizing yourself with the fundamentals—as summarized in Figure 2.5—will pay dividends for you and your brand.

Social Media Legal Tips for Endorsements and Testimonials

DOs	DON'Ts
■ Establish and distribute—within your company and to outside media agencies working on your behalf—a social media policy that requires endorsers to disclose any incentives they receive to promote your company's products or services.	■ Do not falsely assume that you are shielded from liability for the actions of your outside agencies. You are responsible for ensuring that these firms provide guidance and training to their bloggers concerning the need to disclose and to ensure that statements they make are truthful.
■ Clearly and conspicuously disclose—and require that your endorsers so disclose—any and all "material connections" between your company and endorsers in any ad, including whether the endorser is being paid, receiving a free product, or is an employee of your company.	■ Do not be misled into believing there is a *de minimis* exclusion—even if the value of the free product or service is minimal or the product is returned to the advertiser after review, endorsers should disclose the receipt or use of the free product, particularly if the endorser has an ongoing relationship with the advertiser.
■ Instruct bloggers not to make any false or misleading statements about your products or services, and monitor their blogs for compliance.	■ Do not fail to disclose the sponsored relationship for a product or service that was originally provided for free for each subsequent endorsement, even if the free product was provided at a much earlier occasion.
■ Remind bloggers that they may be liable for representations made in the endorsement if they fail to clearly and conspicuously disclose any payment or gift.	■ Do not continue to pay or provide gifts to rogue bloggers—that is, bloggers who fail to adhere to the FTC's disclosure requirements.
■ On Twitter, use hashtags such as #paid-ad, #paid, or #ad to make required disclosures. For blogs and other social networks, post a link on your profile page directing people to a full "Disclosure and Relationships Statement," disclosing how you work with companies in accepting and reviewing products and listing any conflicts of interest that might affect the credibility of your sponsored or paid reviews.	■ Do not place disclosures in inconspicuous places—for example, buried on an "About Us" or "General Info" page, behind a poorly labeled hyperlink ("Disclaimer" or "Legal"), or in a terms of service agreement. The average consumer who visits your site must be able to notice, read, and understand your disclosure.

Figure 2.5 *Social Media Legal Tips for Endorsements and Testimonials.*

CHAPTER 2 ENDNOTES

1   E-tailing group/PowerReviews 2010 Social Shopping Study, available at http://www.e-tailing.com/content/?p=1193

2   http://www.ag.ny.gov/media_center/2009/july/july14b_09.html

3   16 C.F.R. Part 255, available at http://www.ftc.gov/os/2009/10/091005endorsementguidesfnnotice.pdf

4   See FTC Facts for Business: The FTC's Revised Endorsement Guides: What People Are Asking, June 2010, available at http:// www.ftc.gov/bcp/edu/pubs/business/adv/bus71.pdf

5   16 C.F.R. § 255.5 (Example 7)

6   16 C.F.R. § 255.0 (Example 8)

7   16 C.F.R. § 255.5 (Example 8)

8   16 C.F.R. § 255.1 (Example 5)

9   Mary Engle, the FTC's Associate Director for Advertising Practices, reportedly told attendees at a 2010 blogging conference that disclosure of SWAG is not required if it is given to all members of a group, rather than to targeted individuals. In the former case, there is no special relationship between the advertisier and a blogger who got the SWAG. See http://getgood.com/road-maps/2010/06/29/travel-blogs-ethics-and-the-ftc-endorsement-guidelines/.

10 74 FR 53124, at 53127 (Oct. 15, 2009)

11 74 FR 53124, at 53136 (Oct. 15, 2009)

12 See "The FTC's Revised Endorsement Guides: What People Are Asking" (June 23, 2010), available at http://business.ftc.gov/documents/bus71-ftcs-revised-endorsement-guideswhat-people-are-asking

13 See "FTC's Dot Com Disclosures: Information about Online Advertising" (May 3, 2000), available at http://www.ftc.gov/os/2000/05/0005dotcomstaffreport.pdf

14 See, for example, The Word of Mouth Marketing Association Guide to Disclosure in Social Media Marketing (2010), available at http://womma.org/ethics/disclosure/

15 15 U.S.C §§ 41-58 (as amended)

16 15 U.S.C § 45

17 See FTC's 4/20/10 Closing Letter to Kenneth A. Plevan, Esq., Counsel for AnnTaylor Stores Corporation in case of AnnTaylor Stores Corporation (File No. 102 3147) available at http://www.ftc.gov/os/closings/100420anntaylorclosingletter.pdf.

18 In the Matter of Reverb Communications, Inc. et al., FTC File No. 092 3199 (Nov. 26, 2010). A copy of Complaint is available at http://www.ftc.gov/os/caselist/0923199/101126reverbcmpt.pdf.

19 See FTC's 11/16/11 Closing Letter to Christopher Smith, Esq., Counsel for Hyundai Motor America Hyundai in case of Hyundai Motor America (File No. 112 3110) available at http://www.ftc.gov/os/closings/111116hyundaimotorletter.pdf.

20 In the Matter of Legacy Learning Systems, Inc., et al., FTC File No. 102 3055 (Jun. 10, 2011). A copy of the Decision and Order is available at http://www.ftc.gov/os/caselist/1023055/110610legacylearningdo.pdf.

The [Mis]Use of Social Media in Pre-Employment Screening

Historically, employers have researched potential new hires through their applications, interviews, professional and personal references, background checks, and credit checks. With the advent of social media, however, more and more employers are reviewing Facebook, LinkedIn, Twitter, and other internet sites to screen applicants in making hiring decisions. Even a simple Google search can yield a treasure trove of potentially valuable information about an applicant's work history, education, extracurricular activities, and contacts.

According to the 2011 Jobvite Social Recruiting Survey[1]:

- *89% of employers will recruit in social networks this year.*
- *55% of employers will spend more on social recruiting.*
- *64% of employers use two or more networks for recruiting.*
- *78% of employers expect increased competition for hires.*

Likewise, according to a 2009 CareerBuilder Survey[2] of more than 2,600 hiring managers:

- 18% surveyed reported that information online encouraged them to hire candidates (see Figure 3.1).

- 35% reported that information online led them to not hire candidates (see Figure 3.2).

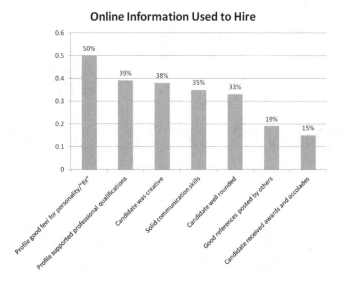

Figure 3.1 *Information found on social media sites sometimes leads employers to make job offers.*

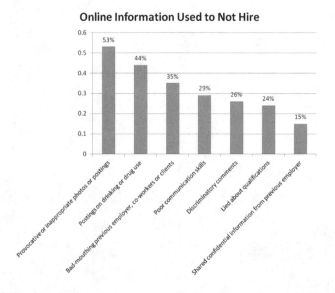

Figure 3.2 *Conversely, information found online often leads to an applicant not getting hired.*

For example, a prospective Cisco employee tweeted, "Cisco just offered me a job! Now I have to weigh the utility of a fatty paycheck against the daily commute to San Jose and hating the work." Reportedly, a self-described Cisco "channel partner advocate" saw the tweet and responded, "Who is the hiring manager. I'm sure they would love to know that you will hate the work. We here at Cisco are versed in the web." Clearly, this applicant failed to appreciate the not-so-"social" nature of her social media communications. Whether it was this tweet or something else that cost her the job, we may never know.

> Clearly, this applicant failed to appreciate the not-so-"social" nature of her social media communications.

Although there are ample *bona fide* business reasons for the use of social media in pre-employment screening, potential pitfalls exist for such screening as well. These pitfalls include obtaining information that is unlawful to consider in any employment decision, such as the applicant's race, religion, national origin, age, pregnancy status, marital status, disability, sexual orientation (some state and local jurisdictions), gender expression or identity (some state and local jurisdictions), and genetic information. Because this information is often prominently displayed on social networking profiles, even the most cautious employer may find itself an unwitting defendant in a lawsuit.

To minimize the likelihood of a charge of discrimination, employers should consider assigning a person not involved in the hiring process to review social media sites (pursuant to a standard written search policy), to filter out any information about membership in a protected class (that is, race, religion, and so on), and to only forward information that may be lawfully considered in the hiring process. Employers should keep records of information reviewed and used in any employment decision, and be sure that any information learned from social media sites in the employment decision process is used consistently.

 Note

An employer who circumvents an applicant's privacy settings on social media sites—by having a colleague "friend" the applicant for purposes of obtaining information they otherwise would not have access to, for example—might be exposing itself to a claim for invasion of privacy. To avoid this potential liability, employers should only view information that is readily accessible and intended for public viewing.

Employers should also familiarize themselves with the "off-duty" laws in each state where their employees are located and refrain from considering any protected activities in their hiring decisions. More than half of the states prohibit employers from taking an adverse employment action based on an employee's lawful conduct *on their own time* (that is, off the job), even if (in many cases) the employee is only a prospective employee. In Minnesota, for example, it is unlawful for an employer to prohibit a prospective employee from using lawful consumable products, such as alcohol and tobacco, during nonworking hours.[3] Further, New York protects all lawful recreational activities, including political activities, during nonworking hours.[4]

While employers can continue to use social media for recruiting purposes, they should take care not to violate existing laws in the hiring process (and be mindful of the various laws developing in this area as well).

The Fair Credit Reporting Act

Employers should also be alerted to the fact that pre-employment social media background checks—if not conducted correctly—might also give rise to liability under the Fair Credit Reporting Act (FCRA),[5] a federal law that protects the privacy and accuracy of the information in consumers' credit reports.

Employment background checks routinely include information from a variety of sources: credit reports, employment and salary history, criminal records, and (with increasing frequency) social media. Companies providing background reports to employers—and employers using such reports—must comply with the FCRA. The FCRA delineates consumers' rights as job applicants and employers' responsibilities when using credit reports and other background information to assess an employment application. Although the FCRA might not come immediately to mind when considering social media background checks, the FRCA does govern consumer reports "used for the purpose of evaluating a consumer for employment, promotion, reassignment, or retention as an employee."[6]

 Note

The FCRA—and similar state consumer protections laws (for example, California Investigative Consumer Reporting Agencies Act)—needs to be observed whenever social media content is used as part of a company's background check process. If your company uses a third party to collect information and provide it to you in a report, the FCRA is triggered. However, the FCRA does *not* apply if the company conducts the background screening entirely internally.

Before the FCRA was passed, little or no protection existed for job applicants who were denied employment or who were later fired because of false, inaccurate, incomplete, or irrelevant information contained in their consumers' reports, which were (then lawfully) obtained without the employee's knowledge or consent from private consumer reporting agencies. Congress enacted the FCRA to ensure that employment decisions, together with other matters (like extension of credit), are based on fair, accurate, and relevant consumer information.[7]

Under the FCRA, a *consumer report* is defined as any written, oral, or other communication of information provided by a consumer reporting agency bearing on a consumer's creditworthiness (and other credit-related) matters and/or his or her "character, general reputation, personal characteristics, or mode of living which is used or expected to be used or collected in whole or in part for the purpose of serving as a factor in establishing the consumer's eligibility for ... employment purposes."[8]

A subclass of consumer reports, called *investigative consumer reports*, contains information obtained through personal interviews with friends, neighbors, associates, and acquaintances of the consumer concerning the consumer's character, general reputation, personal characteristics, or mode of living.[9]

Both types of reports must be obtained through a *consumer reporting agency* ("CRA"), which is defined as "any person who regularly engages in whole or in part in the practice of assembling or evaluating consumer credit information or other information on consumers for the purpose of furnishing consumer reports to third parties."[10] To ensure the accountability of employers who use background information about their employees in making hiring, firing, or promotion decisions, employers must:

- Provide the applicant/employee with notice that a consumer report may be obtained, generally via a clear and conspicuous written disclosure to the consumer, found in a stand-alone document that consists solely of the disclosure,

- Obtain written authorization from the applicant/employee for the employer to obtain a consumer report for employment purposes, and

- Provide certain notices and certifications (detailed below) regarding the basis of any adverse employment decision.[11]

Although no court has yet squarely ruled on the issue, given the FCRA's broad scope, and the expansive definitions of *consumer reporting agency, consumer report,* and *investigative consumer report,* it is almost inevitable that background checks utilizing profiles and information stored with social networking services will be held to fall within FCRA's reach.

For companies that assemble reports about applicants based on social media content and regularly disseminate such reports to third parties (including affiliates), therefore, both the reporting company and the user of the report must ensure compliance with the FCRA, including the following provisions:

> It is almost inevitable that background checks utilizing profiles and information stored with social networking services will be held to fall within FCRA's reach.

- **Notice and authorization**—An employer must get the applicant's written permission before asking for a report about him/her from a CRA or any other company that provides background information. The employer has no further obligation to review the application if permission is withheld.[12]

If an employer intends to use an *investigative consumer report* (that is, a consumer report based on personal interviews by the CRA) for employment purposes, the employer must disclose to the applicant that an investigative consumer report may be obtained, and the disclosure must be provided in a written notice that is mailed, or otherwise delivered, to the applicant no later than three days after the date on which the employer first requests the investigative consumer report.[13] Further, the disclosure must also include a statement informing the applicant of his or her right to request additional disclosures of the "nature and scope" of the investigation.[14] In this regard, the disclosure "must include a complete and accurate description of the types of questions asked, the types of persons interviewed, and the name and address of the investigating agency."[15]

- **Due diligence**—The CRA or other company providing the background information must take reasonable steps to ensure the maximum possible accuracy of what's reported (from social network sites or otherwise) and that it relates to the correct person.

- **Pre-adverse action procedures**—If an employer might use information from a credit or other background report to take an adverse action (for example, to deny your application for employment), the employer must give the applicant a copy of the report and a document called *A Summary of Your Rights Under the Fair Credit Reporting Act* before taking the adverse action.[16] If any inaccurate or incomplete information is found in the report (for example, the report is for the wrong "John Smith", contains a false driving or criminal record, or inaccurately lists salary, job titles, or employers), the job applicant is advised to contact the company that issued the report and dispute the information. Following an investigation, the CRA or other company providing background information must send an updated report to the employer if the applicant asks them to.

- **Adverse action procedures**—If an employer takes an adverse action against an applicant based on information in a report, it must provide the applicant with notice, which can be in writing or delivered orally or by electronic means.[17] The notice must include the name, address, and phone number of the company that supplied the credit report or background information; a statement that the company that supplied the information did not make the decision to take the adverse action and cannot give the applicant any specific reasons for it; and a notice of the applicant's right to dispute the accuracy or completeness of any information in the report and to get an additional free report from the company that supplied the credit or other background information if the applicant asks for it within 60 days after receipt of the notice.[18]

Under the FCRA, companies selling background reports for employment must require that employers certify to the CRA that the report will not be used in a way that would violate federal or state equal employment opportunity laws or regulations. In an effort to reduce the risk of inadvertent discrimination or allegations of discrimination, employers should also require that companies conducting social media background checks remove protected class information (for example, race, religion, disability) from any reports they generate.

Real-World Examples

There is a growing rise in legal and regulatory scrutiny regarding social media background checks. A few illustrative cases are discussed here.

FTC v. Social Intelligence Corp.

On May 9, 2011, the FTC's Division of Privacy and Identity Protection sent a "no action" letter to Social Intelligence Corporation ("Social Intelligence"), "an Internet and social media background screening service used by employers in pre-employment background screening."[19] The FTC found that Social Intelligence is a consumer reporting agency "because it assembles or evaluates consumer report information that is furnished to third parties that use such information as a factor in establishing a consumer's eligibility for employment."[20] The FTC stated that the same rules that apply to consumer reporting agencies—including, notably, the FCRA—apply equally in the context of social networking sites.

The FTC completed its investigation and found that no further action was warranted at that time, but that its decision should "not to be construed as a determination that a violation may not have occurred," and that it "reserves the right to take further action as the public interest may require."[21]

In a letter dated September 19, 2011, Senators Richard Blumenthal (D-Conn) and Al Franken (D-Minn) wrote to Social Intelligence expressing concern that the company's "collection of online and social media information about job applicants and distribution of that information to potential employers may contain inaccurate information, invade consumers' right to privacy online, violate the terms of service agreements of the websites from which your company culls data, and infringe upon intellectual property rights." [22]

The letter raises a series of questions, which should be considered by all businesses that provide, or request, social media background checks, including:

- "How does your company determine the accuracy of the information it provides to employers?"

- "Is your company able to determine whether information it finds on a website is parody, defamatory, or otherwise false?"

- "Is your company able to differentiate among applicants with common names?"

- "Search engines like Google often provide archived versions of websites; these cached web pages may contain false information that was later updated. Search engines also provide "mirrors" of websites, like Wikipedia or blog articles; these mirrored pages may be archives of inaccurate information that has since been corrected. Is your company able to determine whether information it is providing is derived from an archived version of an inaccurate website?"

- "Does your company specify to employers and/or job applicants where it searches for information—e.g., Facebook, Google, Twitter?"

- "Is the information that your company collects from social media websites like Facebook limited to information that can be seen by everyone, or does your company endeavor to access restricted information?"

- "There appears to be significant violations of user's intellectual property rights to control the use of the content that your company collects and sells. .... These pictures [of the users], taken from sites like Flickr and Picasa, are often licensed by the owner for a narrow set of uses, such as noncommercial use only or a prohibition on derivative works. Does your company obtain permission from the owners of these pictures to use, sell, or modify them?"

FTC v. the Marketers of 6 Mobile Background Screening Apps

On January 25, 2012, the FTC sent warning letters to the providers of six mobile applications that can be used to obtain background screening information about individuals, allegedly including criminal history information.[23] The letters raised concern that such information could be used to make decisions about an individual's eligibility for employment, housing, or credit, in violation of the FCRA.

The companies that received the letters are Everify, Inc., marketer of the Police Records app, InfoPay, Inc., marketer of the Criminal Pages app, and Intelligator, Inc., marketer of Background Checks, Criminal Records Search, Investigate and Locate Anyone, and People Search and Investigator apps.

According to the letters, each company had at least one mobile app that involves background screening reports that include criminal histories, which are likely to be used by employers when screening job applicants. The letters explain that, in providing such histories to a consumer's current or prospective employer, the companies are providing "consumer reports" and therefore are acting as a "consumer reporting agency" (CRA) under the FCRA. The FTC reminded the companies of their obligations – and their apps users' obligations – to comply with the FCRA if they had reason to believe their reports were being used for employment or other FCRA purposes. According to the FTC, "[t]his is true even if you have a disclaimer on your website indicating that your reports should not be used for employment or other FCRA purposes," noting that the FTC "would evaluate many factors to determine if you had a reason to believe that a product is used for employment or other FCRA purposes, such as advertising placement and customer lists."[24]

Although the FTC made no determination that the companies were in fact violating the FCRA, it encouraged them to review their apps and their policies and procedures to ensure that they comply with the law, reminding them that a violation of the FCRA may result in legal action by the FTC, in which it is entitled to seek monetary penalties of up to $3,500 per violation.

If you use mobile applications, social media, or any other form of new media and technology to conduct background checks on your current or prospective employees, be aware that such activity will most likely be covered by the FCRA, especially if such information is being used for employment or other FCRA-restricted purposes.

Robins v. Spokeo, Inc.

The case of *Robins v. Spokeo, Inc.*[25] further illustrates the broad scope of the FCRA and how it applies to online entities and scenarios. In this case, Thomas Robins (the plaintiff), *on behalf of himself and others similarly situated* (a bit of legalese required in class-action lawsuits to include all eligible plaintiffs), initiated a class-action lawsuit under the FCRA against a search engine operator for collecting and disseminating false (and unflattering) information about him.

The defendant's website (Spokeo) enables users to connect with family, friends, and business contacts by searching for a name, email address, or phone number. Spokeo provides an in-depth report that displays the searched party's name, phone number, marital status, age, occupation, names of siblings and parents, education, ethnicity, property value, and wealth level.

Further, according to Robins in the complaint initiating the lawsuit, Spokeo markets itself to "human resource professionals, law enforcement agencies, persons and entities performing background checks, and publishes individual consumer 'economic health' assessments," previously referred to by the defendant as "credit estimates."

The court initially dismissed the case because Robins failed to plead actual or imminent harm or injury, which is necessary to achieve *standing*—that is, a personal stake in the outcome of the controversy sufficient to entitle a party to bring the lawsuit.[26] (For purposes of standing, the harm must be "actual" or "imminent", as opposed to conjectural or hypothetical. Allegations of possible future injury are generally insufficient to confer standing.)

Robins (who was unemployed) subsequently filed an amended complaint, wherein he alleged that he suffered actual harm in the form of anxiety, stress, concern and/or worry about his diminished employment prospects due to the incorrect information posted about him by Spokeo, including his age, marital status, "economic health" and "wealth level." The court found that the amended complaint contained sufficient allegations of harm for *standing*: "Plaintiff has alleged an injury in fact—the 'marketing of inaccurate consumer reporting information about Plaintiff'—that is fairly traceable to Defendant's conduct—alleged FCRA violations—and that is likely to be redressed by a favorable decision from this Court."[27]

Surprisingly, after Spokeo sought approval to appeal the district court's finding that Robins had standing, the district court reinstated its initial order (finding that the plaintiff lacked standing) and dismissed the case. The court held that:

> *"Among other things, the alleged harm to Plaintiff's employment prospects is speculative, attenuated and implausible. Mere violation of the Fair Credit Reporting Act does not confer Article III standing, moreover, where no injury in fact is properly pled. Otherwise, federal courts will be inundated by web surfers' endless complaints. Plaintiff also fails to allege facts sufficient to trace his alleged harm to Spokeo's alleged violations. In short, Plaintiff fails to establish his standing before this Court."*[28]

It is important to note that the case was not dismissed on the alternative basis advanced by Spokeo denying that it was a consumer reporting agency under the FCRA. In dismissing the case on standing grounds, the court left open the issue as to what types of online content aggregators fall within FCRA's purview. Prudence dictates, however, that whenever a company assembles and analyzes consumer credit information (including a consumer's character, general reputation, personal characteristics, or mode of living—for example, wealth, credit, lifestyle, home, education, and political persuasion) and markets it to third parties for a fee via the Internet, the company should heed the provisions of FCRA.

Employers who do not fully comply with the FCRA face significant legal consequences.

Employers who do not fully comply with the FCRA face significant legal consequences—for example, if they fail to get an applicant's authorization before getting a copy of their credit or other background report, fail to provide the appropriate disclosures in a timely manner, or fail to provide adverse action notices to unsuccessful job applicants. In addition to civil remedies for those injured by an employer's noncompliance with FCRA—which includes recovery of either actual damages or up to $1,000 plus punitive damages for willful noncompliance,[29] an employer who knowingly or willfully procures a consumer report under false pretenses may also be criminally fined and incarcerated for up to 2 years.[30]

Bottom line: Like traditional consumer reports, when social media consumer reports are used in connection with making employment-related decisions, employers must ensure that the reporting and decision-making were performed in compliance with the FCRA. People involved in the screening and hiring process would be wise to adhere to the best practices summarized in Figure 3.3 in order to stay on the right side of the law.

Social Media Legal Tips for Pre-Employment Screening

DOs	DON'Ts
■ Establish internal procedures for making employment decisions based on social media and web research to avoid running afoul of federal and state anti-discrimination and privacy laws.	■ Do not attempt to bypass a person's privacy settings in collecting social media information—for example, by impersonating a "friend" or creating a profile with the same city and/or alma mater of an applicant, in an attempt to see information restricted by geographical or university network.
■ Use a person not involved in the hiring process to review social media sites, to filter out any information regarding membership in a protected class (for example, race, religion, and national origin), and to only forward information that may be lawfully considered in the hiring process.	■ Do not forget to keep records of information reviewed and used in any employment decision, and be sure that any information learned from social media sites in the employment decision process is used consistently.
■ Be aware that pre-employment social media background checks may give rise to liability under the Fair Credit Reporting Act (FCRA). Companies providing background reports to employers—and employers using such reports—must comply with this law.	■ Do not conduct social media background checks on applicants/employees for any employment purpose without first obtaining their written authorization.
■ Require all job applicants to authorize you to perform background checks under the FCRA as part of the hiring process, as well as at other times during employment.	■ Do not assume that your managers are not using social media to screen applicants or employees, even if your company does not, as a matter of policy, conduct such background checks. Be sure to train your managers regarding the FCRA and its requirements.
■ Require that any third party providing you with social media background checks warrant that no laws—FCRA, privacy, copyright, or other intellectual property laws—have been violated in gathering the information from social networking sites.	■ Do not make employment decisions based upon an applicant's "off-duty" lawful conduct (such as tobacco or alcohol use), which most states prohibit employers from considering.

Figure 3.3 *Social Media Legal Tips for Pre-Employment Screening.*

CHAPTER 3 ENDNOTES

1   http://recruiting.jobvite.com/resources/social-recruiting-survey.php

2   http://www.careerbuilder.com/share/aboutus/pressreleasesdetail.aspx?id=pr519&sd=8%2F19%2F20
    09&ed=12%2F31%2F2009

3   Minn. Stat. Ann. § 181.938

4   N.Y. Lab. Code § 201-d.

5   15 U.S.C. § 1681 *et seq.*

6   15 U.S.C. § 1681a(h)

7   15 U.S.C. §1681(b)

8   15 U.S.C. § 1681a(d)(1)

9   15 U.S.C. § 1681a(e)

10 15 U.S.C. § 1681a(f)

11 15 U.S.C. §§ 1681a(f) and 1681b(b)

12 15 U.S.C. § 1681b(b)

13 15 U.S.C. § 1681d

14 *Id.*

15 *See* 40 Years of Experience with the Fair Credit Reporting Act: An FTC Staff Report with Summary
    of Interpretations (July 2011), available at http://www.ftc.gov/os/2011/07/110720fcrareport.pdf

16 15 U.S.C. § 1681b(b)

17 15 U.S.C. § 1681m(a)

18 *Id.*

19 *See* FTC's 5/9/11 Letter to Renee Jackson, Esq., counsel for Social Intelligence Corporation, available
    at http://ftc.gov/os/closings/110509socialintelligenceletter.pdf

20 *Id.*

21 *Id.*

22 *See* http://blumenthal.senate.gov/newsroom/press/release/blumenthal-franken-call-on-social-intelli-
    gence-corp-to-clarify-privacy-practice

23 *See* FTC Press Release (2/7/12), *FTC Warns Marketers That Mobile Apps May Violate Fair Credit
    Reporting Act,* available at http://www.ftc.gov/opa/2012/02/mobileapps.shtm

24 *See,* for example, FTC Warning Letter to Everify, Inc. (1/25/12), available at http://www.ftc.gov/
    os/2012/02/120207everifyletter.pdf

25 *Robins v. Spokeo, Inc.*, Case 2:10-CV-5306 ODW (AGR) (C.D. Cal. Jul. 20, 2010)

26 *Robins v. Spokeo, Inc.*, Case 2:10-CV-5306 ODW (AGR), slip op. at 2-3 (C.D. Cal. Jan. 27, 2011)
    (Order Granting Defendant's Motion to Dismiss)

27 *Robins v. Spokeo, Inc.*, Case 2:10-CV-5306 ODW (AGR), slip op. at 3 (C.D. Cal. May 11, 2011)
    (Order Granting in Part and Denying in Party Defendant's Motion to Dismiss Plaintiff's First
    Amended Complaint)

28 *Robins v. Spokeo, Inc.*, Case 2:10-CV-5306 ODW (AGR) (C.D. Cal. Sept. 19, 2011) (Order Correcting Prior Ruling and Finding Moot Motion for Certification)

29 15 U.S.C. § 1681n-o

30 15 U.S.C. § 1681q

Monitoring, Regulating, and Disciplining Employees Using Social Media

Social media has been aptly described as a double-edged sword for employers. Despite the obvious work-related benefits, employee use of social media is not without considerable risk. Employees can inadvertently disclose sensitive company information or trade secrets (for example, posting to Facebook about a pending business deal, launch and release dates, or contemplated reorganizations); post wrong or improper company information on social media sites, and thereby dilute the company's control over its own brand and content; send inappropriate messages of a romantic or sexual nature to co-workers, subjecting the employer to a discrimination or harassment lawsuit; compromise the company's data through viruses, malware, and other data security risks; or publicly disparage the employer and its products or services, or suppliers and competitors, and thereby damage the employer's reputation and goodwill.

Given the high potential for damage to an employer's business that can arise from an employee's irresponsible use of social media, employers are increasingly monitoring and disciplining workers over such misuse. As detailed below, such activities, although primarily motivated by sound business-related reasons, are nonetheless subject to legal scrutiny, putting employers at risk of monetary fines, reinstatement of terminated employees, payment of lost wages, and other damages.

Social media has been aptly described as a double-edged sword for employers. Despite the obvious work-related benefits, employee use of social media is not without considerable risk.

Employee Monitoring

Monitoring employee use of social media makes sound business sense, but companies need to keep limits in mind, particularly as they relate to employee's privacy rights under both federal and state law. For instance, accessing password-restricted sites handled by employees can violate many federal and state privacy laws, including the Stored Communications Act (SCA),[1] which makes it an offense to intentionally access stored communications without authorization or in excess of authorization.[2] Note, however, that the statute also provides an exception to liability with respect to conduct authorized by a user with regard to a communication intended for that user—for example, an employee affirmatively authorizes her employer to access her email account or Facebook page.[3]

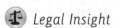 *Legal Insight*

An employer's use of its employees' personal social media accounts—even accounts which are partially used for business purposes—carries significant risk. In *Maremont v. Susan Fredman Design Group*,[4] for example, the employer, an interior design firm headquartered in Chicago, allegedly accessed its Director of Marketing's Twitter account and Facebook page, while she was hospitalized following a serious car accident. Although Maremont asked her employer to refrain from posting updates to her Facebook page and Twitter account while she was in the hospital and on medical leave, the employer refused to honor her request. Maremont filed a lawsuit against her employer for improperly using her identity to promote its services, even though these same accounts were used in the past to market the employer's business. In her Complaint, Maremont asserted, among other claims, false endorsement under the Lanham Act and violations of the SCA. On December 7, 2011, the court refused to dismiss both these claims, reasoning, as to the false endorsement claim, that "Maremont created a personal following on Twitter and Facebook for her own economic benefit and also because if she left her employment with [the interior design firm], she would promote another employer with her Facebook and Twitter followers."[5] In refusing to dismiss Maremont's SCA claim, the Court concluded that there were questions of material fact concerning whether the employer exceeded its authority in obtaining access to Maremont's personal Facebook and Twitter accounts. This case serves as an important reminder that companies should adopt social media policies that squarely address issues such as the distinction between personal and business social media accounts, who owns the accounts, and who is authorized to speak for the company on social media sites.

Pietrylo et al. v. Hillstone Restaurant Group[6] aptly illustrates the limits of employer monitoring of its employees' online activities. In this case, two restaurant employees set up an invitation-only MySpace chat room specifically to "vent about any BS we deal with [at] work without any outside eyes spying in on us." One restaurant manager accessed the chat room through her MySpace profile on an employee's home computer. Other managers were given the password after an employee felt "she would have gotten in some sort of trouble" if she did not comply. The chat room posts included sexual remarks about management and customers, jokes about some of the specifications that the restaurant had established for customer service and quality, and references to violence and illegal drug use. Because the remarks were found to be offensive and violative of company policy, the two employees principally responsible for the chat room were terminated.

The New Jersey Appeals Court rejected the restaurant's argument that the SCA did not apply, as the access was authorized. According to the Appeals Court, it was a jury question as to whether, under the circumstances, the obtaining of the password was coerced. At trial, the jury found that the restaurant did, in fact, violate the SCA, and that the employees' privacy interests were violated as a result of the unauthorized viewing of their chat room posts.[7]

 *Legal Insight*

In 2010, in the case of *City of Ontario v. Quon*,[8] the U.S. Supreme Court unanimously held that a public employer's review of an employee's text messages on an employer-issued pager was a reasonable search under the Fourth Amendment. After noticing that its employee Jeff Quon, a City of Ontario, California Police Sergeant and SWAT team member, had an excessive number of text messages, the city asked its service provider for copies of the text messages from Quon's phone. The city found that many of the messages received and sent on Quon's pager were not work-related, and some were sexually explicit (between Quon and his wife and his mistress). After being allegedly disciplined, Quon filed suit, claiming that his Fourth Amendment privacy rights had been violated.

After a jury trial, a federal district court in California held that the city did not violate Quon's Fourth Amendment rights. A U.S. federal Appeals Court disagreed, concluding that, although the search was conducted for "a legitimate work-related rationale," it "was not reasonable in scope."[9] Notably, the Appeals Court also held that the service provider violated the SCA when it provided the employee's text messages to the employer, without the employee's consent.

As to the alleged Fourth Amendment violation (the SCA claim not being accepted for further appeal), the Supreme Court reversed, holding that the employer had a right to see text messages sent and received on the employer's pager, particularly as the city had a policy providing that text messages would be treated like emails, so employees should have no expectation of privacy or confidentiality when using their pagers. Although the Supreme Court was cautious to narrowly limit its decision (and not to elaborate "too fully on the Fourth Amendment implications of emerging technology before its role in society has become clear"[10]), the case is nonetheless instructive to public and private employers alike, as it serves as a reminder for employers to have clear policies specifically reserving their right to monitor employee usage of Internet, e-mail and text messages, and establishing that employees should have no expectation of privacy in these communications when conducted on company-issued equipment (such as computers and cell phones).

Monitoring employee's off-duty social media conduct may also expose the employer to liability under state privacy laws. Several states have enacted lifestyle protection laws that prevent employers from prying too far into the personal lives of their employees, particularly when the information found has no bearing on the employer's business interest, the employee's job performance, or a bona fide occupational requirement.

Note

For example, Colorado forbids termination of employees based on any lawful activity conducted off employer's business premises during nonworking hours;[11] North Dakota prohibits discharging, and failing or refusing to hire if based on lawful off-duty conduct during nonworking hours;[12] and California provides that "[n]o person shall discharge an employee or in any manner discriminate against any employee or applicant for employment because the employee or applicant engaged in any [lawful conduct occurring during nonworking hours away from the employer's premises]."[13] Note, however, that, except for California, these prohibitions do not apply when an employee's off-duty behavior undermines a bona fide occupational requirement, an employee's job responsibilities, or an employer's essential business interests.

How far an employer may pry into its employees' off-duty social lives is perhaps best illustrated by the case of *Johnson v. Kmart*.[14] In this case, 55 plaintiffs brought an action for invasion of privacy based on an unauthorized (and secret) *intrusion into their seclusion*—that is, a tort which generally consists of an intrusion, offensive to a reasonable person, and in an area where a person is entitled to privacy. Kmart hired private investigators to pose as employees in one of its distribution centers to record employee conversations and activities not only at work, but also at social gatherings outside of the workplace. The reports contained highly personal information, including employee family matters (for example, the criminal conduct of employees' children, incidents of domestic violence, and impending divorces); romantic interests/sex lives (sexual conduct of employees in terms of number/gender of sexual partners); and personal matters and private concerns (employee's prostate problems, paternity of employee's child, characterization of certain employees as alcoholics because they drank "frequently").

The Appellate Court of Illinois denied Kmart's motion for *summary judgment*—that is, Kmart's request for a judgment in its favor as a matter of law—because the court found a *material issue of fact* (requiring jury resolution) existed regarding whether a reasonable person would have found Kmart's actions to be an offensive or objectionable intrusion. Although the employees willingly provided these personal details to the investigators, the means employed by Kmart to induce the employees to reveal this information were deceptive, particularly as Kmart admitted that it had no business justification for gathering information about its employees' personal lives. According to the court, "A disclosure obtained through deception cannot be said to be a truly voluntary disclosure. Plaintiffs had a reasonable expectation that their conversations with 'coworkers' would remain private, at least to the extent that intimate life details would not be published to their employer."[15]

Similarly, employees using social media do not expect their employer to covertly or deceptively peer into their private social lives. Rather, employees have a reasonable expectation of privacy that their employers will not secretly spy on them, whether in the real or virtual world. To avoid a claim of invasion of privacy, employers should generally refrain from monitoring their employees' off-duty social activity.

> To avoid a claim of invasion of privacy, employers should generally refrain from monitoring their employees' off-duty social activity.

 Legal Insight

An employee's reasonable expectation of privacy in an employment setting is a function of a variety of factors, including (most importantly) whether an employer has a policy notifying its employees that the employer monitors their use of internet, email (both web-based, personal email accounts and employer-provided accounts), telephones, and the like, for legitimate work-related reasons. In *Stengart v. Loving Care Agency, Inc.,*[16] for example, the New Jersey Supreme Court ruled that an employee did not waive the protection of the attorney-client privilege with respect to personal emails sent to her attorney from a company-issued laptop because she had a reasonable expectation that the correspondence would remain private. In this case, the plaintiff, Marina Stengart, the former Executive Director of Nursing at the defendant's home care services company, brought a discrimination claim against her former employer.. Prior to her resignation, Stengart communicated with her attorney about a potential action against her employer using her personal, password-protected Yahoo email account. (She never saved her Yahoo ID or password on the company laptop.) After Stengart filed suit, the company extracted and created a forensic image of the hard drive from plaintiff's computer. In reviewing Stengart's Internet browsing history, the employer was able to discover and read numerous email communications between Stengart and her attorney. Although the employer had an electronic communications policy disclosing that it may access and review "all matters on the company's media systems and services at any time," and that all e-mails, Internet communications, and computer files are the company's business records and "are not to be considered private or personal" to employees, the New Jersey Supreme Court found that this was insufficient to vitiate Stengart's reasonable expectation of privacy in the emails she sent to her attorney. According to the court:

- The employer's policy failed to give express notice to employees that messages exchanged on a personal, password-protected, web-based e-mail account are subject to monitoring if company equipment is used. Although the policy states that the employer may review matters on "the company's media systems and services," those terms are not defined.

- The policy does not warn employees that the contents of personal, web-based e-mails are stored on a hard drive and can be forensically retrieved and read.

- The policy creates ambiguity by declaring that e-mails "are not to be considered private or personal," while also permitting "occasional personal use" of e-mail.

The *Stengart* decision triggered a paradigm shift throughout the country dispelling the commonly-held belief that companies automatically own **all** electronic information found on their computers, and can use such information however they desire. Nonetheless, while not full-proof, a clearly worded and consistently enforced policy outlining what electronic communications (including those conducted on social media sites) are subject to employer monitoring is the best means to overcome any expectation of privacy that an employee may have in such communications.

Employer Regulation

As a general rule, courts have found employers will be held liable for the online actions of employees on company computers,[17] except where the employers took proactive steps to prevent misuse.

For example, in *Yath v. Fairview Clinics*,[18] an employee of a clinic disclosed to others that a patient had a sexually transmitted disease and a new sex partner other than her husband. This information was later posted on MySpace. The court declined to hold the employer vicariously liable for the acts of the employee in these circumstances because the employee's actions were not *foreseeable*, particularly as MySpace is a blocked website at the hospital, meaning that employees cannot access the site on the company's computer while at work.

Similarly, in *Delfino et al. v. Agilent Technologies, Inc.*,[19] a California Court of Appeals held that the employer was not liable for its employee's threatening messages (sent by email and posted on Internet bulletin boards), even though the employer's computers were used to send such messages. The court so ruled because the employer promptly terminated the employee upon discovering its computer systems were being used to send the messages. (The court also held that an employer that provided its employees with Internet access was among the class of parties potentially immune under § 230 of the Communications Decency Act [CDA] for cyber-threats transmitted by its employees.) (The CDA's impact on social media communications is discussed in Chapter 6, "Managing the Legal Risks of User-Generated Content.")

 Legal Insight

> Social media posts can also give rise to hostile work environment claims, even if the posts were made during off-work hours. Employers have a duty to prevent such misconduct (via policies and training), and to take prompt and reasonable corrective action when they learn of it. For the majority of courts, an employer is deemed to have *notice* (actionable awareness) of hostile/harassing conduct taking place in any company-sponsored online forum (for instance, an intranet chat room) even if the employer is unaware of such conduct in fact. With regard to private employee conduct online, employers do not have an obligation to persistently monitor or ferret out inappropriate conduct on the Web. However, an employer may be deemed to be on *constructive notice* (legal term for could have had and should have had actionable awareness) of what is taking place on private social media sites if its managers have access to these sites (for example, a manger is Facebook friends with several of the company's employees).

Employee Discipline for Social Media Use

Reprimanding or firing employees for comments they make in social networks is justifiable in some circumstances, but illegal in others. Understanding the differences between these scenarios when disciplining your employees for inappropriate conduct in social networks is therefore imperative.

The National Labor Relations Board's (NLRB) emerging position that employee discipline over social media usage may

Reprimanding or firing employees for comments they make in social networks is justifiable in some circumstances, but illegal in others.

violate Section 7 of the National Labor Relations Act (NLRA),[20] a federal labor law that prohibits companies from violating a worker's right to engage in protected, "concerted activity" with co-workers to improve working conditions,[21] presents employers with increasing danger when disciplining employees over their use of social media. Although *concerted activity* generally refers to two or more employees acting together to address a common employment-related concern, the NLRA also protects instances of concerted activity wherein a single employee's actions, on behalf of others, are a reasonable form of protest that will affect other employees.

 Note

> The NLRA prohibits employers from disciplining employees for discussing working conditions (such as wages, benefits, and the like), *regardless of whether or not the employee is a member of a labor union*. In other words, employers of nonunion workforces also have to ensure that adverse employment decisions comply with the law.

The following is a summary of the recent enforcement actions brought by the NLRB regarding possible violations of the NLRA arising from employer discipline for alleged employee misuse of social media. The lesson to be gleaned is that such discipline needs to be conducted with care.

Ambulance Service Provider

In October 2010, the NLRB filed a complaint[22] against American Medical Response of Connecticut, Inc. (AMR), an ambulance service, alleging that the company violated Section 7 of the NLRA when it discharged an emergency medical technician for violating the company's social media policy, which provided, in relevant part, as follows:

- "Employees are prohibited from posting pictures of themselves in any media, including but not limited to the Internet, which depicts the Company in any way, including but not limited to a Company uniform, corporate logo or an ambulance, unless the employee receives written approval from the [Company] in advance of the posting."

- "Employees are prohibited from making disparaging, discriminatory or defamatory comments when discussing the Company or the employee's superiors, co-workers and/or competitors."

In this case, the discharged employee posted disparaging comments on her Facebook page about her supervisor and criticized the company for its decision to make that person a supervisor in the first place, insinuating that the company allowed a "psychiatric patient" to be a supervisor. The Facebook posting drew comments from the employee's co-workers, to which the employee responded.

The NLRB took the position that the company's social media policy, along with the discharge of the employee, violates the NLRA because the employee and her co-workers were simply discussing their working conditions. As the NLRB observed, the policy was impermissibly overbroad, in so far as it restricted employees from engaging in protected activities, such as "posting a picture of employees carrying a picket sign depicting the Company's name, or wearing a t-shirt portraying the company's logo in connection with a protest involving the terms and conditions of employment."[23]

The case was subsequently settled, as part of which AMR agreed to narrow the scope of its social media policy so that it does not improperly restrict employees from discussing their wages, hours, and working conditions with co-workers and others while not at work.

Chicago Luxury Car Dealer

In May 2011, the NLRB issued an unfair labor practice complaint against a Chicago-area luxury car dealer alleging that the company illegally terminated a salesman after he posted photos and comments on Facebook criticizing the dealership for only offering its customers hot dogs and bottled water at a sales promotional event.[24] Even after he removed the posts at the dealership's request, the salesman was still terminated the following week. The NLRB alleged that the employee's post was voicing the "concerted protest and concerns" of several employees "about Respondent's handling of a sales event which could impact their earnings."[25]

However, on September 28, 2011, an administrative law judge (ALJ) with the NLRB issued an opinion holding that, while the NLRA protected the employee's sarcastic post, the dealership's termination decision was still lawful because it was based on other, unprotected Facebook content.[26] In the opinion, the ALJ noted that the NLRB had previously rejected the same argument in cases where employees' protected speech and tone were disparaging, unpleasant, mocking, sarcastic, satirical, ironic, demeaning, or even degrading. The decision is an important reminder for employers that when protected and unprotected content appear on the same social media site the protected content does not immunize the employee from discipline based on the unprotected content, provided that the unprotected speech was the real reason for the disciplinary decision.

⚖ *Legal Insight*

Employee rants are hardly a recent phenomenon. However, the proliferation of social media sites targeted at disgruntled employees—such as www.jobvent.com, www.hateboss.com, www.fthisjob.com, and so on—represents a particularly thorny dilemma for employers wanting to curtail such speech. While social media policies often include broad provisions to limit negative, offensive, or disparaging statements related to employment, employers should review their policies for overbroad statements regarding employee speech. Because the NLRA prohibits employers from disciplining employees for discussing working conditions, regardless of whether the employees are members of a labor union (or not), all employers need to reexamine their social media policies to make sure they comply with the law.

Not every job-related grievance an employee may post on the Internet is protected. The NLRB continues to require that the employee's *speech* posted on social media be related to *protected concerted activity* (that is, encouraging workers to engage in activity to better the terms and conditions of their employment) before it will protect that speech from employer discipline. To be considered *concerted*, the activity must have been engaged in with or on the authority of other employees, and not solely by and on behalf of the employee himself.[27] While this is a highly fact-specific determination, concerted activity has been found when the circumstances involve group activities, whether the activity is formally authorized by the group or otherwise.[28] Individual activities that are the "logical outgrowth of concerns expressed by the employees collectively"[29] are also considered concerted.

Advice Memoranda

In July 2011, the NLRB's Office of the General Counsel issued three advice memoranda that clarified the NLRB's position on when it is appropriate to discipline an employee who engages in misconduct through social media.

Advice Memorandum 1: JT's Porch Saloon

The first advice memoranda, *JT's Porch Saloon*,[30] addressed a charge filed by a bartender at an Illinois restaurant. Under the employer's tipping policy, waitresses do not share their tips with the bartenders even though the bartenders help the waitresses serve food. During his employment, the aggrieved employee complained to a fellow bartender about the tipping policy, and she agreed that it "sucked."

However, neither of them, or any other bartender, ever raised the issue with management. Instead, several months later, the aggrieved bartender had a Facebook conversation with his stepsister, a nonemployee, wherein the bartender complained that he had not had a raise in 5 years and was doing the waitresses' work without the benefit of tips. He also posted derogatory comments about the restaurant's customers, calling them rednecks and stating that he hoped they choked on glass as they drove home drunk.

Although the bartender's Facebook comments did address terms and conditions of his employment, the NLRB found that this Internet activity was not concerted in nature and therefore was not protected. The memorandum pointed out that the bartender did not discuss the social media posting with any of his co-workers either before or after it was written and that none of his colleagues responded to the posting. Further, the bartender made no attempt to initiate group action to change the tipping policy or to raise his complaints with management. The comments were simply to his stepsister. The NLRB therefore concluded that the employer's decision to terminate the employee (via Facebook, ironically enough) was not an unfair labor practice.

Advice Memorandum 2: Wal-Mart

In the second advice memorandum, *Wal-Mart*,[31] the NLRB held that a customer service employee's Facebook postings criticizing his manager were not concerted action, where the posting included vulgar terms for the manager and subsequent messages of support from fellow employees. In this case, the employee's postings stated, "I swear if this tyranny doesn't end in this store they are about to get a wakeup call because lots are about to quit!" The employee also commented, in a posting riddled with expletives, that he would be talking to the store manager about his grievances. A few co-workers responded to his Facebook postings and made supportive replies, such as "hang in there."

The NLRB General Counsel concluded that even though these posts addressed the employee's terms and conditions of employment and were directed to co-workers, they did not constitute protected activity. More than "mere griping" is needed. Here, the employee was merely expressing his personal "frustration regarding his individual dispute with the Assistant Manager over mispriced or misplaced sale items." Therefore, there was no outgrowth of collective concerns, and the employee was not seeking to initiate or induce collective action. The General Counsel also concluded that the co-workers' humorous and sympathetic responses did not convert the posts to group action because the responses demonstrated their belief that the employee was only speaking on his own behalf.

⚖ Legal Insight

Concerted activities lose their protection under the NLRA if they are sufficiently *opprobrious* (outrageously disgraceful or shameful) or if they are disloyal, reckless, or *maliciously untrue* (that is, made with knowledge of their falsity or with reckless disregard for their truth or falsity). This test may produce seemingly inconsistent and sometimes surprising results. For instance, statements have been found to be unprotected where they are made "at a critical time in the initiation of the company's" business and where they constitute "a sharp, public, disparaging attack upon the quality of the company's product and its business policies, in a manner reasonably calculated to harm the company's reputation and reduce its income."[32] But, stating that a company's president does his "dirty work ... like the Nazis during World War II"[33] or that a supervisor is a "dick" and "scumbag"[34] (when not accompanied by verbal or physical threats) was held to be protected.

As a general rule, whether the employee has crossed the line depends on the following:

- Whether the statement was made outside of the workplace and/or during nonworking hours;

- The subject matter of the statement (that is, whether it discusses terms and conditions of employment); and

- Whether the employee's outburst was provoked by the employer's unfair labor practices.

Advice Memorandum 3: Martin House

The third advice memorandum, *Martin House*,[35] involved a recovery specialist who worked at a residential facility for homeless people, including those with significant mental health issues. While working an overnight shift, the employee engaged in a conversation with friends on her Facebook wall in which she stated that it was "spooky" to work at night in a "mental institution" and joked about hearing voices and popping pills with the residents. None of the individuals who replied to the recovery specialist's postings were co-workers, nor was the recovery specialist a Facebook friend with any of her colleagues. She was a Facebook friend, however, with a former client of her employer, who reported her concerns to the employer after she saw the postings. The recovery specialist was discharged for her Facebook postings, which inappropriately used a client's illness for her personal amusement and which disclosed confidential information about clients.

The NLRB General Counsel determined that the recovery specialist had not engaged in any protected concerted activity. Instead, she had merely communicated with her personal friends about what was happening on her work shift. She did not discuss her Facebook posts with her fellow employees, and only personal friends responded to the posts. The aggrieved employee was not seeking to induce or prepare for group action and her activity did not grow out of employees' collective concerns. In light of these facts, the employer was within its rights to discharge the employee.

 Note

> Can an employee's disparaging 140-character tweet against an employer ever constitute concerted activity protected by the NLRA? In one recent case,[36] a Thomson Reuters reporter—in response to a supervisor's alleged invitation to send Twitter posts about how to "make Reuters the best place to work"—posted the following to Twitter: "One way to make this the best place to work is to deal honestly with Guild members." This tweet allegedly violated a company policy that prohibited employees from saying anything that would "damage the reputation of Reuters News or Thomson Reuters." After the reporter was reprimanded for the tweet, the NLRB threatened it would file a case against Thomson Reuters, claiming the employer's policy and its application to this journalist violated the NLRA because it would reasonably tend to chill employees in the exercise of their right to engage in concerted activity. Rather than face a trial, Reuters agreed to settle the case by adopting a new social media policy that included language referencing employees' right to engage in "protected concerted activity."

Lawfully Disciplining Employees

Recognizing the need to clarify when an employer can lawfully discipline an employee for social networking misconduct without violating the NLRA, on August 18, 2011, the NLRB's Acting General Counsel published a 24-page memorandum summarizing the outcome of investigations into 14 cases involving employee use of social media and employer's policies governing such use.[37] The findings are highly fact specific, but the memorandum emphasized the fact that many of the policies at issue were impermissibly broad, as employees could reasonably construe them to prohibit protected conduct. In other words, a social media policy prohibiting employees from making disparaging remarks when discussing the company or supervisors may be overly broad, whereas the same policy with limiting language informing employees that the policy did not apply to NLRA-protected activity would more likely pass muster.

Further, on January 24, 2012, the NLRB's Acting General Counsel released a second report[38] describing social media cases reviewed by its office, seven of which address issues regarding employer social media policies, and another seven of which involve discharges of employees after they posted comments to Facebook.

The report reconfirms:

- Employer policies should not be so sweeping that they prohibit the kinds of activity protected by federal labor law, such as the discussion of wages or working conditions among employees

- An employee's comments on social media sites are generally not protected if they are mere gripes not made in relation to group activity among employees.

Based on the continuing wave of legal challenges against social media policies and employment practices, companies should tread carefully before disciplining employees for social networking misconduct. Before an adverse employment decision is made, the following factors (none of which alone are dispositive) should be considered:

- Whether the social media post was submitted during working hours or on the employee's own time

- Whether the employee is using a social media platform to comment on wages, benefits, performance, staffing levels, scheduling issues, or other terms and conditions of employment

- Whether the social media activity appears to initiate, induce, or prepare for group action (versus mere griping)

- Whether the employee's co-workers had access to the social media postings

- Whether co-workers responded to or otherwise participated in the social media postings and, if so, whether their responses suggest group action

Note

A policy precluding employees from pressuring co-workers to "friend" them does not violate the NLRA, because such a prohibition is designed to prevent harassment and cannot reasonably be interpreted to preclude social media communications that are protected concerted activity.

In the wake of the first NLRB memorandum, on September 2, 2011, a ruling in the first-ever adjudicated social media firing case was reached in *Hispanics United Of Buffalo, Inc. v. Ortiz.*[39] In this case, an NLRB administrative law judge (ALJ) ruled that Hispanics United of Buffalo, Inc. (HUB) violated the NLRA when it terminated five employees for criticizing a sixth co-worker's job performance on Facebook, even though the Facebook postings were made on the employees' own computers outside of working hours.

The first challenged Facebook posting read as follows:

> "Lydia Cruz, a coworker feels that we don't help our clients enough at HUB I about had it! My fellow coworkers how do u feel?"

The co-workers responded through Facebook by making such postings as these:

> "What the f. .. Try doing my job I have 5 programs;" What the H..., we don't have a life as is, What else can we do???;" Tell her to come do mt [my] f...ing job n c if I don't do enough, this is just dum;" I think we should give our paychecks to our clients so they can "pay" the rent, also we can take them to their Dr's appts, and served as translators (oh! We do that). Also we can clean their houses, we can go to DSS for them and we can run all their errands and they can spend their day in their house watching tv, and also we can go to do their grocery shop and organized the food in their house pantries ... (insert sarcasm here now)"

The original poster responded:

> "Lol. I know! I think it is difficult for someone that its not at HUB 24-7 to really grasp and understand what we do ... I will give her that. Clients will complain especially when they ask for services we don't provide, like washer, dryers stove and refrigerators, I'm proud to work at HUB and you are all my family and I see what you do and yes, some things may fall thru the cracks, but we are all human love ya guys"

After the targeted employee, Lydia Cruz-Moore, brought the postings to her director's attention, HUB terminated the employees involved in the posts as they allegedly constituted bullying and violated HUB's policy on harassment. In concluding that the terminations violated the NLRA, the ALJ stated:

> "Employees have a protected right to discuss matters affecting their employment amongst themselves. Explicit or implicit criticism by a co-worker of the manner in which they are performing their jobs is a subject about which employee discussion is protected by Section 7. That is particularly true in this case, where at least some of the discriminatees had an expectation that Lydia Cruz-Moore might take her criticisms to management. By terminating the five discriminatees for discussing Ms. Cruz-Moore's criticisms of HUB employees' work, Respondent violated Section 8(a)(1) [which prohibits employers from interfering with, restraining, or coercing employees in the exercise of their Section 7 rights to engage in concerted protests or complaints about working conditions]."[40]

Notably, the ALJ further concluded, "It is irrelevant to this case that the [terminated employees] were not trying to change their working conditions and that they did not communicate their concerns to [HUB]." [41] According to the ALJ, just as employee complaints to each other concerning schedule changes constitute protected activity, so are discussions about criticisms of their job performance.

 Note

Unlike private employers, government employers have the additional obligation of avoiding violating their employees' First Amendment (and similar) rights by disciplining them for content posted on social media sites, particularly if the online speech is of public concern.

When it comes to mitigating your company's social media risks, employee monitoring alone is not enough. Here, an ounce of prevention is really worth a pound of cure. Arming employees with social media training and best practices (see Figure 4.1) will not only reduce your company's legal risks, but also increase the effectiveness of your company's social media programs and initiatives. Employee social media training therefore makes sense from both a return-on-investment and a legal-compliance perspective.

Legal Tips for Monitoring, Regulating, and Disciplining Employees Using Social Media

DOs	DON'Ts
■ When monitoring employee use of social media, companies need to keep limits in mind, particularly as they relate to employee's privacy rights under both federal and state law.	■ Do not adopt social media policies, which include broad prohibitions against damaging the employer's reputation, embarrassing the employer, or which otherwise broadly prohibit employees from discussing the company, its management, employees or competitors, or from making any disparaging remarks, or engaging in any inappropriate discussions, without providing limiting language explicitly stating that such prohibitions do not apply to activity protected by Section 7 of the NLRA.
■ Establish proper training and guidelines to minimize the adverse risks arising from employee use of social media. Guidelines should prohibit the posting of comments about coworkers, supervisors, customers, third-party vendors or the employer that are vulgar, obscene, threatening or intimidating, or a violation of the employer's policies against discrimination or harassment on account of age, race, religion, sex, ethnicity, nationality, disability, or any other protected class.	■ Do not monitor employee's off-duty social media conduct. Doing so may expose the employer to liability under state privacy laws. Several states have enacted lifestyle protection laws that prevent employers from prying too far into the personal lives of their employees, particularly when the information found has no bearing on the employer's business interest, the employee's job performance, or a bona fide occupational requirement.
■ Prohibit employees from representing in any way that they are speaking on the company's behalf without prior written authorization to do so.	■ Do not require employees to avoid identifying themselves as employees of the employer unless discussing the terms and conditions of employment in an "appropriate" manner, without defining "appropriate"—either through specific examples of what is covered or through limiting language that would exclude Section 7 NLRA activity.
■ Employers may discipline employees for their postings to social media sites that do NOT relate to the terms and conditions of employment (such as wages, benefits, and so on) and/or that are NOT directed at or do not involve other employees. However, individual gripes not made in relation to group activity among employees are not protected.	■ Do not discipline or fire employees for their postings to social media sites that discuss the terms and conditions of employment with, or seek advice from, other employees regarding job performance, staffing levels, supervisory actions, wages, salary, and commissions, or concerns about workplace responsibilities or policies, even if the postings contain insulting or offensive language.

- Include a disclaimer in your social media policy that it will not be construed or applied to limit employees' rights under the NLRA or applicable law, even for discussions the employer may consider unprofessional or inappropriate.

- Do not rely exclusively upon a disclaimer to comply fully with the NLRA, as provisions elsewhere in your policy may be ambiguous and reasonably interpreted as restricting the exercise of NLRA rights.

- Prohibit employees from using the company's name or logo when engaging or depicting in social media any conduct which violates the company's policies or is unlawful.

- Do not adopt "no name/logo" prohibitions that do not make it clear that the use of the company's name and logo is permitted while engaging in protected concerted activity.

- Remind employees that they may not disclose the employer's (or its customers') confidential, proprietary, or non-public information, or trade secrets, on any social networking site. Be sure to provide examples of the types of information deemed confidential, proprietary, and non-public (e.g., personal health information about customers or patients) and clarify that the policy does not prohibit Section 7 NLRA activity (such as discussing wages with family members, for example).

- Do not allow employees to promote the company's business on the employees' personal media accounts, absent an agreement specifying that the employer own the social media account and any followers related to the account.

- Draft policies that clearly and unambiguously describe any employer monitoring of employee use of work computers and other electronic devices, and clearly disclose that such use is not private. Be sure to also include an explanation of how employee web activity can be captured in temporary internet files or otherwise stored on a work computer's hard drive and may be later "forensically retrieved" and reviewed by the employer. Obtain a signed acknowledgment of receipt of the policy from each employee.

- Do not forget to specify in your social media and electronic communications policy that emails and social media messages sent or received on a personal, web-based account on a work computer (or via a company server) are subject to employer monitoring, whenever it furthers the employer's legitimate business interests.

- Enforce your social media policies uniformly, particularly as they relate to employee discipline for social networking activity. Also, draft your social media policies from the perspective of what conduct a "reasonable" employee would construe as being limited.

- Avoid policies that include overly broad, ambiguous or undefined prohibitions against "offensive conduct," "rude and discourteous behavior;" or "inappropriate discussions," wherever such prohibitions do not include limiting language to remove potential ambiguities regarding whether Section 7 NLRA activity is prohibited.

Figure 4.1 *Legal tips for Monitoring, Regulating, and Disciplining Employees Using Social Media.*

CHAPTER 4 ENDNOTES

1   18 U.S.C. § 2701 *et seq.*

2   18 U.S.C. § 2701(a)(1):

"(a) Offense. -Except as provided in subsection (c) of this section whoever -

(1) intentionally accesses without authorization a facility through which an electronic communication service is provided;… shall be punished as provided in subsection (b) of this section."

3   18 U.S.C. § 2701(c)(2):

(c) Exceptions. - Subsection (a) of this section does not apply with respect to conduct authorized -
…

(2) by a user of that service with respect to a communication of or intended for that user;…"

4   *Maremont v. Susan Fredman Design Group, Ltd. et al.*, Case No. 1:10-CV-07811 (N.D.Il. Dec. 9, 2010)

5   See Memorandum Opinion and Order (Document No. 58) (Dec. 7, 2011), in *Maremont v. Susan Fredman Design Group, Ltd. et al.*, Case No. 1:10-CV-07811 (N.D.Il. Dec. 9, 2010)

6   *Pietrylo et al. v. Hillstone Restaurant Group*, 2008 U.S. Dist. LEXIS 108834 (D.N.J. 2008)

7   *Pietrylo v. Hillstone Rest. Group*, 2009 U.S. Dist. LEXIS 88702, *; 29 THAT ISR. Cas. (BNA) 1438

8   *City of Ontario et al. v. Quon et al.*, 130 S. Ct. 2619 (2010)

9   *City of Ontario et al. v. Quon et al.*, 529 F. 3d 892, 908 (9th Cir. 2008)

10 *City of Ontario et al. v. Quon et al.*, 130 S. Ct. 2619, at 2629 (2010)

11 COLO. REV. STAT. 24-34-402.5 (2006)

12 N.D. CENT. CODE §14-02.4-03 (2004)

13 CAL. LAB. CODE §98.6(a) (2003)

14 *Johnson v. Kmart Corp.*, 723 N.E.2d 1192 (Ill. App. 2000)

15 *Id.* at 1196

16 *Stengart v. Loving Care Agency, Inc.*, 990 A.2d 650 (N.J. 2010)

17 *See*, for example, *Doe v. XYZ Corp.*, 382 N.J. Super. 122 (App. Div. 2005) (where employer sued for negligence arising from an employee's use of company's computers to post naked pictures of his minor stepdaughter on a child-pornography website, court allowed case to go to trial even though employer had policy against monitoring of or reporting the Internet activities of its employees)

18 *Yath v. Fairview Clinics*, N. P., 767 N.W.2d 34 (Minn. App. Ct.) (2009)

19 *Delfino et al. v. Agilent Technologies, Inc.*, 145 Cal. App. 4th 790 (Ct. of Appeals of Calif., 6th App. District 2006), *cert. denied*, 52 U.S. 817 (2007)

20 The National Labor Relations Act, Pub.L. 74-198, 49 Stat. 449, codified as amended at 29 U.S.C. §§ 151–169.

21   Section 7 of the NLRA provides in relevant part:

"Employees shall have the right to self-organization, to form, join, or assist labor organization, to bargain collectively through representatives of their own choosing, and to engage in other concerted activities for the purpose of collective bargaining or other mutual aid or protection, and shall also have the right to refrain from any or all of such activities...." (29 U.S.C. § 157)

22   *American Medical Response of Connecticut, Inc.,* Case No. 34-CA-12576 (Region 34, NLRB) (Oct. 27, 2010)

23   *Id.*

24   *NLRB v. Knauz BMW,* Div. of Advice No. 13-CA-045452 (Jul. 21, 2011)

25   *Id.*

26   A copy of the ALJ's opinion is available at http://mynlrb.nlrb.gov/link/document.aspx/09031d45

27   *Meyers Industries (Meyers I),* 268 NLRB 493 (1984), *revd. sub nom Prill v. NLRB,* 755 F.2d 941 (D.C. Cir. 1985), *cert. denied* 474 U.S. 948 (1985), *on remand Meyers Industries (Meyers II),* 281 NLRB 882 (1986), *affd. sub nom Prill v. NLRB,* 835 F.2d 1481 (D.C. Cir. 1987), *cert. denied* 487 U.S. 1205 (1988)

28   *Meyers II,* 281 NLRB at 887

29   *See,* for example, *Five Star Transportation, Inc.,* 349 NLRB 42, 43-44, 59 (2007), *enforced,* 522 F.3d 46 (1st Cir. 2008) (Drivers' letters to school committee raising individual concerns over a change in bus contractors was a logical outgrowth of concerns expressed earlier at a group meeting.)

30   *JT's Porch Saloon,* NLRB Div. of Advice No. 13-CA-46689 (Jul. 7, 2011)

31   *Wal-Mart,* NLRB Div. of Advice No. 17-CA-25030 (Jul. 19, 2011)

32   *Endicott Interconnect Technologies, Inc. v. NLRB,* 453 F.3d 532, 537 (D.C. Cir. 2006)

33   *Konop v. Hawaiian Airlines, Inc.,* 302 F.3d 868 (Ct. App., 9th Cir. 2002)

34   *American Medical Response of Connecticut, Inc.,* Case No. 34-CA-12576 (Region 34, NLRB) (Oct. 27, 2010)

35   *Martin House,* NLRB Div. of Advice No. 34-CA-12950 (Jul. 19, 2011)

36   http://www.nytimes.com/2011/04/30/business/media/30contracts.html?_r=1&scp=1&sq=Zabarenko&st=nyt

37   Report of the Acting General Counsel Concerning Social Media Cases Within the Last Year (Memorandum OM 11-74) (August 18, 2011), *available at* https://www.nlrb.gov/news/acting-general-counsel-releases-report-social-media-cases

38   Updated Report of the Acting General Counsel Concerning Social Media Cases Within The Last Year (Memorandum OM 12-31) (Jan. 24, 2012), *available at* http://mynlrb.nlrb.gov/link/document.aspx/09031d45807d6567

39   *Hispanics United Of Buffalo, Inc. v. Ortiz,* NLRB Case No. 3-CA-27872 (Sept. 2, 2011)

40   *Id.*

41   *Id.*

5

Social Media in Litigation and E-Discovery: Risks and Rewards

Given the ubiquity of social media in the modern world, it is little wonder that social media content has become an increasingly common (and vital) component of litigating business disputes.

Why should businesses care about the role social media plays in litigation? First and foremost, what companies and their employees say on social media sites can be used against them. Conversely, your adversaries' posts, blogs, or Tweets can potentially be used against them as well. As social networking sites become more popular, courts and litigants are increasingly confronted with challenges surrounding the discoverability and admissibility of the information posted on those sites.

This chapter discusses the growing use of social media in the courtroom, and the steps companies need to take to properly discover, preserve, and authenticate such evidence.

Note

Social media presents unique challenges to businesses trying to manage their litigation risks. Indeed, an employee who responds to an online complaint regarding its company's products—even without the company's authorization —might be exposing (albeit, unwittingly) its employer to potential liability. If the employee posts something that is not accurate, for example, or that is otherwise inconsistent with the employer's official stance, this may undermine the employer's litigation position. What companies and their employees (even when not speaking in an official capacity) say online matters.

E-Discovery of Social Media

Users of social networks typically share personal information, pictures and videos, thereby creating a virtually limitless depository of potentially valuable, discoverable evidence for litigants.

Indeed, there is growing number of court cases where social media is playing a key role. For example:

- In *Offenback v. LM Bowman, Inc. et al.*,[1] the plaintiff was ordered to turn over Facebook account information that contradicted his claim of personal injury; namely, despite claims that his motor vehicle accident prevented him from riding a motorcycle or being in traffic or around other vehicles, his Facebook postings showed that he continued to ride motorcycles, even on multistate trips.

- In *EEOC v. Simply Storage Mgmt., LLC*,[2] a court in Indiana ordered the plaintiffs to produce social media postings, photographs, and videos "that reveal, refer, or relate to any emotion, feeling, or mental state" in a sexual harassment case where plaintiffs alleged severe emotional distress injuries, including post-traumatic distress disorder.

- In *Largent v. Reed*,[3] a Pennsylvania court granted defendant's motion to compel plaintiff to produce her Facebook username and password as her public Facebook profile included status updates about exercising at a gym and several photographs showing her enjoying life with her family that contradicted her claim of damages—that is, depression, leg spasms, and the need to use a cane.

- In *Barnes v. CUS Nashville, LLC*,[4] a magistrate judge in Tennessee created a Facebook account and requested that the witnesses accept

the judge as a Facebook friend "for the sole purpose of reviewing photographs and related comments *in camera*" for discoverable materials
relating to plaintiff's personal injury claim.

The wealth of social media information has recently raised the issue of whether
parties are entitled to discovery of an adversary's social networking data, even
when that data is designated as *private*.

Under federal and state laws governing procedures in civil courts, *discovery* is
the pretrial phase in a lawsuit in which each party can obtain evidence from the
opposing party (via requests for answers to interrogatories, requests for production of documents, requests for admissions, and depositions) and from nonparties
(via depositions and subpoenas). Generally, a party can obtain discovery regarding
any nonprivileged matter that is relevant to any part's claim or defense, or that
is reasonably calculated to lead to the discovery of admissible evidence.[5] Several
courts have ruled that the content of social media is generally discoverable, despite
privacy objections.[6]

 Note

"Privileged" matters, such as confidential communications between an
attorney and his/her client, or a doctor and his/her patient, are generally
afforded special legal protection, such that the person holding the privilege
(for example, the client or patient) may refuse to disclose, and prevent
any other person from disclosing, any privileged communications. In most
circumstances, given the relatively public nature of social media platforms,
it's not likely that any communications taking place thereon would be
deemed "privileged."

Under state and federal court rules, parties to a lawsuit are required to disclose
(without awaiting a discovery request) a copy of all electronically stored information (ESI) that the disclosing party has in its possession, custody, or control and
which it may use to support its claims or defenses.[7] Businesses must take measures
to preserve ESI not only at the inception of a lawsuit, but whenever litigation is
reasonably anticipated (that is, the time before litigation when a party should have
known that the evidence may be relevant to likely future litigation). In this regard,
parties are required to initiate a *litigation hold*, halting the destruction of potentially relevant documents.

The duty to preserve ESI, therefore, might include requesting third-party providers, such as social media providers, to segregate and save relevant data. Whether
the case involves a commercial dispute, employment litigation, or personal
injury—postings, pictures and messages transmitted through social media sites can
be a valuable source of discovery.

Note

ESI generally presents more challenges in discovery and litigation holds than traditional hard-copy information, and the use of social media only increases those challenges. For example, given the inherently dynamic nature of social media, a risk exists that information held on a social media site may be changed or removed at any given moment for any number of reasons. Therefore, the legal hold requirement may mean downloading the information and retaining it in another format (such as a screen capture or PDF printout). Both Facebook and Twitter have procedures for the preservation and procurement of information from the sites, should a litigation hold be required. Care must be taken, however, to capture sufficient data so that it may be properly authenticated at trial and admitted into evidence.

Because discovery of social media communications can be used against a company in a lawsuit, employers should remind their employees that their postings might not be protected and that anything they say may be used against the company. Certainly, in the event of pending or anticipated litigation, employers should ensure that their employees do not post anything that might undermine the company's legal position.

Companies should also be mindful of the serious penalties that exist for certain failures to produce ESI. Is the loss of ESI due to a routine, *good faith* operation of an electronic system? If not, significant sanctions may be imposed for failure to produce ESI—including dismissal of your case, or a default judgment in favor of your opponent. A company's retention policies, together with its routine destruction cycles, must be well documented to avoid the possible inference that any loss of ESI (including information placed on a company's branded social networking sites) was the result of *bad faith*—such as the deliberate destruction, mutilation, alteration or concealment of evidence. In this regard, whenever litigation is *reasonably anticipated*, the destruction of a company's ESI should be immediately suspended to avoid the negative inference.

> Employers should remind their employees that their postings might not be protected, and that anything they say may be used against the company.

 *Legal Insight*

While there do not appear to be any court decisions directly addressing the issue of whether a litigant can be sanctioned for failing to proactively preserve information on a social networking site, companies should consider sending their opponents a preservation letter specifically including such information and seek sanctions if they fail to abide. Because parties have control over what information is posted (and deleted) on their social media networking sites, court may be willing to consider sanctioning parties for failing to produce a copy of their communications on such sites.

In *Katiroll Co. v. Kati Roll and Platters, Inc.*,[8] for example, a federal district court found that a spoliation inference was not appropriate—and sanctions were therefore not warranted—where a party changed his social media profile picture during the course of litigation as he had not been explicitly requested to preserve such evidence. This case involved a trademark infringement claim between two restaurants that sell a similar food called kati rolls (a type of Indian kebab wrapped in flatbread). Although the owner of one restaurant changed his profile picture on Facebook from a picture displaying the infringing trade dress without preserving that evidence, the court found that it would not have been immediately clear to him that changing his profile picture would undermine discoverable evidence and that any spoliation was therefore unintentional.

The Stored Communications Act

Information placed on social networking sites such as Facebook, YouTube, and Twitter is increasingly being sought by adversaries in a lawsuit. Access to this information can often make or break a case because such information may contain details that contradict (or weaken) the claims being asserted in the litigation. Limits apply to accessing this information, however, particularly as the Stored Communications Act (SCA)[9] relates to discovery requests.

 *Legal Insight*

There is no expectation of privacy in information available to the public, whether posted on- or off-line. Applying this concept in the social media context, one California appellate court found that the plaintiff did not have a reasonable expectation of privacy in an article she posted on MySpace because it was "available to any person with a computer" and thus open for public viewing (and republication).[10] As felicitously noted by another court, "[t]he act of posting information on a social networking site, without the poster limiting access to that information, makes whatever is posted available to the world at large."[11] Such information should be freely accessible without giving rise to an invasion of privacy claim.

The SCA was enacted because the advent of the Internet presented a host of potential privacy breaches that the Fourth Amendment's prohibition against unreasonable governmental searches and seizures does not address. It creates a set of Fourth Amendment-like privacy protections by statute, regulating the relationship between government investigators and service providers in possession of users' private information, including email and other digital communications stored on the Internet:

- First, the statute limits the government's right to compel providers to disclose information in their possession about their customers and subscribers.

- Second, the statute limits the right of an Internet service provider (ISP) to disclose information about customers and subscribers to the government voluntarily.

- Among the most significant privacy protections of the SCA is the ability to prevent a third party from using a subpoena in a civil case to get a user's stored communications or data directly from an electronic communication service (ECS) provider or a remote computing service (RCS) provider.[12]

 Note

The SCA distinguishes between a remote computing service (RCS) provider and an electronic communication service (ECS) provider, establishing different standards of care for each. The SCA defines an ECS as any service which provides to users thereof the ability to send or receive wire or electronic communications—such as, for example, email and text messaging services providers. With certain enumerated exceptions, the SCA prohibits an ECS provider from knowingly divulging to any person or entity the contents of a communication while in "electronic storage" by that service.[13]

The SCA defines RCS as the provision to the public of computer storage or processing services by means of an electronic communications system, and in turn defines an electronic communications system (as opposed to an electronic communication service) as any wire, radio, electromagnetic, photo-optical or photoelectronic facilities for the transmission of wire or electronic communications, and any computer facilities or related electronic equipment for the electronic storage of such communications. An electronic bulletin board is an example of an RCS. The SCA prohibits an RCS provider from knowingly divulging to any person or entity the contents of any communication which is carried or maintained on that service, if the provider is not authorized to access the contents of the communications for purposes of providing services other than storage or computer processing.[14]

Because the SCA is silent on the issue of compelled third party disclosure, courts have interpreted the absence of such a provision to be an intentional omission reflecting Congress's desire to protect user data, in the possession of a third-party provider, from the reach of private litigants.

For instance, in *Crispin v. Audigier, Inc.*,[15] a California federal district court determined that the SCA applies to social media posts, provided that the poster had established privacy settings intended to keep other users from viewing the content without authorization.

In this case, the defendants issued third-party subpoenas to Facebook and MySpace, among others, to obtain all messages and wall postings that referred to the defendants. The court held that the plaintiff was entitled to *quash the subpoenas* (that is, have them declared void), finding that the SCA applied to these communications because the social media site providers were electronic communication services.

According to the court, the content in question was electronically stored within the meaning of the SCA and therefore could not be accessed without authorization. As a result, messages sent using the sites and content posted but visible only to a restricted set of users (that is, Facebook friends) were both subject to the SCA, and the court disallowed the defendants' discovery request. The *Crispin* court drew a distinction, however, between plaintiff's private messages and wall postings because wall postings are generally public, unless specifically protected by the user. Accordingly, the *Crispin* court remanded the case back to the magistrate judge for a determination of whether the plaintiff's privacy settings rendered these wall postings unprotected by the SCA.

Although *Crispin* suggests that a user's efforts to make communications on social networking sites private is a key factor in determining whether a user's communications are protected by the SCA, some courts have still required parties to provide access to this purportedly private information.

In *Romano v. Steelcase*,[16] for example, a New York Supreme Court ordered a plaintiff to execute a consent and authorization form providing defendants access to information on the social networking sites she utilized, including Facebook and MySpace. The defendants were entitled to this information because it was believed to be inconsistent with plaintiff's claims concerning the extent and nature of her injuries. Indeed, the plaintiff's public profile page on Facebook showed her smiling happily in a photograph outside her home despite her claim that she sustained permanent injuries and is largely confined to her house and bed. The information on these social networking sites further revealed that the plaintiff enjoyed an active lifestyle and traveled out of state during the time period she alleges that her injuries prohibited such activity.

Note

As it relates to the discovery process, courts generally do not permit parties to conduct a *fishing expedition*—that is, to throw the discovery net
indiscriminately wide hoping to find something, somewhere.[17] Accordingly,
a litigant will most likely not be entitled to another party's social network
information without an adequate showing of relevancy to the claims and
defenses in the litigation.

For litigants seeking the contents of an adversary's private social networking
account, *Crispin* and *Romano* provide important guidance. In certain cases, as in
Romano, litigants may be ordered to relinquish access to their entire social networking sites that may be *relevant and material*—that is, sufficiently related to, and
tending to prove or disprove—the issues in the pending case, notwithstanding the
party's privacy settings. In other cases, like *Crispin*, access to an adversary's social
networking pages can be obtained directly by the social networking site, not by a
subpoena (which the SCA generally prohibits), but rather with the consent of the
user, which can be compelled by a court order.

Legal Insight

In *Crispin,* the court quashed those portions of the Facebook and MySpace
subpoenas to the extent they sought private messaging, finding such content to be protected by the SCA. However, as to the portions of the subpoenas that sought Facebook wall postings and MySpace comments, the
court required additional information regarding plaintiff's privacy settings
and the extent to which he allowed access to his social media postings and
comments.

Presumably, disclosure would be permitted if public access were allowed
since the SCA does not apply to an "electronic communication [that] is
readily accessible to the general public."[18] Importantly, *Crispin* addressed
only the private messaging aspects of social networking websites; it did not
consider whether other content on a user's page, such as photos, videos,
"likes," subscription lists, "follows," lists of "friends," *etc.*, could be disclosed in response to a subpoena.

In this regard, it should be noted that the SCA only protects "communications" from disclosure. Whether a court will interpret this term broadly
enough to encompass all of the user's information on a social media website (and not just "communications" as traditionally understood) remains
to be seen.

Authenticating Social Networking Site Evidence at Trial

Documents may not be admitted into evidence at trial unless they are properly *authenticated* (that is, proven to be genuine, and not a forgery or fake).[19] Given the anonymous nature of social networking sites, and the relative ease in which they can be compromised or hijacked, authenticating social networking site evidence is particularly challenging.

In *Griffin v. Maryland*,[20] for example, the Court of Appeals of Maryland ordered a new trial of a criminal conviction. The court based the new trial order solely on the prosecutor's failure to properly authenticate certain social media pages used during trial.

> Authenticating social networking site evidence is particularly challenging.

During the defendant, Antoine Levar Griffin's trial, the state sought to introduce his girlfriend's MySpace profile to demonstrate that she had allegedly threatened a key witness prior to trial. The printed pages contained a MySpace profile in the name of Sistasouljah (a pseudonym), listed the girlfriend's age, hometown, and date of birth, and included a photograph of an embracing couple, which appeared to be that of Griffin and his girlfriend. The printed pages also contained the following posting, which substantiated the witness's intimidation claim:

> "JUST REMEMBER SNITCHES GET STITCHES!! U KNOW WHO YOU ARE!!"

Griffin was convicted of second-degree murder, first-degree assault, and illegal use of a handgun, and was sentenced to 50 years in prison.[21]

On appeal, Griffin objected to the admission of the MySpace pages because "the State had not sufficiently established a connection" between Griffin's girlfriend and these documents.[22] The intermediate appellate court denied the appeal and concluded that the documents contained sufficient indicia of reliability because the testimony of the lead investigator and the content and context of the pictures and postings properly authenticated the MySpace pages as belonging to her.[23]

The Maryland Court of Appeals reversed this holding, finding instead that the picture of the girlfriend, coupled with her birth date and location, were not sufficient *distinctive characteristics* on a MySpace profile to authenticate its printout.[24]

First, as the court observed, although MySpace typically requires a unique username and password to establish a profile and access, "[t]he identity of who generated the profile may be confounding, because 'a person observing the online profile of a user with whom the observer is unacquainted has no idea whether the profile is legitimate.' ... The concern arises because anyone can create a fictitious account and masquerade under another person's name or can gain access to another's account by obtaining the user's username and password."[25]

Second, the court noted the potential for user abuse and manipulation on social media sites:

- Fictitious account profiles and fake online personas (spoofing)
- Relative ease of third-party access and source of information
- Potential manipulation of photographs through Photoshop

These risks require a *greater degree of authentication* than merely a date of birth or picture to establish the identity of the creator or user of a social networking site.[26]

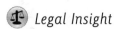 *Legal Insight*

Courts in other jurisdictions have also wrestled with the issue of authenticating social media evidence in light of how relatively easy it is to manipulate such "evidence". For example, in *People v. Lenihan*,[27] a New York criminal judge refused to admit MySpace photos of the prosecution's witnesses depicting them (together with the deceased victim) as gang members in part because of the potential manipulation of the images through Photoshop.

Likewise, in *State v. Eleck*,[28] the Appellate Court of Connecticut agreed with the trial court's decision to exclude from evidence a printout documenting messages allegedly sent to the defendant (Robert Eleck) by the victim from her Facebook account. Despite evidence that the victim added Eleck to her Facebook "friends" before sending the messages and removed him after testifying against him, this was insufficient to establish that the messages came from the victim, and not simply from her Facebook account.

Similarly, in *Commonwealth v. Williams*,[29] the Supreme Judicial Court (SJC) in Massachusetts found that the trial judge erred in admitting into evidence the contents of several MySpace messages from the criminal defendant's brother—urging a witness not to testify against the defendant or to claim a lack of memory about the events at her apartment the night of the murder—without proper authentication. According to the SJC, "[a]lthough it appears that the sender of the messages was using [defendant] Williams's MySpace Web "page," there is no testimony ... regarding how secure such a Web page is, who can access a Myspace Web page, whether codes are needed for such access, etc. Analogizing a Myspace Web page to a telephone call, a witness's testimony that he or she has received an incoming call from a person claiming to be "A," without more, is insufficient evidence to admit the call as a conversation with "A." ... Here, while the foundational testimony established that the messages were sent by someone with access to Williams's MySpace Web page, it did not identify the person who actually sent the communication." [30]

The *Griffin* court proposed three methods by which social media evidence could be properly authenticated (in both criminal and civil cases):

- **Deposition testimony**—At deposition, the purported creator can be asked if he/she created the profile and the posting in question. Although the Fifth Amendment's protection against self-incrimination precludes a criminal defendant from being forced to testify, no similar restrictions exist in the civil context.

- **Forensic investigation**—The purported creator's computer's Internet history and hard drive can be examined to determine whether that computer was used to originate the social networking profile and posting in question. An inspection of a computer's and mobile phone's *evidentiary trail* is a valuable means of establishing whether the subject hardware included the actual devices used in originating the profile/posting.

- **Subpoena third-party social networking website**—A subpoena to the social networking website provider can be issued to obtain information related to the purported users' accounts and profiles, and that "links the establishment of the profile to the person who allegedly created it and also links the posting sought to be introduced to the person who initiated it."[31]

Businesses—and their attorneys—should move to preclude any adverse postings allegedly from their employees that are not properly authenticated.

Businesses can cite the following factors as additional grounds to challenge the authenticity (and thereby seek to preclude the admissibility) of potentially damaging social networking site evidence:

- Whether the social networking site allows users to restrict access to their profiles or portions thereof

- Whether the account in question is password protected

- Whether others have access to the account

- Whether the account has been hacked in the past

- Whether the account is generally accessed from a public or private computer

- Whether the account is generally accessed from a secured or unsecured network

- Whether the posting in question came from a public or private area of the social networking site

- Whether the appearance, contents, substance, internal patterns, or other distinctive characteristics of the posting, considered in light of the circumstances, show it came from a particular person

The challenges associated with an increase in legal liability arising from ESI and social media information (and their preservation and proper destruction) may be painful, particularly for companies with limited resources. The tips outlined in Figure 5.1 serve as actionable guidelines for mitigating the risks social media may present in the litigation of business disputes.

Social Media Legal Tips for Litigation and E-Discovery

DOs	DON'Ts
■ Remind your employees that their social media postings might not be protected, even if their accounts are set as "private." Anything they post online may be used against the company.	■ Do not allow employees to discuss sensitive business content online. Social postings, which give away delicate information, may derail business dealings and your litigation position.
■ Thoroughly mine social media sites for potential evidence to use against your opponent. Be sure to conduct a social media search of your company as well, to ascertain what information your opponent may discover about you.	■ Do not use deceptive tactics to obtain social network content, such as impersonating a "friend" to gain access to a user's private profile information.
■ Be sure to request at the outset of litigation, or of anticipated litigation, that your opponent preserve social media content in its current state, and that any such information not be removed or altered in any way. Failure to do so may result in any claimed spoliation being deemed unintentional.	■ Do not seek indiscriminate and unfettered access to your opponents'—or their witnesses'—private social media accounts. Requests that are less intrusive and narrowly tailored to address relevant content and date ranges have a greater chance of being enforced.
■ Whenever litigation is reasonably anticipated, issue an immediately-effective and comprehensive litigation hold notice to all your and employees agents to identify and preserve any documents that may be relevant to the dispute, including electronically stored information (ESI) and content on social media sites.	■ Do not allow your opponent to introduce into evidence any social media (or other online) content that is not properly authenticated—that is, shown to be what it purports to be and from whom it purports to be from.
■ Educate all employees about the risks of sanctions and adverse inferences if ESI is lost or destroyed.	■ Do not forget to suspend the routine destruction of your company's ESI whenever litigation is reasonably anticipated—otherwise, you face possible dismissal of your case, an automatic judgment in favor of your opponent, and payment of your opponents' attorneys' fees and costs.

Figure 5.1   *Social Media Legal Tips for Litigation and E-Discovery.*

CHAPTER 5 ENDNOTES

1   *Offenback v. LM Bowman, Inc. et al.*, Case No. 1:10-CV-1789 (M.D. Pa. June 22, 2011)

2   *EEOC v. Simply Storage Mgmt., LLC*, 270 F.R.D. 430 (S.D. Ind. 2010)

3   *Largent v. Reed*, 2009-1823 (Pa. C.P. Franklin Co. Nov. 8, 2011) ("There is no reasonable expectation of privacy in material posted on Facebook." "Only the uninitiated or foolish could believe that Facebook is an online lockbox of secrets.")

4   *Barnes v. CUS Nashville, LLC*, Case No. 3:09-CV-00764 (M.D. Tenn. June 3, 2010)

5   *See,* for example, Federal Rules of Civil Procedure, Rule 26(b)

6   *See,* for example, *Romano v. Steelcase*, 907 N.Y.S.2d 650 (N.Y. Sup. Ct., Suffolk Co. 2010); *Patterson v. Turner Construction Co.*, 931 N.Y.S.2d 311 (N.Y. App. Div. 2011) ("The postings on plaintiff's online Facebook account, if relevant, are not shielded from discovery merely because plaintiff used the service's privacy settings to restrict access…, just as relevant matter from a personal diary is discoverable.")

7   *See,* for example, Federal Rules of Civil Procedure, Rule 26(a)(1)(A)(ii)

8   *Katiroll Co. v. Kati Roll and Platters, Inc.*, Case No. 3:2010-CV-03620, Docket No. 151, Memorandum Order (D.N.J. Aug. 3, 2011)

9   18 U.S.C. § 2701 *et seq.*

10 *Moreno v Hartford Sentinel, Inc.*, 91 Cal. App. 4th 1125 (2009)

11 *Independent Newspapers, Inc. v. Brodie*, 966 A.2d 432, 438 n 3 (Md. 2009)

12 *See* 18 U.S.C. §§ 2702(a)(1) and 2702(a)(1)(a)(2)

13 *See* 18 U.S.C. § 2702(a)(1)

14 See 18 U.S.C. § 2702(a)(2)

15 *Crispin v. Audigier, Inc.*, 717 F.Supp.2d 965 (C.D. Calif. May 26, 2010)

16 *Romano v. Steelcase,* 907 N.Y.S.2d 650 (N.Y. Sup. Ct., Suffolk Co. 2010)

17 *See,* for example, *Caraballo v. City of New York*, 2011 N.Y. Misc. LEXIS 1038, at *6 (N.Y. Sup. Richmond County, Mar. 4, 2011) (Defendant's motion to compel discovery of plaintiff's social networking site information denied because "digital 'fishing expeditions' are no less objectionable than their analog antecedents.")

18 18 U.S.C. §2511(2)(g)

19 *See,* for example, Federal Rules of Evidence, Rule 901(a), which provides: "The requirement of authentication or identification as a condition precedent to admissibility is satisfied by evidence sufficient to support a finding that the matter in question is what its proponent claims."

20 *Griffin v. Maryland*, 19 A.3d 415 (Md. Apr. 28, 2011)

21 *Griffin v. Maryland*, 995 A.2d 791 (Md. Ct. Spec. App. 2010)

22 *Id.* at 796

23 *Id.* at 806–807

24 *Griffin v. Maryland*, 19 A.3d 415, 424 (Md. Apr. 28, 2011). Note: Under Federal Rules of Evidence, Rule 901(b)(4), a piece of evidence may be authenticated through its "appearance, contents, substance, internal patterns, or other distinctive characteristics, taken in conjunction with circumstances."

25 *Id.* at 421

26 *Id.* at 424

27 *People v. Lenihan*, 911 N.Y.S.2d 588 (N.Y. Sup. Queens Cty. 2010)

28 *State v. Eleck*, 130 Conn. App. 632 (Conn. App. Ct. 2011)

29 *Commonwealth v. Williams*, 456 Mass. 857, 926 N.E.2d 1162 (Mass. 2010)

30 *Id.* at 869

31 *Griffin v. Maryland, supra*, at 428

Managing the Legal Risks of User-Generated Content

Unlike paid media, user-generated content (UGC), also known as consumer-generated media (CGM), describes a wide range of digital media created and shared by consumers. UGC consists of materials that users post to a website for public consumption, and is often inspired by product or service experiences. UGC can take on a wide variety of forms, including reviews, feedback, testimonials, ratings, Twitter tweets, Facebook postings, photos, comments, and videos posted on social networks, blogs, forums, clubs, groups, wikis, review sites and e-commerce sites (such as Amazon.com, which hosts a number of customer product reviews).

UGC can be a key driver of website traffic, thereby increasing the site's value and its organic search engine page rank. Because this type of content is regularly updated, it is an instrumental ingredient for search engine optimization (SEO) purposes. UGC also serves as an effective and influential means to capture leads, and increase website conversion rates and sales based on positive reviews, testimonials, and endorsements.

Despite these benefits, however, UCG should not be viewed only as a corporate asset. The use of UGC also presents a number of legal challenges concerning potential copyright infringement, defamation, invasion of privacy, and the like which makes it a significant source of potential liability as well. Whenever UGC is involved, businesses need to remain vigilant against hosting content that is defamatory (against a person or another business, employee, competitor, or vendor), offensive, pornographic, racist, sexist, or otherwise discriminatory, or that infringes another's IP or privacy rights.

Fortunately, important legal safeguards exist which serve to shield businesses hosting impermissible UGC from such potential liability. This chapter examines these safeguards, in particular, the Digital Millennium Copyright Act (DMCA), and the Communications Decency Act (CDA). Generally speaking, the DMCA protects website operators against claims of copyright infringement associated with UCG it hosts; and the CDA protects website operators from claims of defamation and invasion of privacy rights arising from UGC hosted on their sites.

To enjoy the protections offered by the DMCA and CDA, however, businesses are required to fully comply with a very detailed set of legal requirements, leaving little room for error. Because the law imposes an extremely high level of detail upon businesses seeking DMCA and CDA "safe harbor" protection, the descriptions contained in this chapter are necessarily highly detailed as well. Strict compliance with these requirements (albeit, exacting) nevertheless should allow businesses harnessing UGC to do so without losing their statutory immunity.

Copyright in the Age of Social Media

Because social media sites are not exempt from traditional copyright laws, copyright infringement is unquestionably the greatest intellectual property (IP) legal issue facing UGC providers. Even uploading another's picture onto the company's Facebook page without the author's consent might violate the author's copyright. To avoid civil and criminal law sanctions for copyright infringement, care should be taken to ensure that all necessary rights for publication on social networking sites have been properly assigned and that any uploaded content is noninfringing of another's copyright.

 Note

Australia's Virgin Mobile phone company's recent high-profile dispute regarding its alleged misuse of UGC is a helpful reminder that companies should obtain permission from all relevant parties before using another's photo (or other UGC), including the subjects depicted in the photo as well as its author. In that case, Virgin Mobile—as part of its "Are You With Us Or What?" marketing campaign to promote free text messaging and other services—allegedly grabbed a picture of teenager Alison Chang from Flickr (a popular photo-sharing website), and plastered her photo on billboards throughout Australia without her consent. (See Figure 6.1.) In the ad, Virgin Mobile printed one of its campaign slogans, "Dump your pen friend," over Alison's picture. Further, to 16-year-old Chang's great embarrassment, at the bottom of the ad was also printed "Free text virgin to virgin." Chang (through her mother since Chang was a minor) filed suit against Virgin Mobile in the U.S., alleging invasion of privacy (misappropriating her name and likeness without her consent) and libel (false statements subjecting her to public humiliation).[1] The photographer, Justin Ho-Wee Wong, also a plaintiff in the suit, brought an action for, among other matters, copyright infringement and breach of contract for Virgin Mobile's alleged failure to properly attribute him as the photographer.

Although the case is still pending (and no final decision has yet been reached), Virgin Mobile serves as a helpful lesson to other businesses using UGC to be sure to have all necessary permissions in place before such content is used.

Copyright infringement is traditionally divided into three categories: direct infringement, contributory infringement, and vicarious infringement.

Figure 6.1 *Virgin Mobile ad using another's photo and likeness allegedly without permission. (Original photo by Justin Ho-Wee Wong from his Flickr photo-sharing web page.)*

Direct Infringement

In a claim for *direct copyright infringement*,[2] the injured party must show that it owns the copyright in the work and that the defendant violated one or more of the plaintiff's exclusive rights under the Copyright Act,[3] including the rights to:

- Reproduce the copyrighted work[4]

- Prepare derivative works based on the copyrighted work[5]

- Distribute copies of the copyrighted work[6]

- Publicly perform copyrighted literary, musical, dramatic, and choreographic works, pantomimes, and motion pictures and other audiovisual works[7]

- Publicly display copyrighted literary, musical, dramatic, and choreographic works, pantomimes, and pictorial, graphic, or sculptural works, including the individual images of a motion picture or other audiovisual work[8]

- Publicly perform copyrighted sound recordings by means of a digital audio transmission[9]

A company may be liable for direct infringement whenever it uses a copyrighted work of another without permission. While such conduct may appear innocuous, uploading another's song or photo onto your site—even those found on the web "for free"—without permission are examples of direct copyright infringement.

Contributory Infringement

To prevail under a claim of *contributory copyright infringement*, a plaintiff must show that the defendant (a) has knowledge of the infringing activity; and (b) induces, encourages, or materially contributes to the infringing conduct of the direct infringer.[10]

In other words, just as selling burglary tools to a burglar may expose you to liability, if you provide the means (for example, software) that allows users to share copyrighted works with the objective of promoting infringement, you may be held "contributorily" liable for the direct infringement of those third parties.

Vicarious Infringement

Finally, in the case of *vicarious copyright infringement*, the defendant may be held liable for another's direct infringement if the defendant (a) had the right and ability to monitor and control the direct infringer; and (b) profits from the infringing activity.[11]

By way of example, the operator of a flea market in which counterfeit recordings were regularly sold was found to be a vicarious infringer because he could have monitored the vendors who rented booths from him (but failed to do so). Also, the flea market operator made money from that booth rental as well as from admission and parking fees from the flea market attendees (many of whom paid such fees in order to gain access to the counterfeit recordings).[12]

Digital Millennium Copyright Act

Hosting infringing copyrighted content can create liability for contributory or vicarious infringement, as noted above. To avoid liability, online companies that enable their users to upload content must strictly comply with the federal Digital Millennium Copyright Act (DMCA),[13] which provides a *safe harbor* (that is protection and immunity) for online service providers against claims of any alleged copyright infringement committed by their users.

The DMCA, signed into law on October 28, 1998, was passed to address the growing threat of digital copyright infringement. It criminalizes the production and dissemination of technology designed to circumvent measures that control access to copyrighted works, while simultaneously shielding service providers from liability for copyright infringement by their users. According to President Bill Clinton, who signed the bill into law, the DMCA "grant[s] writers, artists, and other creators of copyrighted material global protection from piracy in the digital age."[14]

Title II of the DMCA (known as the Online Copyright Infringement Liability Limitation Act) generally protects online "service providers,"[15] which include all website owners, from all monetary damages and most injunctive and other equitable relief for copyright infringement where a third party initiated the delivery of the allegedly infringing content and the service provider did not modify or selectively disseminate the content.

 Note

The DMCA protects from liability the owners of Internet services, not the users (including marketers) who access them. Marketers utilizing UGC are not shielded under the DMCA with respect to uploading onto a third-party's website copyright-infringing content.

As a general rule, to qualify for DMCA's safe harbor protection, online service providers (OSPs) that store content uploaded by users must, among other things:

- Adopt (and reasonably implement) a policy of terminating the accounts of subscribers who repeatedly infringe copyrights of others

- Designate an agent registered with the U.S. Copyright Office to receive notifications of claimed copyright infringement

- Expeditiously remove or block access to the allegedly infringing content upon receiving notice of the alleged infringement

- Not receive a financial benefit directly attributable to the infringing activity, in a case in which the service provider has the right and ability to control such activity

- Not have actual knowledge of the infringement, not be aware of facts or circumstances from which infringing activity is apparent (the so-called red flag test[16]), or upon gaining such knowledge or awareness, respond expeditiously to take the material down or block access to it[17]

⚖️ *Legal Insight*

Are DMCA's requirements of direct financial benefit and the red flag test anachronistic in light of the present-day proliferation of social media sites whose *raison d'être* is UGC? In *A&M Records, Inc. v. Napster, Inc.*,[18] the court held that copyrighted material on Napster's site created a "draw" for customers that resulted in a "direct financial benefit" because Napster's future revenue was "directly dependent" on the size and increase in its user base. Indeed, Napster's primary purpose was to facilitate the distribution of copyrighted media files (primarily music) across a network of millions of users.

By contrast, in *Ellison v. Robertson*,[19] the court held that AOL did not receive a "direct financial benefit" when a user stored infringing material on its server because the copyrighted work did not "draw" new customers. AOL neither "attracted [nor] retained ... [nor] lost ... subscriptions" because of the infringing material; instead, AOL's service (which allowed users to store messages from various online discussion groups, including the alleged infringing message) was simply an "added benefit" to customers. For social media sites hosting UGC, the exact contours of what constitutes *drawing* in new customers to receive a *direct financial benefit* will have to be elucidated on a case-by-case basis.

To qualify for the protection against liability for taking down material, the online service provider must promptly notify the subscriber that it has removed or disabled access to the material and provide the subscriber with the opportunity to respond to the notice and takedown by filing a counter notification.[20] If the subscriber serves a counter notification complying with the DCMA's statutory requirements, including a statement under penalty of perjury that the subscriber believes in good faith that the material was removed or disabled through mistake or misidentification, then unless the copyright owner files an action seeking a court order against the subscriber, the service provider must put the material back up within 10 to 14 business days after receiving the counter notification.[21] Penalties are provided for knowingly making material misrepresentations in either a notice or a counternotice. Any person who knowingly materially misrepresents that the challenged content is infringing, or that it was removed or disabled through mistake or misidentification, is liable for any resulting damages (including costs and attorneys' fees) incurred by the alleged infringer, the copyright owner or its licensee, or the service provider.[22]

Copyright holders must also consider *fair use*[23] (that is, statutorily permitted use of a copyrighted work in a non-infringing manner) before issuing DMCA takedown notices for allegedly infringing content posted on the Internet. Whether a particular use of copyrighted materials constitutes *fair use* depends upon the following factors:

- The purpose and character of the use, including whether such use is of a commercial nature or is for nonprofit educational purposes

- The nature of the copyrighted work

- The amount and substantiality of the portion used in relation to the copyrighted work as a whole

- The effect of the use upon the potential market for or value of the copyrighted work.

For example, in *Lenz v. Universal Music Corp.*,[24] the plaintiff posted on YouTube a home video of her children dancing to Prince's song "Let's Go Crazy." Universal Music Corporation (Universal) sent YouTube a DMCA takedown notice alleging that plaintiff's video violated its copyright in the song. Lenz (the plaintiff) claimed fair use of the copyrighted material and sued Universal for misrepresentation of its DMCA claim. In denying Universal's motion to dismiss, the court held that Universal had not in good faith considered fair use when filing a takedown notice and that the plaintiff was therefore entitled to monetary damages.

The case of *UMG Recordings, Inc. v. Veoh Networks, Inc.*[25] provides additional guidance to OSPs seeking insulation under the "safe harbor" provisions of the DMCA. In this case, UMG, one of the world's largest record labels (including Motown and Def Jam) and music publishing companies, sued Veoh, an operator of a video sharing website, for direct and contributory copyright infringement. Despite the various procedures implemented by Veoh on its website to prevent copyright infringement (including third-party filtering solutions), Veoh's users were still able to make numerous unauthorized downloads of songs for which UMG owned the copyright. UMG claimed, however, that Veoh's actions were insufficient due to Veoh's late adoption of the filtering technology to detect infringing material and because Veoh removed only the specific videos identified in DMCA takedown notices, but not other infringing material that the filter detected.

In affirming the lower's court dismissal of the case, the U.S. Court of Appeals for the Ninth Circuit found that Veoh was entitled to protection under the DMCA's safe harbor for the following reasons:

- Veoh did not have actual knowledge of the infringing activity. "[M]erely hosting a category of copyrightable content ... with the general knowledge that one's services could be used to share infringing material, is insufficient to meet the actual knowledge requirement." To hold otherwise would render the safe harbor provisions "a dead letter." Rather, "specific knowledge of particular infringing activity" is required for an OSP to be rendered ineligible for safe harbor protection.

- Veoh did not have the right and ability to control infringing activity (which would otherwise disqualify it for safe harbor protection). "[T]he 'right and ability to control' ... requires control over specific infringing activity the provider knows about" and "a service provider's general right and ability to remove materials from its services is alone insufficient." Here, Veoh only had the necessary right and ability to control infringing activity once it had been notified of such activity. It would be a "practical impossibility for Veoh to ensure that no infringing material is ever uploaded to its site, or to remove unauthorized material that has not yet been identified to Veoh as infringing."

- Veoh did not lose DMCA safe harbor protection because it did more than merely store uploaded content. For example, it automatically converted the videos into smaller "chunks" and "transcoded" the video into a format that would make the videos more easily accessible to other users. The DMCA's safe-harbor provisions are not limited only to web host services (versus the web services themselves). Rather, such provisions also "encompass the access-facilitating processes that automatically occur when a user uploads a video." "Veoh has simply established a system whereby software automatically processes user-submitted content and recasts it in a format that is readily accessible to its users." Veoh does not actively participate in or supervise file uploading, "[n]or does it preview or select the files before the upload is completed."

- Veoh did not receive a financial benefit directly attributable to the infringing activity (which would otherwise render it ineligible for safe harbor protection). Rather, Veoh took down infringing material as soon as it was notified of the infringement.

Note

Interestingly, even though UMG presented evidence of emails sent to Veoh executives and investors by copyright holders regarding infringing activity—including one sent by the CEO of Disney to Michael Eisner, a Veoh investor, representing that the movie *Cinderalla III* and certain episodes from the television series *Lost* were available on Veoh without Disney's permission—the Ninth Circuit Appeals Court held that this was insufficient to create actual knowledge of infringement on Veoh's part (and therefore an obligation to remove infringing content). Rather, Disney, as an alleged infringed copyright holder, was subject to the DMCA's notification requirements, which these informal emails failed to meet. In any event, Veoh reportedly removed this offending material immediately upon learning of it.

As the Ninth Circuit's decision in UMG Recordings makes clear, when statutorily compliant and specific DMCA takedown notices are received, a website operator or service provider should act swiftly to remove the specifically identified infringing content. Such prompt action should help shield website operators and service providers from liability under the DMCA's safe harbor provisions that would otherwise arise from hosting infringing UGC.

 *Legal Insight*

Social media site *Pinterest*, which enables users to "pin" interesting photos to a virtual pinboard to share with others (such as clothing, jewelry, honeymoon destinations, "yummy desserts," and anything else that strikes a person's fancy), has become the focus of mounting concern that the site encourages unauthorized sharing of copyrighted materials. To help allay such fears, Pinterest is allowing website owners (and copyright holders) to opt-out of being featured on the site, by adding a "nopin" meta tag to their site. Pinterest users attempting to share images or other material from a site with the "nopin" code will be presented with the following message (also shown in Figure 6.2):

"This site doesn't allow pinning to Pinterest. Please contact the owner with any questions. Thanks for visiting!"

Further, Pinterest's Terms of Use includes a provision requiring its members to indemnify (read: pay or reimburse) Pinterest for any monetary loss in the event infringing copyrighted material is "pinned:" *"You agree to defend, indemnify, and hold [Pinterest], its officers, directors, employees and agents, harmless from and against any claims, liabilities, damages, losses, and expenses, including, without limitation, reasonable legal and accounting fees, arising out of or in any way connected with (i) your access to or use of the Site, Application, Services or Site Content, (ii) your Member Content, or (iii) your violation of these Terms."*

Whether Pinterest's "nopin" code will be sufficient to shield it from liability—leaving its members holding the bag for any infringing content they upload—remains to be seen.

Figure 6.2   *Even photos of cute kittens are copyright protected. Attempting to "pin" this photo displayed on Flickr resulted in a warning message.*

Defamation, Invasion of Privacy, and CDA Immunity

Although likely the most costly, copyright issues are not the only legal concerns related to UGC. The posting of allegedly defamatory materials has also given rise to a series of lawsuits against UGC service providers. In *Carafano v. Metrosplash. com, Inc.,*[26] for example, the plaintiff sued an Internet-based dating service (Matchmaker.com) for allegedly false content contained in her dating profile. According to the plaintiff (a popular actress who goes by the stage name Chase Masterso and who had a prominent recurring role in the TV show *Star Trek: Deep Space Nine*), the profile was posted by an imposter and contained a number of false statements about her, which characterized her as licentious. The case was ultimately dismissed based on immunity provided by the Communications Decency Act.

The federal Communications Decency Act of 1996 (CDA) [27] immunizes website operators and other interactive computer service providers from liability for third parties' *tortious* (legally wrongful) acts, including defamation, invasion of privacy, and intentional infliction of emotional distress. Section 230 of the CDA shields providers and users of interactive computer services from responsibility for third-party content. The CDA was specifically passed to help "promote the continued development of the Internet and other interactive computer services and other interactive media" and "to preserve the vibrant and competitive free market that presently exists for the Internet and other interactive computer services, unfettered by Federal or State regulation."[28]

Section 230(c)(1) of the CDA states that "no provider or user of an interactive computer service shall be treated as the publisher or speaker of any information provided by another information content provider."[29] The statute further provides that "no cause of action may be brought and no liability may be imposed under any State or local law that is inconsistent with this section."[30] Accordingly, the provider, so long as not participating in the creation or development of the content, will be immune from defamation and other, nonintellectual property,[31] state law claims arising from third-party content.

 Note

Courts have broadly interpreted the term *interactive computer service* provider under the CDA to cover a wide range of web services, including online auction websites, online dating websites, operators of Internet bulletin boards, and online bookstore websites.[32] At least one court has held that corporate employers that provide their employees with Internet access through the company's internal computer systems are also among the class of parties potentially immune under the CDA.[33]

The potential breadth of CDA immunity can appear quite staggering. For example, in *Doe II v. MySpace, Inc.*,[34] plaintiffs, young girls aged 13 to 15, were sexually assaulted by adults they met through the defendant's Internet social networking site, MySpace. Through their parents or guardians, the plaintiffs brought four separate cases against the site, asserting claims for negligence. Underscoring the breadth of CDA immunity, the California Court of Appeals affirmed the lower court's finding, holding that MySpace was not liable for what third parties posted on its site:

> "Given the general consensus to interpret section 230 immunity broadly, ... we also conclude that section 230 immunity shields MySpace in this case. That appellants characterize their complaint as one for failure to adopt reasonable safety measures does not avoid the immunity granted by section 230. It is undeniable that appellants seek to hold MySpace responsible for the communications between the Julie Does and their assailants. At its core, appellants want MySpace to regulate what appears on its Web site. Appellants argue they do not 'allege liability on account of MySpace's exercise of a publisher's traditional editorial functions, such as editing, altering, or deciding whether or not to publish certain material, which is the test for whether a claim treats a website as a publisher under Barrett.' But that is precisely what they allege; that is, they want MySpace to ensure that sexual predators do not gain access to (i.e., communicate with) minors on its Web site. That type of activity—to restrict or make available certain material—is expressly covered by section 230."

It has been long held that lawsuits seeking to hold service providers liable for the exercise of a publisher's traditional editorial functions (such as deciding whether to publish, withdraw, postpone, or alter content) are generally barred.[35] The 2010 to 2011 class-action lawsuit against consumer review site Yelp! Inc. further highlights the scope of the protection afforded interactive service providers under the CDA. In *Levitt v. Yelp! Inc.,*[36] the defendant was accused of manipulating its consumer reviews to extort the plaintiff businesses to purchase advertising on its site. In particular, the plaintiffs alleged that Yelp relocated or removed positive reviews from its site, resulting in a lowered overall "star" rating for a business (whereas businesses purchasing advertising on Yelp were given prominent ratings); that it retained negative reviews, even if those reviews violated Yelp's terms of service; and that employees of Yelp said they would manipulate reviews favorably for businesses that paid for advertising on the site.

Despite these allegations, the complaint against Yelp was dismissed because decisions to remove or reorder user content traditionally fall within the scope of Section 230 CDA immunity. According to the court, this is true even if Yelp had an improper motive in including certain reviews and excluding others. As to the policy of protecting possible bad faith exercises of editorial functions, the court observed:

> *"Furthermore, it should be noted that traditional editorial functions often include subjective judgments informed by political and financial consider- ations... Determining what motives are permissible and what are not could prove problematic. Indeed, from a policy perspective, permitting litigation and scrutiny motive could result in the 'death by ten thousand duck-bites' against which the Ninth Circuit cautioned in interpreting § 230... As illustrated by the case at bar, finding a bad faith exception to immunity under [§ 230] could force Yelp to defend its editorial decisions in the future on a case by case basis and reveal how it decides what to publish and what not to publish. Such expo- sure could lead Yelp to resist filtering out false/unreliable reviews (as someone could claim an improper motive for its decision), or to immediately remove all negative reviews about which businesses complained (as failure to do so could expose Yelp to a business's claim that Yelp was strong-arming the business for advertising money). The Ninth Circuit has made it clear that the need to defend against a proliferation of lawsuits, regardless of whether the provider ultimately prevails, undermines the purpose of section 230."[37]*

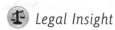 Legal Insight

The Internet is awash with message boards, review sites, and customer feedback forums that provide a public platform to bad-mouth a company and its employees behind a cloak of anonymity. Based on a single defama- tory comment, a company's good will, customer relations, and profits can be seriously affected. Companies that are harmed in this way should not despair, however, as there are means to ferret out the defamer's identity. A "John Doe suit," for example, allows a company to name the website or internet service provider as defendants (together with the fictitiously- named "John Doe"), and to compel them to turn over the identity of the offending online speaker.

While there is no universal standard for discovery of anonymous Internet users' real identities, courts generally consider the following factors (or a permutation thereof) in assessing whether the companies' need for com- pelled disclosure outweighs the online poster's First Amendment right to anonymous speech:[38]

- Whether the plaintiff has sufficiently stated a cause of action for defamation

- Whether the discovery request is sufficiently specific to lead to identifying information

- Whether there are alternative means to obtain the subpoenaed information

- Whether there is a central need for the subpoenaed information to advance the claim

- Whether the anonymous Internet user has a reasonable expectation of privacy.[39]

Of course, learning the identity of the anonymous poster is one thing (for example, a rival company, an ex-employee); getting the website to take down the offending content is something else altogether. The latter potential remedy is discussed in greater detail in Chapter 8.

Limitations of CDA Immunity

Despite its broad breadth, CDA immunity does not *attach* (apply) if the host exercises editorial control over the content and the edits materially alter the meaning of the content. For companies that operate their own blogs, bulletin boards, YouTube channels, or other social media platforms, therefore, it is imperative that they avoid contributing to the "creation or development"[40] of the offensive content so that their immunity is not revoked.

 Legal Insight

Does re-tweeting impermissible (say, defamatory) content fall within the grant of CDA immunity? Probably yes, because CDA immunity depends on the source of the information in the injurious statement, not the source of the statement itself, and the CDA protects both the provider and user of an interactive computer service. Reposting (or re-tweeting) such statements is most likely protected under the statute, provided the person reposting/re-tweeting did not actually take part in creating the original content.

The line demarking where content host ends and content creator begins is often blurry. In 2006, the franchisor for the popular Subway restaurants filed a lawsuit against Quiznos related to two television commercials and an online contest that invited consumers to submit videos comparing the competitors' sandwiches, demonstrating "why you think Quiznos is better."[41] Perhaps inevitably, various allegedly disparaging videos were submitted, including one wherein a Subway sandwich is portrayed as a submarine unable to dive because it does not have enough meat.

Despite the defendant's Section 230 CDA immunity objections, the court declined to dismiss the case because an issue existed as to whether Quiznos merely published information provided by third parties or instead was "actively responsible for the creation and development of disparaging representations about Subway contained in the contestant videos."[42] According to the court:

> *"Here, the Defendants invited contestants to submit videos comparing Subway and Quiznos and demonstrating 'why you think Quiznos is better.' The domain name used to solicit entrants for the Contest, 'meatnomeat.com,' is arguably a literal falsity because it implies that the Subway sandwich has 'no meat.' In addition, the four 'sample videos' designed by the Defendants to shape the Contest submissions arguably contain false representations because they depict the Subway sandwich as having no meat or less meat than a Quiznos sandwich. In these circumstances, the Court cannot conclude, as a matter of law, that the Defendants are not responsible for the creation and development of the contestant materials. Whether the Defendants are responsible for creating or developing the contestant videos is an issue of material fact, best submitted to the jury after viewing all of the relevant evidence. A reasonable jury may well conclude that the Defendants did not merely post the arguably disparaging content contained in the contestant videos, but instead actively solicited disparaging representations about Subway and thus were responsible for the creation or development of the offending contestant videos."[43]*

 Note

> There are important comparative advertisement lessons to be taken away from this case as well. As discussed in greater detail in Chapter 7, businesses should take care that the statements made in their promotional messages are true, regardless of whether the statements are made in traditional or new media, and regardless of whether the statements are made directly by the business or by others on the business behalf, or which were created or developed with the businesses' active participation.

The case of *Fair Housing Council v. Roommates.com, LLC,*[44] is further illustrative of the fact that the immunity afforded by the CDA is not absolute and may be forfeited if the site owner invites the posting of illegal materials or makes actionable postings itself. The defendant operates a website to match people looking to share a place to live. As part of the registration process, subscribers had to create a profile that required them to answer a series of questions, including his/her sex, sexual orientation, and whether he/she would bring children to a household. The appellate court found that because the operator created the discriminatory questions and choice of answers and designed its online registration process around them, it was the "information content provider"[45] as to the questions and could claim no CDA immunity for posting them on its website, or for forcing subscribers to answer them as a condition of accessing its services. By these actions, the defendant was found to be more than a passive transmitter of information provided by others; rather, it "created or developed," at least in part, that information, and accordingly, lost its CDA immunity.

 Note

A blog or chat room operator is not protected under CDA if it hosts content that infringes the intellectual property rights of others, including their trademarks and copyrights. In the latter case, to be shielded from liability, the operator must conform to the notice, take down, and other procedures of the DMCA, as detailed earlier in this chapter.

Further, the CDA carves out its own exception to its grant of statutory immunity. While under Section 230 of the CDA "no provider or user of an interactive computer service shall be treated as the publisher or speaker of any information provided by another information content provider" and "no cause of action may be brought and no liability may be imposed under any State or local law that is inconsistent with this section," Section 230(e)(2)states that the CDA should not "be construed to limit or expand any law pertaining to intellectual property." Accordingly, the CDA will not bar IP claims asserted against a site operator.

In *Doe v. Friendfinder Network, Inc. et al.*,[46] for example, a federal district court in New Hampshire ruled that the CDA does not preclude a state law right of publicity claim against operators of a "sex and swinger" online community who reposted— as advertisements on other third-party websites—naked photos and a sexual profile "reasonably identified" as the plaintiff without the plaintiff's knowledge or consent. The plaintiff brought eight claims against the defendants, including for defamation, invasion of privacy, and false designation in violation of Section 43(a) of the Lanham Act.[47]

The plaintiff's invasion of privacy claim was predicated on four separate theories:

- The defendants intruded on the plaintiff's solitude (by exposing intimate—albeit, non-factual—details of her life to the public)

- The defendants publicly disclosed private "facts" about the plaintiff

- The defendants cast the plaintiff in a false light (by implying, for example, that she was a "swinger" or engaged in a "promiscuous sexual lifestyle")

- The defendants appropriated plaintiff's identity for their own benefit.

According to the court, only the fourth theory (the right of publicity) was a widely recognized IP right exempt from CDA immunity. "The other three torts encompassed by the 'right of privacy' rubric, however, do not fit that description. Unlike a violation of the right to publicity, these causes of action—intrusion upon seclusion, publication of private facts, and casting in false light—protect 'a personal right, peculiar to the individual whose privacy is invaded' which cannot be transferred like other property interests."[48] In applying the CDA's grant of immunity, therefore, the court allowed the defendant's motion to dismiss the plaintiff's state tort claims (defamation, invasion of privacy, and so on) but permitted her state and federal IP claims (violation of right to publicity and false designation) to proceed.

 Legal Insight

> The CDA and DMCA safe harbor are not the only legal protections available to online hosts of UGC. As violations of a terms of service may constitute "exceeding authorized access" under the Computer Fraud and Abuse Act (CFAA),[49] a terms of service explicitly prohibiting uploading or posting infringing or defamatory content, and a prominent click-wrap agreement requiring the user to read and actively accept the terms and conditions by clicking an I Accept button, for example (versus a terms of service accessible via a link), are also advisable. The terms of service should also require that all appropriate representations, warranties, and indemnities from users submitting UGC are given.

Although the use of UGC presents a number of legal issues concerning copyright infringement, defamation, and privacy rights violations, there are important legal protections available to businesses to immunize them from such claims. However, strict compliance with the DMCA and CDA's statutory requirements is mandated if a business does not want to lose its statutory immunity. Figure 6.3 provides a summary of some of these key requirements, as well as other practical tips for businesses hosting UGC.

Social Media Legal Tips for Managing the Legal Risks of User-Generated Content

DOs	DON'Ts
■ To insulate yourself from liability associated with users uploading infringing materials onto your site, familiarize yourself with and adhere to the safe harbor requirements of the Digital Millennium Copyright Act (DMCA).	■ Do not allow your employees to upload onto third-party's websites copyright-infringing content. The DMCA protects from liability the owners of Internet services, not the users (including marketers) who access them.
■ Be sure to obtain all necessary third-party permissions before using UGG, including from the content's creator (for example, the photographer, videographer, or songwriter), as well as from any parties depicted in the photos, videos, or other UGC material.	■ Do not assume that making only minor changes to someone else's UGC shields you from liability. Copyright infringement can occur whenever you reproduce any part of someone else's work if the part you use is an important or distinct part of the original—regardless of size.
■ While you are under no duty to police sites for potential acts of infringement, you should expeditiously remove any copyright infringing materials once you receive DMCA-compliant takedown notices, and terminate the accounts of repeat infringers.	■ Do not forget to designate an agent registered with the U.S. Copyright Office to receive notifications of claimed copyright infringement. Overlooking this requirement will void any DMCA safe-harbor protection to which you may otherwise be entitled.
■ Establish an internal data log policy to keep record of any takedown notices you receive (DMCA-compliant or otherwise) and maintain records of any responsive actions you take.	■ Do not invite the posting of illegal materials, condition accessing your services upon answering impermissible questions, or make actionable postings yourself. If you become more than a passive transmitter of information provided by others—by creating or developing, at least in part, that information—you will lose your statutory (CDA) immunity.
■ Be sure to explicitly prohibit the uploading or posting of infringing, defamatory, privacy-invading, or other legally impermissible content in your Terms of Service. The TOS should also require that all appropriate representations, warranties, and indemnities from users submitting UGC are given.	■ For companies that operate their own blogs, bulletin boards, YouTube channels, or other social media platforms, do not contribute to the "creation or development" of defamatory, harassing, or other wrongful content. Statutory (CDA) immunity does not apply if the host exercises editorial control over the content and the edits materially alter the meaning of the content.

Figure 6.3   *Social Media Legal Tips for Managing the Legal Risks of User-Generated Content.*

CHAPTER 6 ENDNOTES

1   *Chang et al. v. Virgin Mobile USA, LLC et al.*, Case No 3:07-CV-01767-D (N.D. Tex., Oct. 19, 2007). The action was dismissed without prejudice on jurisdictional grounds, as the challenged conduct allegedly occurred primarily in Australia. The case was subsequently refilled, and is currently pending in the U.S. District Court, California Northern District. *See Chang et al. v. Virgin Mobile USA, LLC et al.*, Case No. 5:08-MC-80095-JW (N.D. Tex., May 8, 2008)

2   17 U.S.C. § 501(a)-(b)

3   17 U.S.C. §101 *et seq.*

4   17 U.S.C. § 106(1)

5   17 U.S.C. § 106(2)

6   17 U.S.C. § 106(3)

7   17 U.S.C. § 106(4)

8   17 U.S.C. § 106(5)

9   17 U.S.C. § 106(6)

10 *See*, for example, *MGM Studios Inc. v. Grokster, Ltd.*, 545 U.S. 913 (2005)

11 *Id.* at 930

12 *Fonovisa Inc. v. Cherry Auction*, 76 F.3d 259, 37 USPQ2d 1590 (9th Cir. 1996)

13 Pub. L. No. 105-304, 112 Stat. 2860 (Oct. 28, 1998)

14 Statement by the President on Digital Millennium Copyright, 1998 WL 754861 (Oct. 29, 1998)

15 As it relates to providing online transitory communications, *service provider* is defined in section 512(k)(1)(A) of the Copyright Act as "an entity offering the transmission, routing, or providing of connections for digital online communications, between or among points specified by a user, of material of the user's choosing, without modification to the content of the material as sent or received."

For purposes of service providers providing storage of information on websites (or other information repositories) at the direction of users, *service provider* is more broadly defined as "a provider of online services or network access, or the operator of facilities therefore." Title 17 U.S.C., § 512(k)(l) (B)

16 According to the legislative history of § 512(c)(1)(A)(ii) of the DMCA, the *red flag* test (to determine whether an infringing activity is "apparent") contains both a subjective and an objective element. The subjective element examines the OSP's knowledge during the time it was hosting the infringing material. The objective element requires that the court examine all relevant facts to determine if a "reasonable person operating under the same or similar circumstances" would find that infringing activity was apparent See H.R. Rep. No. 105-551(II) at 53 (1998).

17 17 U.S.C., §§ 512(c) and 512(i)

18 *A&M Records, Inc. v. Napster, Inc.*, 239 F.3d 1004 (9th Cir. 2001)

19 *Ellison v. Robertson*, 357 F.3d 1072 (9th Cir. 2004)

20 17 U.S.C. § 512(g)(2)

21 17 U.S.C. §§ 512(g)(2) and 512(g)(3)

22 17 U.S.C. § 512(f)

23 17 U.S.C. § 107

24 *Lenz v. Universal Music Corp. et al*, 572 F. Supp. 2d 1150 (N.D. Cal. 2008)

25 *UMG Recordings, Inc., et al. v. Veoh Networks, Inc.*, Case No. 10-55732 (9th Cir., Dec. 20, 2011)

26 *Carafano v. Metrosplash.com, Inc.*, 339 F.3d 1119 (9th Cir. 2003)

27 Public Law No. 104-104 (Feb. 8, 1996), codified at 47 U.S.C. §230

28 47 U.S.C. § 230(b)

29 47 U.S.C. § 230(f)(2) defines *interactive computer service* as "any information service, system, or access software provider that provides or enables computer access by multiple users to a computer server, including specifically a service or system that provides access to the Internet and such systems operated or services offered by libraries or educational institutions."

   Similarly, 47 U.S.C. § 230(f)(3) defines *information content provider* as "any person or entity that is responsible, in whole or in part, for the creation or development of information provided through the Internet or any other interactive computer service."

30 47 U.S.C. § 230(e)(3)

31 47 U.S.C. § 230(e)(2) removes intellectual property law claims from the scope of immunity provided by the statute.

32 *See*, respectively, *Gentry v. eBay, Inc.*, 99 Cal. App. 4th 816, 2002 Cal. App. LEXIS 4329; *Carafano v. Metrosplash.com, Inc.*, 339 F.3d 1119 (9th Cir. 2003); *Chicago Lawyers' Comm. for Civil Rights Under the Law, Inc. v. Craigslist, Inc.* (N.D.Ill. 2006) 461 F. Supp. 2d 681; and *Schneider v. Amazon. com, Inc.* 108 Wn. App. 454, 31 P.3d 37, 40–41] (2001)

33 *Delfino v. Agilent Technologies, Inc.*, 145 Cal. App. 4th 790 (2006)

34 *Doe II, a Minor, etc., et al., v. MySpace Incorporated*, 175 Cal. App. 4th 561 (2009)

35 *Zeran v. America Online, Inc.*, 129 F.3d 327, 330 (4th Cir. 1997)

36 *Levitt et al., v. Yelp! Inc.*, Case No. 3:10-CV-01321-EMC (N.D. Cal. Mar. 29, 2010)

37 *See* Order Granting Defendant's Motion to Dismiss (Chen, J.) (Oct. 26, 2011) in *Levitt et al., v. Yelp! Inc.*, Case No. 3:10-cv-01321-EMC (N.D. Cal. Oct. 26, 2011) (Document 89) [Note: The case is currently on appeal.]

38 It is well-settled that the First Amendment's protection extends to the Internet, even to anonymous speech. *See, e.g., Reno v. ACLU*, 521 U.S. 844, 870, 117 S.Ct. 2329 (1997) ("Through the use of chat rooms, any person with a phone line can become a town crier with a voice that resonates farther than it could from any soapbox."); *Doe v. 2TheMart.Com, Inc.*, 140 F.Supp.2d 1088, 1097 (W.D.Wash.2001) ("Internet anonymity facilitates the rich, diverse, and far ranging exchange of ideas ... [;] the constitutional rights of Internet users, including the First Amendment right to speak anonymously, must be carefully safeguarded.").

39 *See, e.g., Sony Music Entertainment Inc. v. Does 1-40*, 326 F.Supp.2d 556 (S.D.NY 2004); and *Columbia Insurance Company v. Seescandy.com*, 185 F.R.D. 573 (N.D. Cal. 1999).

40 47 U.S.C § 230(f)(3) defines *information content provider* as "any person or entity that is responsible, in whole or in part, for the *creation* or *development* of information provided through the Internet or any other interactive computer service."

41 *Doctor's Associates, Inc. v. QIP Holder LLC, et al.*, Case No. 3:06-CV-1710 (D. Conn.) (Oct. 27, 2006)

42 *Doctor's Associates, Inc. v. QIP Holder LLC, et al.*, Case No. 3:06-CV-1710 (D. Conn.) (Oct. 27, 2006) (Document 271) (order denying defendants' motion for summary judgment entered Feb. 19, 2010)

43 *Id.*

44 *Fair Housing Council v. Roommates.com, LLC*, 521 F.3d 1157 (9th Cir. 2008) *(en banc)*

45 47 U.S.C. § 230(f)(3)

46 *Doe v. Friendfinder Network, Inc. et al.*, 540 F.Supp.2d 288 (D.N.H. 2008)

47 *See* Section 43(a) of Lanham Act, 15 U.S.C. § 1125(a)

48 *Doe v. Friendfinder Network, Inc. et al.*, 540 F.Supp.2d 288 (D.N.H. 2008) *(internal citations omitted)*

49 18 U.S.C. § 1030. *See*, in particular, § 1030(a)(4), which provides that "whoever knowingly and with intent to defraud, accesses a protected computer without authorization, or exceeds authorized access, and by means of such conduct furthers the intended fraud and obtains anything of value, unless the object of the fraud and the thing obtained consists only of the use of the computer and the value of such use is not more than $5,000 in any 1 year period … shall be punished as provided in subsection (c) of this section."

The Law of Social Advertising

There are two sides to the social network coin: the organic side, which comprises the unadulterated conversations taking place in social platforms; and the advertising side, where social networks are leveraged as promotional channels. Social advertising is comprised of any online advertising conducted on social networks. Advertising on social platforms such as Facebook, YouTube, LinkedIn, and Twitter have become an integral part of campaign planning. This is in large part driven by the hyper-targeting capabilities of social ads powered by the user demographic data contained within users' social profiles, including their location, education, language, age, gender, relationship status, likes, and interests. Social network advertising tends to focus on three primary objectives: building awareness, driving sales, and increasing the number of social followers, subscribers, fans, and so forth. But that is just scratching the surface. Social advertising can also help businesses engage existing customers, reach new ones, change the market sentiment of a brand, generate leads, gather customer feedback, and drive traffic to a landing page. Although varied and evolving, the most common types of social ads include banner ads, branded business profiles, give/get widgets, branded quiz apps, and sponsored content. The messaging employed within online ads also vary, ranging from blunt, hard-hitting sales messages (such as "Buy Now, Save 50%") to more subtle, gated content lures (such as offering a free downloadable e-book in exchange for an email address).

Despite the wide range of social media advertising techniques, common threads bind them together. First, they are all designed to capture leads (that is, to acquire friends, followers, subscribers, email addresses, and the like), convert them into sales (that is, to migrate audiences from social platforms into, and through the conversion funnel), and cultivate a cadre of brand evangelists. Further, all social media advertising, regardless of platform, is governed by the same laws, policies, and ethics which govern the advertising industry as a whole. Practitioners who engage in social media promotions and advertising, therefore, need to be aware of, and operate within these legal constraints.

> All social media advertising, regardless of platform, is governed by the same laws, policies, and ethics which govern the advertising industry as a whole. Practitioners who engage in social media promotions and advertising, therefore, need to be aware of, and operate within these legal constraints.

In addition to the rules governing online sweepstakes and promotions (discussed in Chapter 1), online endorsements and testimonials (discussed in Chapter 2), web host immunity under the Communications Decency Act (CDA) (discussed in Chapter 6), and data privacy and security (discussed in Chapter 10), this chapter highlights a few more key laws impacting social media advertising, and provides best practice tips for businesses using social media advertisements. In particular, this chapter examines the FTC Act (regarding false advertising vis-à-vis consumers); section 43 of the Lanham Act (regarding false advertising vis-à-vis business competitors); the CAN-SPAM Act of 2003 (regarding electronic solicitations); and the Children's Online Privacy Protection Act (COPPA) (regarding advertising and other business practices directed toward children).

Note

> This chapter does not discuss all the laws and regulations impacting social media advertising, as such a discussion would be beyond the intended scope of this book. The reader should note, however, that there are many laws and regulations with are potentially implicated in this space, including those relating to pricing, use of the terms "free" and "rebate," guarantees and warranties, "Made in the U.S.A." labels, telemarketing, mail orders, group-specific target marketing (for example, senior citizens, Hispanic citizens), advertising in specific industries (for example, food, alcohol, medical products, funeral, jewelry, motor vehicles, retail food stores, and drugs), and labeling (for example, clothing, appliances, cosmetics, drugs, food, furs, hazardous materials, and tires).

The FTC Act

As discussed in Chapter 2, advertisements are principally governed by Section 5 of the FTC Act[1] (and the associated regulations promulgated under FTC's authority) (and the corresponding state "mini-FTC Acts"[2]), which generally requires that advertisements be truthful, non-deceptive, adequately substantiated, and not be unfair.

Section 5 of the FTC Act prohibits "unfair or deceptive acts or practices" affecting commerce. "Unfair" practices are those that cause or are "likely to cause substantial injury to consumers which [are] not reasonably avoidable by consumers themselves and not outweighed by countervailing benefits to consumers or to competition."[3]

In determining whether a particular advertisement (or other business practice) is unfair or deceptive for Section 5 purposes, courts generally consider the following factors:

- Whether the representation or omission is likely to mislead the consumer

- The reasonableness of the consumer's reaction to the representation or omission, determined from the total impression the advertisement creates in the mind of the consumer, not by isolating words or phrases within the advertisement

- The materiality of the representation or omission in terms of whether it is "likely to affect the consumer's conduct or decision with regard to a product or service." If inaccurate or omitted information is material, consumer injury is likely (and in many instances presumed), because consumers are likely to have chosen differently but for the deception.

Best Practices for Social Media Advertising

At a minimum, businesses advertising via social media should therefore observe the following required (and best) practices:

- **Be truthful in your social media advertising**—Any claims that you make, through social media or otherwise, must be truthful. A false ad for purposes of Section 5 is one which is "misleading in a material respect."[4] Businesses should be mindful not only of the honesty of their own practices, but of the practices of those whom they rely on to spread their advertising message on their behalf—including outside ad agencies, PR and marketing firms, affiliate marketers, and so on.

- **Make sure your social media advertising claims aren't unfair or deceptive**—To comply with the FTC Act, advertisements also need to be fair and non-deceptive. Examples of misleading or deceptive practices include "false oral or written representations, misleading price claims, sales of hazardous or systematically defective products or services without adequate disclosures, failure to disclose information regarding pyramid sales, use of bait and switch techniques, failure to perform promised services, and failure to meet warranty obligations."[5]

  Similarly, the FTC considers the following factors in assessing whether an advertisement is unfair:

  - Whether the practice injures consumers
  - Whether it violates established public policy
  - Whether it's unethical or unscrupulous[6]

  Examples of unfair practices include withholding or failing to generate critical price or performance data, for example, leaving buyers with insufficient information for informed comparisons; and exercising undue influence over highly susceptible classes of purchasers, as by promoting fraudulent "cures" to seriously ill cancer patients.[7]

- **Substantiate your social media advertising claims (and those made on your behalf)**—For social media advertisements (like advertisements in traditional media), it is incumbent upon the advertiser to have adequate substantiation of all claims (both expressed and implied) depicted in the ad—that is, advertisers must have a reasonable basis for advertising claims before they are disseminated.[8] It is important to note that companies may face liability not only for the unsubstantiated claims they make, but also for claims made on their behalf, including by sponsored endorsers, such as the blogger in the following example (even though she was not paid for her review):

> *"The advertiser requests that a blogger try a new body lotion and write a review of the product on her blog. Although the advertiser does not make any specific claims about the lotion's ability to cure skin conditions and the blogger does not ask the advertiser whether there is substantiation for the claim, in her review the blogger writes that the lotion cures eczema and recommends the product to her blog readers who suffer from this condition. The advertiser is subject to liability for misleading or unsubstantiated representations made through the blogger's endorsement. The blogger also is subject to liability for misleading or unsubstantiated representations made in the course of her endorsement. The blogger is also liable if she fails to disclose clearly and conspicuously that she is being paid for her services. The advertiser should also monitor bloggers who are being paid to promote its products and take steps necessary to halt the continued publication of deceptive representations when they are discovered."[9]*

Section 43(a) of the Lanham Act

While the FCT Act governs advertiser liability *to consumers* for false or misleading advertising, advertisers may equally face liability *to business competitors* under Section 43(a) of the Lanham Act[10] for such conduct. The Lanham Act—a piece of federal legislation that governs trademark law in the U.S., and which prohibits trademark infringement, trademark dilution, and false advertising—defines false advertising as "any false designation of origin, false or misleading description of fact, or false or misleading representation of fact, which…in commercial advertising or promotion, misrepresents the nature, characteristics, qualities, or geographic origin of his or her or another person's goods, services, or commercial activities."

In order to establish a claim of false or misleading advertising under the Lanham Act, a plaintiff must prove that:

- The defendant made a false or misleading statement of fact about its or plaintiff's products or services

- The false or misleading statement actually deceived or tended to deceive a substantial portion of the intended audience

- The statement is material in that it will likely influence the deceived customer's purchasing decision

- The defendant has been or is likely to be injured as a result of the false statement, either by direct diversion of sales from itself to defendant or by a loss of goodwill associated with its products or services.

- The advertisements were introduced into interstate commerce.

 Note

With literally false statements, the plaintiff need not prove that the audience is actually deceived or is likely to be deceived by the literally false representation. The law presumes that a literally false advertisement deceives the intended audience. In the case of claims that are literally true but misleading (that is, claims that prove misleading, in the overall context of the advertisement, because they convey a false impression or fail to disclose important qualifying information), the plaintiff is required to prove that the challenged statement actually deceived (or tends to deceive) the intended audience.

Doctor's Assocs., Inc. v. QIP Holders, LLC.[11] is one of the first cases brought under the Lanham Act relating to social media and user-generated content (UGC) comparative advertisement marketing campaigns. In 2006, the operators of the *Subway* sandwich chain sued the operators of the *Quiznos* sandwich chain over certain UGC advertisements created as part of a nationwide contest called "Quiznos v. Subway TV Ad Challenge." In this contest, Quiznos encouraged contestants to upload videos to a dedicated site comparing a Subway sandwich to the Quiznos Prime Rib Cheesesteak sandwich using the theme "meat, no meat." Predictably, videos unfavorable to Subway were submitted.

Subway sued Quiznos, claiming that the contestant-created entries contained false and misleading advertising in violation of the Lanham Act, among other laws.

Although the videos at issue were not directly created by Subway, the court denied Quiznos' motion for summary judgment, finding that Quiznos could be found to have actively participated in the creation or development of the submitted UGC.[12]

The case shortly settled after this ruling. (The implications of this case on the scope of immunity under the Communications Decency Act—which generally protects hosts from liability for the content that others post on their site—are discussed in greater detail in Chapter 6.)

Although the settlement prevented further development of the law relating to false advertising claims and UGC marketing messages, the case underscores the fact that advertisers could potentially face liability from competitors if false or misleading advertising claims are distributed through social media channels.

Indeed, on August 2, 2010, Ocean Spray Cranberries, Inc. filed a lawsuit against, amongst others, Decas Cranberry Products, Inc., alleging that Decas orchestrated "an unlawful and malicious campaign" against Ocean Spray designed to harm the company's reputation, frustrate its relationships with its customers, and undermine its dealings with grower-owners and other cranberry growers in the industry.[13]

The complaint alleged violations of the Agricultural Fair Practices Act, Section 43(a) of the Lanham Act, and the Massachusetts Unfair and Deceptive Trade Practices Act.

According to Ocean Spray's complaint, Decas used a variety of methods to disseminate its "smear campaign," including widely distributed letters and emails, internet blogs and websites, Facebook accounts, YouTube videos and Twitter postings, which falsely accused Ocean Spray of the following:

- Creating "a significant oversupply of cranberries" in the industry and contributing to that surplus by reducing the amount of cranberries in its products

- Mislabeling its Choice® sweetened dried cranberry product, a lower-cost alternative for industrial customers, and harming the cranberry industry by selling a product that takes fewer barrels of cranberries to create

- Harming the industry and "abandoning the cranberry," and of introducing Choice solely for "corporate greed" and with a "blind focus on profits."

- Producing the Choice product for its own corporate profit, and that the "favorable return" relating to Choice is only for Ocean Spray, and not for its "growers"

Allegedly, these same representations were variously repeated on a YouTube video called "The Scamberry" (see Figure 7.1), as well as on a Twitter account called @ Scamberry and a Facebook page called Scamberry (allegedly created by "Michele Young," who posed as a "consumer advocate").

Figure 7.1 *A YouTube video on "Scamberry" channel discussing Ocean Spray.*

The case settled on December 12, 2011. Although the settlement denied us an important legal precedent regarding the interplay between social media and Section 43(a) of the Lanham Act, the case further highlights the need for companies to tread carefully when making claims about their competitors in any medium.

Northern Star Industries, Inc., v. Douglas Dynamics LLC[14] is another new media case involving false advertising, and apparently provides the first instance in which a party was ordered to use social media to remedy a social media advertising "wrong."

In 2011, Northern Star, the manufacturer of "Boss" brand snow plows, filed suit against its direct competitor, Douglas Dynamics, the manufacturer of "Fisher" and "Western" brand snowplows. According to the complaint, Douglas Dynamics conducted an advertising campaign (via print, video, web, and social media) which made false comparisons between the two company's products, including:

- A print ad (appearing in stand-alone and print-based media) showing a photograph of a man with a bloody face holding a piece of raw meat against an eye, and another of a shattered windshield, both stating, "IF YOUR V-PLOW DOESN'T COME WITH A TRIP EDGE, IT BETTER COME WITH A CRASH HELMET."

- Another ad containing a large headline stating, "IF YOUR V-PLOW ISN'T A WESTERN, YOU MAY NEED TO GET YOUR HEAD EXAMINED," combined with a picture of a doctor reviewing two skull x-rays (one with a fracture and with "Boss" written on it in stylized letters), a statement that with [Northern Star's] V-plow trip blades "you'll experience bone-jarring windshield-banging, steering wheel smacking wake up calls with every obstacle you encounter," and a statement that the Western snow plow is "just what the doctor ordered."

- A video link page stating "If your V-plow has a trip blade, you know the story. There you are, plowing along, feeling good, saving the rest of the world from the storm, when BAM you're in the crash zone wondering what the #@!* you hit. That's because when a trip blade hits a hidden obstacle in vee or scoop, it can't trip. And the results aren't pretty. Good thing FISHER® XtremeV™ V-plow comes with a trip edge, which trips over hidden obstacles in any configuration. It can save you a lot of headaches."

Douglas Dynamics published these allegedly false and misleading print ads (and links) on its Fisher and Western Facebook pages.

On January 26, 2012, the court granted Northern's Star request for a preliminary injunction, preliminarily finding that, amongst other matters, Douglas Dynamics' claims—implying and/or stating that users of Northern Star's blade-trip plows will be physically injured but users of Fisher/Western edge-trip plows will not—were not true.[15]

After giving the parties a chance to agree upon a proposed order, on February 15, 2012 the court ordered Douglas Dynamics to publicly withdraw such claims. Of particular interest, Douglas Dynamics was ordered to post a retraction notice on its Fisher/Western Facebook pages and various industry blogs, for one year. See Figure 7.2.

The *Northern Star* decision reminds advertisers that, while the legal standards expressly governing social media marketing are relatively in their infancy, advertisers using social media must still comply with existing laws governing traditional models of advertising. As the law catches up with the technology, it is safe to say that existing legal framework will continue to be asked to absorb, accommodate, and proscribe new methods of advertising.

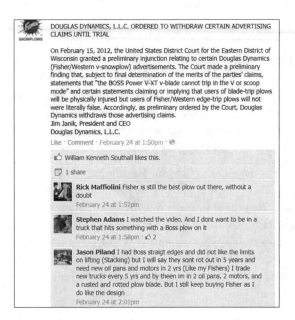

Figure 7.2   *Retraction posted by Douglas Dynamics on its Fisher Facebook page, as ordered by the U.S. District Court for the Eastern District of Wisconsin.*

The CAN-SPAM Act of 2003

The Controlling the Assault of Non-Solicited Pornography and Marketing Act of 2003 (CAN-SPAM Act)[16] establishes the United States' first national standards for the sending of commercial email, provides recipients the right to opt out of future emails, and imposes tough penalties for violations.

The CAN-SPAM Act makes it "unlawful for any person to initiate the transmission, to a protected computer, of a commercial electronic mail message, or a transaction or relationship message, that contains, or is accompanied by, header information that is materially false or materially misleading."[17] An *electronic mail message* is defined as "a message that is sent to a unique electronic mail address,"[18] and an *electronic mail address* means a "destination, commonly expressed as a string of characters, consisting of a unique user name or mailbox and a reference to an Internet domain (commonly referred to as a 'domain part'), whether or not displayed, to which an electronic mail message can be sent or delivered."[19]

Despite its name, the CAN-SPAM Act does not apply only to bulk email; it also covers all *commercial electronic messages*, which the law defines as "any electronic mail message the primary purpose of which is the commercial advertisement or promotion of a commercial product or service (including content on an Internet website operated for a commercial purpose)."[20] Both business-to-business and business-to-consumer email must comply with the law, as must commercial solicitations transmitted through social media sites.

On March 28, 2011, in *Facebook, Inc. v. MaxBounty, Inc.*,[21] the Ninth Circuit District Court held that unwanted commercial solicitations transmitted through Facebook to friends' walls, news feeds, inboxes, or external email addresses registered with Facebook are electronic messages subject to the requirements of the CAN-SPAM Act. In this case, Facebook alleged that MaxBounty created fake Facebook pages intended to redirect unsuspecting Facebook users to third-party commercial sites through a registration process that required a Facebook user to become a fan of the page and to invite all of his or her Facebook friends to join the page. The invitations were then routed to the user's wall, the news feeds, or home pages of the user's friends, Facebook inboxes of the user's friends, or external email addresses. Adopting an expansive interpretation of the scope of the CAN-SPAM Act, the court concluded that these communications were electronic messages and, therefore, subject to the Act's restrictions.

 Note

In a subsequent motion to dismiss filed in the case,[22] the court held that a user who violates Facebook's terms of service may thereby violate the Computer Fraud and Abuse Act (CFAA),[23] on the theory that the user exceeded his or her "authorized access" to the site. By the same logic, therefore, a CFAA violation (and the resulting civil and criminal penalties) may be triggered anytime a user violates any website's terms of service, not just Facebook's, and obtains anything of value.

The Ninth Circuit's holding in *Facebook, Inc. v. MaxBounty* is consistent with the rulings of other courts refusing to limit the reach of the CAN-SPAM Act to traditional email messages.[24] In *MySpace v. The Globe.Com, Inc.*,[25] for example, a California District Court observed that the "overarching intent of this legislation is to safeguard the convenience and efficiency of the electronic messaging system, and to curtail overburdening of the system's infrastructure." The court concluded that limiting "the protection to only electronic mail that falls within the narrow confines set forth by Defendant does little to promote the Congress's overarching intent in enacting CAN-SPAM."[26]

To be safe, particularly in light of the severe civil and criminal penalties for violations of the statute,[27] all social network messages that are commercial in nature, whether submitted by an advertiser or by a consumer who has been induced by the advertiser to send a message, should be considered electronic communications subject to the CAN-SPAM Act.

In determining whether an online message is subject to the CAN-SPAM Act, regard must be paid to the *primary purpose* of the message. If the message contains only commercial content, its primary purpose is commercial, and it must comply with the requirements of the CAN-SPAM Act. If it contains only *transactional or relationship*[28] content (for instance, content that facilitates an already agreed-upon transaction or updates a customer about an ongoing transaction), its primary purpose is transactional or relationship. In that case, it is exempt from most provisions of the CAN-SPAM Act, although it may not contain false or misleading routing information.

 Note

> If the message combines commercial content and transactional or relation-
> ship content, the primary purpose of the message is decided by a reason-
> ableness test. If a recipient reasonably interpreting the subject line would
> likely conclude that the message contains an advertisement or promotion
> for a commercial product or service, the primary purpose of the message
> is commercial. Likewise, if the majority of the transactional or relationship
> part of the message does not appear at the beginning of the message, it is
> a commercial message under the CAN-SPAM Act.

Commercial electronic messages must adhere to the following CAN-SPAM Act requirements:

- The message cannot contain header information that is materially false or misleading. Your From, To, Reply-To, and routing information—including the originating email address, domain name, or IP address—must be accurate and identify the person or business who initiated the message.[29]

- The message cannot contain deceptive subject headings. The subject heading must accurately reflect the contents or subject matter of the message.[30]

- The message must clearly and conspicuously identify that the message is an advertisement or solicitation.[31]

- The message must provide a valid physical postal address of the sender.[32]

- The message must include a clear and conspicuous explanation of how the recipient can opt out of getting future emails from the sender.[33]

- The sender must be able to process opt-out requests for at least 30 days after it sends the message,[34] and it must honor the opt-out requests within 10 business days.[35]

Although the *Facebook, Inc. v. MaxBounty* court did not give any guidance as how to achieve compliance with CAN-SPAM Act with respect to Facebook transmissions like wall postings, messages, and news feed updates, best practices include, at a minimum, identifying the communication as an advertisement and providing an opt-out option for future messages. In light of the Federal Trade Commission's

(FTC) increased enforcement actions against violators of the CAN-SPAM Act, those who use social media to send what have now been defined as electronic mail messages without complying with the Act's requirements do so at their own peril.

The Children's Online Privacy Protection Act (COPPA)

Companies using social media in advertising campaigns (or for other business purposes) should also be aware of legal restrictions on their privacy and data security practices as regards to minors.

The COPPA Rule,[36] issued pursuant to the Children's Online Privacy Protection Act (COPPA),[37] imposes certain requirements on operators of websites or online services directed to children under 13 years of age, and on operators of other websites or online services that have actual knowledge that they are collecting personal information online from a child under 13 (collectively, *operators*). The Rule became effective on April 21, 2000.

 Note

Some sites obviously target children (for example, games, cartoons, school-age educational material). Nonetheless, operators of websites publishing content that may attract children also need to observe COPPA. Whether a website is directed to children under 13 is determined objectively based on whether the site's subject matter and language are child-oriented, whether advertising appearing on the site targets children, or whether the site uses animated characters, famous teen idols, or other similar kid-friendly devices. Simply stating that your site is not directed to children under 13 is insufficient to achieve COPPA immunity.

Further, while not necessarily required by COPPA, companies which sell products not suitable for or legally available to minors (for example, alcohol or tobacco) have a separate set of legal obligations regarding restricting access to their web (and social media) sites. Various service providers are beginning to offer products to allow companies to restrict their marketing messages (and followers) to consumers above a certain age. For example, social relationship management platform company, Vitrue, created a fictitious Twitter account (@BrookstrutAle) to showcase its new "Twitter Gate" feature to screen followers (see Figure 7.3). After attempting to follow a brand, Twitter Gate sends a direct message to the would-be follower: "We only allow people who are of legal drinking age to follow us. Please click this link to verify your age: pub.vitrue.com/kFH." The link in turn brings you to a page where the consumer's age can be verified.

Figure 7.3   *A fictitious Twitter account designed to showcase Vitrue's "Twitter Gate."*

Among other things, the Rule requires operators to meet specific requirements prior to collecting, using, or disclosing personal information from children, including, but not limited to, the following:

- **Post a privacy policy** on the home page of its website or online service and a link to the privacy policy everywhere personal information from children is collected.[38]

- **Provide notice to parents** about the site's information collection practices and, with some exceptions, obtain verifiable parental consent before collecting, using or disclosing personal information from children.[39]

- **Give parents the choice to consent** to the collection and use of a child's personal information for internal use by the website or online service, and give them the chance to choose not to have that personal information disclosed to third parties.[40]

- **Provide parents with reasonable access** to their child's information and the opportunity to delete the information and opt out of the future collection or use of the information.[41]

- **Not condition a child's participation in a game**, the offering of a prize, or another activity on the disclosure of more personal information than is reasonably necessary to participate in the activity.[42]

- **Establish and maintain reasonable procedures** to protect the confidentiality, security and integrity of the personal information collected from children.[43]

Note

Take care to design your age-collection input screen in a manner that does not encourage children to provide a false age to gain access to your site. Visitors should be asked to enter their age in a neutral, nonsuggestive manner. In particular, visitors should not be informed of adverse consequences prior to inputting their age (that is, that visitors under 13 cannot participate or need parental consent in order to participate), because this might simply result in untruthful entries. Cookies should also be used to prevent children from back-arrowing to enter a false age when they discover they do not qualify.

Neither COPPA nor the Rule defines *online service*, but it has been interpreted broadly to include any service available over the Internet or that connects to the Internet or a wide area network, including mobile applications that allow children to

- Play network connected games

- Engage in social networking activities

- Purchase goods or services online

- Receive behaviorally targeted advertisements

- Interact with other content or services[44]

Likewise, Internet-enabled gaming platforms, Voice over IP (VoIP) services, and Internet-enabled location-based services, are also online services covered by COPPA and the Rule.[45] In addition, retailers' premium texting and coupon texting programs that register users online and send text messages from the Internet to users' mobile phone numbers are online services.[46]

COPPA Enforcement

The FTC has brought a number of cases alleging violations of COPPA in connection with social networking services, including the following:

- ***U.S. v. Sony BMG Music Entertainment:***[47] In this case, the FTC alleged that, through its music fan websites, Sony BMG Music Entertainment enabled children to create personal fan pages, review artists' albums, upload photos or videos, post comments on message boards and in online forums, and engage in private messaging, in violation of COPPA. Sony BMG was fined $1 million in civil penalties.

- **U.S. v. Industrious Kid, Inc.:**[48] In this case, Industrious Kid, Inc. was fined $130,000 for operating a web and blog-hosting service that permitted children to message, blog, and share pictures without first obtaining verifiable parental consent prior to collecting, using, or disclosing personal information from children online.

- **U.S. v. Godwin (d/b/a skidekids.com):**[49] Skidekids, operator of self-proclaimed "Facebook and Myspace for Kids," was fined $100,000 for obtaining children's birth date, gender, username, password, and email without prior parental consent.

- **U.S. v. Xanga.com, Inc.:**[50] Xanga.com, which provides free or premium log template software to its registered members and publishes the members' blogs on the Internet, was fined $1 million in civil penalties for collecting date-of-birth information from users who indicated that they were under the age of 13.

On August 12, 2011, in its first case (*U.S. v. W3 Innovations, LLC*[51]) involving the applicability of COPPA to child-directed mobile apps (specifically games for the iPhone and iPod touch), the FTC filed a complaint against W3 Innovations, LLC. The FTC said W3 Innovations, a mobile app developer and owner, violated the COPPA Rule by illegally collecting and disclosing information from children under the age of 13 without their parents' prior verifiable consent.

In its complaint, the FTC alleged that the defendants—owner Justin Maples and W3 Innovations, doing business as Broken Thumbs Apps—collected and permanently maintained more than 30,000 email addresses from users of their Emily's Girl World and Emily's Dress-Up apps. The apps also included features such as a blog, which invites users to post "shout-outs" to friends and family members, ask advice, share embarrassing "blush" stories, submit art and pet photographs, and write comments on blog entries that provided users the chance to freely post personal information.

According to the FTC, the defendants failed to provide notice of their information-collection practices and did not obtain verifiable consent from parents prior to collecting, using, or disclosing their children's personal information, all in violation of the COPPA Rule.

The defendants agreed to pay a $50,000 civil penalty to settle the charges. The defendants further agreed to refrain from future violations of COPPA, agreed to delete all personal information collected and maintained in violation of the Rule, and consented to compliance monitoring for a 3-year period.

⚖ Legal Insight

Best practices dictate that all websites post privacy policies regarding the website operator's information practices. This is a requirement as it relates to collecting personally identifiable information from children under 13 years old. For such companies, their privacy policy should include the name, address, telephone number, and email address of each operator collecting or maintaining personal information from children through their sites; the types of personal information collected from children; and how that information is collected (for example, directly inputted, cookies, GUIDs, IP addresses).

The privacy policy also should detail how such personal information is or might be used, and it should explain whether such personal information is disclosed to third parties, providing parents the option to deny consent to disclosure of the collected information to third parties.

Finally, the policy should also state that the operator cannot condition a child's participation in an activity on the disclosure of more information than is reasonably necessary to participate; that parents can access their child's personal information to review or have the information deleted; and that parents have the opportunity to refuse to permit further use or collection of the child's information.

Proposed Changes to COPPA

On September 15, 2011, in the face of rapid technological and marketing developments and the growing popularity of social networking and interactive gaming with children, the FTC announced proposed amendments to the COPPA Rule.[52] The proposed changes, if adopted by the FTC, will profoundly impact websites and other online services, including mobile applications, that collect information from children under 13 years old, even if the operator merely prompts or encourages (versus requires) a child to provide such information.[53]

Definition Changes

The proposed amendment changes key definitions to information from children. The most important definitional changes are examined here:

- **Personal information:** The proposed amendment expands the definition of *personal information* to include IP addresses, geolocation information, screen names, instant messenger names, video chat names, and other usernames (even when not linked to an email address), and additional types of persistent identifiers (that is, codes and cookies that recognize specific IP addresses)—other than those collected solely for the purpose of internal operations—such as tracking cookies used for behavioral advertising. Accordingly, personal information includes not just personally identifiable information provided by a consumer, but information that identifies the user's computer or mobile device. As an additional measure to avoid tracking children, and which would have far-reaching impact for many companies using social media contests and marketing, photographs, videos and audio files that contain a child's image or voice may also be added to the definition of personal information because of the metadata (in particular, location data) that they store.

- **Collection:** The FTC proposes broadening its definition of *collection* to include circumstances both where an operator requires the personal information and when the operator merely prompts or encourages a child to provide such information. The revised definition also enables children to participate in interactive communities, without parental consent, provided that the operator takes reasonable measures to delete "all or virtually all" children's personal information from a child's postings before they are made public, and to delete it from its records.

- **Online contact information:** The FTC proposes expanding the definition of *online contact information* to encompass all identifiers that permit direct contact with a person online, including instant messaging user identifiers, VoIP identifiers, and video chat user identifiers.

⚖ *Legal Insight*

In its initial Request for Public Comment, the FTC noted that it sought public input on the implications for COPPA enforcement raised by technologies such as mobile communications, interactive television, interactive gaming, and other evolving media. In this regard, the FTC specifically requested comments on the terms *website*, *website located on the Internet*, and *online services*, which are used, but not defined, in COPPA and the Rule.

Following the initial comment period, the FTC found participant consensus that COPPA and the Rule are "written broadly enough to encompass many new technologies without the need for new statutory language."[54] Accordingly, the FTC concluded that *online service* is broad enough to "cover any service available over the Internet, or that connects to the Internet or a wide-area network."[55] The FTC further concluded that the term *website located on the Internet*, covers "content that users can access through a browser on an ordinary computer or mobile device."[56]

In the FTC's view, COPPA and the Rule apply to "mobile applications that allow children to play network-connected games, engage in social networking activities, purchase goods or services online, receive behaviorally targeted advertisements, or interact with other content or services."[57] Further, "Internet-enabled gaming platforms, voice-over–Internet protocol services, and Internet-enabled location-based services also are online services covered by COPPA and the Rule."[58]

Parental Notice

COPPA currently requires that parents be notified via online notice and direct notice of an operator's information-collection and information-use practices. The FTC proposes changes to both kinds of notice:

- **On the operator's website or online service (the *online notice*, usually in the form of a posted privacy policy):** For online notice, the FTC would require that parental notification take place in "a succinct 'just-in-time' notice, and not just a privacy policy." In other words, key information about an operator's information practices would have to be presented in a link placed on the website's home page and in close proximity to any requests for information.

- **In a notice delivered directly to the parent whose child seeks to register on the site or service (the *direct notice*):** For direct notice, the FTC would require operators to provide more detail about the personal information already collected from the child (for example, the parent's online contact information either alone or together with the child's online contact information); the purpose of the notification; action that the parents must or may take; and what use, if any, the operator will make of the personal information collected.

Parental Consent Mechanisms

The proposed Rule would also significantly change the mechanisms for obtaining verifiable parental consent before collecting children's information. One such change eliminates the less-reliable "email plus" method of consent, which currently allows operators to obtain consent through an email to the parent, provided an additional verification step is taken, such as sending a delayed email confirmation to the parent after receiving consent. Instead, the proposed Rule provides for new measures to obtain verifiable parental consent, including consent by video conference, scanned signed parental consent forms, and use of government-issued identification, provided that the identification information is deleted immediately after consent is verified.

Confidentiality and Security Requirements

The FTC also proposes tightening the Rule's current security and confidentiality requirements. In particular, operators of sites that collect children's information would be required to ensure that:

- Any third parties receiving user information have reasonable security measures in place

- Collected information is retained for only as long as is reasonably necessary

- The information is properly and promptly deleted to guard against unauthorized access to, or use in connection with, its disposal.

 Note

In February 2012, the FTC released a staff report—*Mobile Apps for Kids Current Privacy Disclosures are DisAPPointing*[59]— detailing its concerns regarding the privacy failures in many mobile apps directed towards children and with the lack of information available to parents prior to downloading such apps. According to the FTC, "[p]arents should be able to learn what information an app collects, how the information will be used, and with whom the information will be shared"—prior to download. The study recommends, among other steps, that App developers provide this information through simple and short disclosures or icons that are easy to find and understand on the small screen of a mobile device, and alert parents if the app connects with any social media, or allows targeted advertising to occur through the app. Connection to social media sites could pose a problem, because the terms of most social media sites, including Facebook, specifically prohibit access if the user is under 13. The report indicates that, in the coming months following the report's release, the FTC "will conduct an additional review to determine whether there are COPPA violations and whether enforcement is appropriate." In light of the FTC's vigorous enforcement of COPPA and the Rule, app developers and other businesses which target children are reminded to have compliance measures in place prior to collecting personal information from children.

Safe Harbor Programs

The COPPA Rule encourages industry groups to create their own COPPA programs, seek FTC approval, and help website operators to comply with the Rule by using the programs (known as *safe harbor programs*). The FTC proposes strengthening its oversight of self-regulatory safe harbor programs by incorporating initial audits and annual reviews. Under the revised Rule, the FTC would also require industry groups seeking to create programs to verify their competence to create and oversee such programs, and it would require groups that run safe harbor programs to oversee their members.

The FTC's proposed revisions are a means to catch the COPPA Rule up with evolving technologies. All entities operating websites or mobile games directed to children or websites or mobile games that are used by (or attract) children should be aware of the COPPA Rule and the FTC's proposed changes. Noncompliance carries with it a very high price tag—up to $1,000 per violation (that is, per child), an amount that can rapidly balloon into hundreds of thousands of dollars (or more) for even a moderately popular website, mobile game, or app.

As of the date of publication, there are five safe harbor programs approved by the FTC. Generally speaking, operators that participate in a COPPA safe harbor program will be subject to the review and disciplinary procedures provided in the safe harbor's guidelines in lieu of formal FTC investigation and law enforcement.

Currently, to be approved by the FTC, self-regulatory guidelines must: (1) require that participants in the safe harbor program implement substantially similar requirements that provide the same or greater protections for children as those contained in the Rule; (2) set forth an effective, mandatory mechanism for the independent assessment of safe harbor program participants' compliance with the guidelines; and (3) provide effective incentives for safe harbor program participants' compliance with such guidelines.[60]

On February 24, 2012, Aristotle International, Inc. became the fifth FTC-approved safe harbor program.[61] Embracing new and evolving technologies, Aristotle's safe harbor program allows participants to obtain parental consent throughhe "use of electronic real-time face-to-face verification"[62] via Skype and similar video-conferencing technologies, and by e-mailing an electronically signed consent form along with a scanned copy of a government-issued identification document.

Summation

Ignoring the legal issues and lessons surrounding social media advertising is fraught with peril and can expose advertisers (and they brands they represent) to significant penalties. Businesses and their advertisers using social media would do well to heed the legal tips outlined in this chapter, and summarized in Figure 7.4.

Social Media Legal Tips for Advertisement

DOs	DON'Ts
■ Ensure your social media advertising claims are truthful, fair, and non-deceptive, and that any employees or agents working on your behalf as social media advertisers are familiar with the FTC Act, Lanham Act, CAN-SPAM Act, and COPPA to minimize risk of legal violations.	■ Do not include in your ads any representations that are deceptive, misleading, or unsubstantiated. If you don't have proof that the claimed experience represents what consumers will achieve by using you product, the ad must clearly and conspicuously disclose the generally expected results in the depicted circumstances. Disclaimers like "Results not typical" or "Individual results may vary" are not sufficient.
■ Train your employees—and outside media providers—that the traditional rules of advertising equally apply in the social media context. Be sure to avoid making false statement (express or implied) about your products, or those of a competitor, in any medium.	■ Do not assume that you never bear responsible for statements made by others regarding your products or services. Companies may face liability not only for the false or unsubstantiated claims they make, but also for such claims made on their behalf.
■ Be aware that commercial messages sent through social media must comply with the CAN-SPAM Act, including the requirement to clearly and conspicuously identify that the message is an advertisement or solicitation.	■ Do not send unsolicited commercial messages via Facebook (or other social media networks) without providing a clear and conspicuous explanation of how the recipient can opt out of getting future messages from you.
■ Realize that social media communications directed to children under 13 are subject to COPPA, including the requirement to obtain verifiable parental consent before collecting, using, or disclosing any personal information from children.	■ Do not condition a child's participation in a game, the offering of a prize, or any other activity on the disclosure of more personal information than is reasonably necessary to participate in the activity.
■ Keep abreast of changes in COPPA, particularly as it relates to what personal information is protected (for example, geo-location information and screen names) and whether "email plus" will remain an authorized parental consent mechanism.	■ In advertisements which collect information from children, do not design your age-collection input screen in a manner that encourages children to provide a false age to participate. Visitors should not be informed of adverse consequences prior to inputting their age (that is, that visitors under 13 cannot participate or need parental consent in order to participate), because this might result in untruthful entries.

Figure 7.4   *Social Media Legal Tips for Advertising.*

CHAPTER 7 ENDNOTES

1   15 U.S.C. §§ 45 and 52

2   A number of states have modeled their consumer protection statutes on the FTC Act. *See*, for example, California Unfair Competition Act, CAL. BUS. & PROF. CODE. § 17200; Connecticut Unfair Trade Practices Act, CONN. GEN. STAT. § 42-110b; Florida Deceptive and Unfair Trade Practices Act, FLA. STAT. § 501.204; Georgia Fair Business Practices Act, GA. CODE ANN. § 10-1-391; Hawaii's Antitrust and Consumer Protection Laws, HAW. REV. STAT. § 480-2; Louisiana Unfair Trade Practices and Consumer Protection Law, LA. REV. STAT. ANN. §§ 51:1401-1426; Maine Unfair Trade Practices Act, ME. REV. STAT. tit. 5, §§ 207-214; Massachusetts Consumer Protection Act, MASS. GEN. LAWS ch. 93A § 2; Montana Unfair Trade Practices and Consumer Protection Act, MONT. CODE ANN. §§ 30-14-103 to -104; Nebraska Consumer Protection Act, NEB. REV. STAT. §§ 59-1601 to -1623; New York Consumer Protection Act, N.Y. GEN. BUS. LAW § 349; North Carolina Monopolies, Trusts and Consumer Protection Act, N.C. GEN. STAT. § 75-1.1; Ohio Consumer Sales Practices Act, OHIO REV. CODE ANN. § 1345.02; Rhode Island Deceptive Trade Practices Act, R.I. GEN. LAWS §§ 6-13.1-2 to .1-3; South Carolina Unfair Trade Practices Act, S.C. CODE ANN. § 39-5-20; Vermont Consumer Fraud Statute, VT. STAT. ANN. tit. 9, §§ 2451-2453; and Washington Consumer Protection Act, WASH. REV. CODE § 19.86.920.

3   15 U.S.C. § 45(n)

4   15 U.S.C. § 55(a)(1)

5   *See* FTC's *Policy Statement on Deception* (Oct. 14, 1983), appended to *Cliffdale Associates, Inc.*, 103 F.T.C. 110, 174 (1984), available at http://www.ftc.gov/bcp/policystmt/ad-decept.htm

6   *See* FTC's *FTC Policy Statement on Unfairness* (Dec. 17, 1980), appended to *International Harvester Co.*, 104 F.T.C. 949, 1070 (1984), available at http://www.ftc.gov/bcp/policystmt/ad-unfair.htm

7   *Id.*

8   *See* FTC's *Policy Statement Regarding Advertising Substantiation* (Aug. 2, 1984), appended to *Thompson Medical Co.*, 104 F.T.C. 648, 839 (1984), *aff'd*, 791 F.2d 189 (D.C. Cir. 1986), cert. denied, 479 U.S. 1086 (1987), available at http://www.ftc.gov/bcp/guides/ad3subst.htm

9   16 C.F.R. § 255.1 (Example 5)

10   15 U.S.C. § 1125(a)

11   *Doctor's Associates, Inc. v. QIP Holder LLC, et al.*, Case No. 3:06-CV-1710 (D. Conn.) (Oct. 27, 2006)

12   *Doctor's Associates, Inc. v. QIP Holder LLC, et al.*, Case No. 3:06-CV-1710 (D. Conn.) (Oct. 27, 2006) (Document 271) (Order denying defendants' Motion for Summary Judgment entered Feb. 19, 2010)

13   *Ocean Spray Cranberries, Inc. v. Decas Cranberry Prods., Inc.*, Case No. 1:10-CV-11288-RWZ . Mass.) (Aug. 2, 2010)

14   *Northern Star Industries, Inc., V. Douglas Dynamics, LLC*, Case No. 2:11-CV-1103-RTR (E.D. Wis.) (Dec. 5, 2011)

15   *Northern Star Industries, Inc., V. Douglas Dynamics, LLC*, Case No. 2:11-CV-1103-RTR (E.D. Wis.) (Jan. 26, 2012)(Document 38) (Decision and Order)

16   15 U.S.C. § 7701 *et seq.*

17   15 U.S.C § 7704(a)(1)

18 15 U.S.C. § 7702(6)

19 15 U.S.C. § 7702(5); *MySpace v. Wallace*, 498 F.Supp.2d 1293, 1300 (C.D. Cal. 2007)

20 15 U.S.C. § 7702(2)(A)

21 *Facebook, Inc. v. MaxBounty, Inc.*, Case No. 5:10-CV-4712-JF, Order Granting in Part and Denying in Part Motion to Dismiss (Docket No. 35) (Mar. 28, 2011)

22 *Facebook, Inc. v. MaxBounty, Inc.*, Case No. 5:10-CV-4712-JF, Order Denying Motion to Dismiss (Docket No. 46) (Sept. 14, 2011)

23 18 U.S.C. § 1030. *See*, in particular, § 1030(a)(4), which provides that "Whoever knowingly and with intent to defraud, accesses a protected computer without authorization, or exceeds authorized access, and by means of such conduct furthers the intended fraud and obtains anything of value, unless the object of the fraud and the thing obtained consists only of the use of the computer and the value of such use is not more than $5,000 in any 1 year period ... shall be punished as provided in subsection (c) of this section."

24 *See*, for example, *MySpace v. Wallace*, 498 F.Supp.2d 1293, 1300 (C.D. Cal. 2007); *see also MySpace v. The Globe.Com, Inc.*, 2007 WL 168696, at *4 (C.D. Cal. Feb. 27, 2007)

25 *MySpace v. The Globe.Com, Inc.*, 2007 WL 168696 (C.D. Cal. Feb. 27, 2007)

26 *Id.*, at *4

27 Each separate electronic message sent in violation of the CAN-SPAM Act is subject to penalties of up to $16,000. Further, the CAN-SPAM Act has certain aggravated violations that may give rise to additional civil and criminal penalties, including imprisonment.

28 The primary purpose of an email is transactional or relationship if it consists only of content that:

   (i)   Facilitates, completes, or confirms a commercial transaction that the recipient already has agreed to enter into with the sender

   (ii) Provides warranty, product recall, safety, or security information about a product or service used or purchased by the recipient

   (iii) Provides information about a change in terms or features or account balance information regarding a membership, subscription, account, loan or other ongoing commercial relationship

   (iv) Provides information directly related to an employment relationship or employee benefit plan in which the recipient is currently participating or enrolled

   or

   (v)   Delivers goods or services as part of a transaction that the recipient is entitled to receive under the terms of a preexisting agreement with the sender.

   See 15 U.S.C. § 7702(17)(A)

29 15 U.S.C. § 7704(a)(1)

30 15 U.S.C. § 7704(a)(2)

31 15 U.S.C. § 7704(a)(5)(A)(i)

32 15 U.S.C. § 7704(a)(5)(A)(iii)

33 15 U.S.C. § 7704(a)(5)(A)(ii)

34 15 U.S.C. § 7704(a)(3)(A)(ii)

35 15 U.S.C. § 7704(a)(4)(A)

36 16 C.F.R. Part 312

37 15 U.S.C. § 6501 *et seq.*

38 16 C.F.R. §§ 312.4(b)

39 16 C.F.R. §§ 312.4(b) and 312.5

40 16 C.F.R. § 312.5

41 16 C.F.R. § 312.6

42 16 C.F.R. § 312.7

43 16 C.F.R. § 312.8

44 See the FTC's Request for Public Comment to Its Proposed Amendments to COPPA, "COPPA Rule Review, 16 CFR Part 312, Project No. P-104503," available at http://www.ftc.gov/os/2011/09/110915coppa.pdf

45 *Id.*

46 *Id.* (wherein the FTC stated, by way of example, that text alert coupon and notification services offered by retailers such as Target and JC Penney are online services)

47 *U.S. v. Sony BMG Music Entertainment*, Case No. 1:08-CV-10730 (S.D.N.Y, filed Dec. 10, 2008). You can find a copy of the consent decree and order at http://www.ftc.gov/os/caselist/0823071/081211consentp0823071.pdf.

48 *U.S. v. Industrious Kid, Inc.*, Case No. 3:08-CV-0639 (N.D. Cal., filed Jan. 28, 2008). You can find a copy of the consent decree and order at http://www.ftc.gov/os/caselist/0723082/080730cons.pdf.

49 *U.S. v. Godwin (d/b/a skidekids.com)*, Case No. 1:11-CV-03846-JOF (N.D. Ga., filed Nov. 8, 2011). You can find a copy of the consent decree and order at http://www.ftc.gov/os/caselist/1123033/111108skidekidsorder.pdf.

50 *U.S. v. Xanga.com, Inc.*, Case No. 1:06-CV-6853-SH (S.D.N.Y., filed Sept. 7, 2006). You can find a copy of the consent decree and order at http://www.ftc.gov/os/caselist/0623073/xangaconsentdecree_image.pdf.

51 *U.S. v. W3 Innovations LLC*, Case No. CV-11-03958 (N.D. Cal., filed Aug. 12, 2011). You can find a copy of the consent decree and order at http://www.ftc.gov/os/caselist/1023251/110815w3order.pdf.

52 *See* Request for Public Comment to the Federal Trade Commission's Proposed Amendments to COPPA, 76 FR 59804 ("COPPA Rule Review") (Sept. 27, 2011), available at http://www.ftc.gov/os/2011/09/110915coppa.pdf.

53 The FTC accepted comments on the proposed amendments to the COPPA Rule until December 23, 2011.

54 *See* Request for Public Comment to the Federal Trade Commission's Proposed Amendments to COPPA, 76 FR 59804, at 59807 ("COPPA Rule Review") (Sept. 27, 2011), available at http://www.ftc.gov/os/2011/09/110915coppa.pdf.

55 *Id.*

56 *Id.*

57 *Id.*

58 *Id.*

59 *See* FTC's *Mobile Apps for Kids: Current Privacy Disclosures are DisAPPointing* (Feb. 2012), available at http://www.ftc.gov/os/2012/02/120216mobile_apps_kids.pdf.

60 16 C.F.R. § 312.10(b)

61 *See* FTC's Letter Approving Aristotle, Inc.'s Safe Harbor Program Application Under the Children's Online Privacy Protection Rule (Feb. 24, 2012), available at http://www.ftc.gov/os/2012/02/120224aristotlecoppa.pdf.

62 *See* Revised Request for Safe Harbor Approval by the Federal Trade Commission for Aristotle International, Inc.'s Integrity Safe Harbor Compliance Program Under Section 312.10 of the Children's Online Privacy Protection Rule, available at http://www.ftc.gov/os/2012/02/120224aristotleapplication.pdf.

Trademark Protections from Brandjacking and Cybersquatting in Social Networks

A company's most valuable commercial asset is often its brand. Further, a brand's ability to communicate directly with its customers is crucial in today's social business climate. Controlling your business's social network usernames, handles and domain names is therefore critical. After all, you do not want your company's image (or message) to be hijacked by spammers, brandjackers, cybersquatters, impersonators, or competitors.

Generally speaking, "brandjacking" (a clever neologism combining the words "brand" and "hijacking") is the action of acquiring or assuming the online identity of another for purposes of capturing that person's or business's brand equity.

> You do not want your company's image (or message) to be hijacked by spammers, brandjackers, cybersquatters, impersonators, or competitors.

Brandjackers operate in a variety of ways, usually by attempting to leverage the reputation of their target for their own gain, or working to destroy the reputation of their target for malicious reasons. Regardless of the brandjacker's motive (be it financial or otherwise), the effect on the victim's brand can be quite devastating, causing significant PR and financial damage, including lost clients, sales, and market share (and potential stock price plummet for public companies), and an erosion of a brand's reputation and goodwill.

Cybersquatting, or domain squatting, is a similar tactic employed to misappropriate another's brand equity. Cybersquatting is usually defined as the registering, trafficking in, or using a domain name with bad faith intent to profit from the goodwill of a trademark belonging to someone else. Cybersquatting can also wreak havoc on a company looking to "own" a certain domain (in connection with a new product release, for example) only to find that the domain is already being "squatted" upon (and being ransomed by the cybersquatter).

This chapter discusses strategies and best practices for minimizing your exposure to these risks, as well as available remedies should you find yourself the victim of brandjacking or cybersquatting. In particular, this chapter examines the platform-specific complaint mechanisms to remove brand-damaging activity, and details additional redress available to companies under the federal Lanham (Trademark) Act, which includes the Anticybersquatting Consumer Protection Act.

Notable Cases of Brandjacking and Cybersquatting

One of the more well-publicized cases of *brandjacking* involved the manager of the St. Louis Cardinals, Tony La Russa. On May 6, 2009, La Russa filed a lawsuit[1] against Twitter, alleging that the company allowed an imposter to register the domain, twitter.com/TonyLaRussa, which contained an unauthorized photograph of La Russa and written statements impliedly written by La Russa, when in fact they were not. According to the complaint, the tweets originating from this handle were derogatory and demeaning, and therefore damaged La Russa's trademark rights in his name. One tweet, for example, following the death of two Cardinals pitchers, stated that there were no drunk-driving incidents on the St. Louis Cardinals' latest road trip. (The case settled within a month, and the real Tony La Russa appears to now "own" the @TonyLaRussa handle.)

Businesses, of course, are also susceptible to brandjacking and cybersquatting on social networking sites. BP, for instance, found itself the target of a fake Twitter account (http://twitter.com/BPGlobalPR) (see Figure 8.1) that was created in response to the damage caused by the 2010 Gulf of Mexico oil spill. The spoof account includes BP's logo, soiled with oil dripping down its side, and regular tweets such as the following:

- "Very excited to report that there is a Sheen in the Gulf of Mexico!"

- "BP never used false numbers to downplay the severity of the spill. Also, it happened like 100 years ago, get over it."

This spoofed account has more than 150,000 followers (that is, approximately 120,000 more than the official BP America twitter account) as of the time of this writing.

Figure 8.1 *Spoof BP Twitter page.*

🍷 *Legal Insight*

Netflix's recent pricing fiasco also included a comical Twitter account blunder. In 2011, Netflix, the popular DVD-by-mail and online streaming service company, announced that it was increasing its combo plan from $10 per month to $16 per month. Following a huge uproar among its customers (and a 50% drop in its stock price), Netflix decided that it would split the DVD and streaming businesses into two separate entities, forcing customers who wanted both services to maintain two accounts, one for the DVD service (to be named Qwikster) and the other for the streaming service. Miscalculating the anger that this decision would incite, and the power of social media to communicate customer dissatisfaction and ridicule, Netflix was inundated with a vocal online backlash. To exacerbate matters, before introducing its new DVD service, Netflix failed to secure the Twitter handle for Qwikster—which Netflix later discovered was already being used by a pot-smoking Elmo posting obscene tweets (see Figure 8.2). Suffice it to say that Qwikster was quickly abandoned. Lesson: Be sure to secure your Twitter handle (and other social media account names) before launching a new product or business.

Figure 8.2   *Netflix must have been quite surprised to learn that its new product's eponymous Twitter handle, @Qwikster was already taken by "Elmo," who now apparently tweets from @ThisBeQwikster.*

Similarly, in June 2011, Coventry First, a "leading company in the life settlement industry" sued anonymous individuals (or group of individuals) tweeting from the @coventryfirst twitter account.[2] Coventry apparently became the target of this twitterjacking because of its (to some, controversial) alleged business practices: buying life insurance policies and receiving payment of the insurance proceeds (hopefully at a profit) when the insured dies.

The complaint claimed, among other things, that by establishing and using the domain, twitter.com/coventryfirst, the defendants infringed Coventry First's trademark rights. Approximately one month after filing suit, Coventry withdrew its case. As to the Twitter account holder ("Doe"), this person added a parody disclaimer, and an "in" to the username (see Figure 8.3), to keep from running afoul of Twitter's parody guidelines, which requires, among other things, that a username not be the exact name of the subject of the parody.[3]

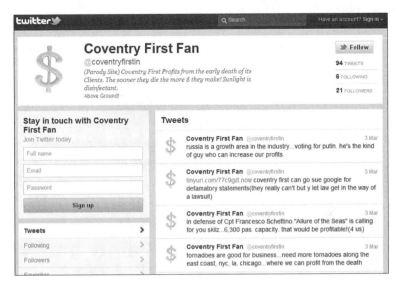

Figure 8.3   *Coventry First "parody site"*

Likewise, in 2009, ONEOK, Inc., a natural gas distributor and Fortune 500 company, also found itself the victim of twitterjacking. After unsuccessfully attempting to have the twitter account @ONEOK transferred to it, ONEOK, Inc. sued Twitter for trademark infringement for assigning this twitter handle to a third party.[4] According to the complaint, the ONEOK Twitter account holder had tweeted at least twice with information regarding ONEOK, Inc., passing off such tweets to unsuspecting recipients as official company statements. The day after filing the complaint, ONEOK, Inc. voluntarily dismissed its action against Twitter, and the Twitter account was transferred to the company.

As the above cases suggest, businesses that become victims of username jacking have several options available to protect their valuable trademarks, including reporting violations to the social media platforms themselves, and (as necessary) filing suit under the Lanham (Trademark) Act for trademark infringement and cybersquatting. These options are discussed in detail in the following sections.

Note

At the time of this writing, Twitter no longer verifies Twitter accounts.[5] Previously, in an effort to prevent imposter accounts, Twitter used a Verified Accounts system to establish the authenticity of identities on Twitter. An account that was verified indicated that Twitter had contacted the person/entity the account is representing and had verified their authenticity so that "users can trust that a legitimate source is authoring their tweets."

Currently, if a person or company is being impersonated, Twitter requests that users submit a *ticket request* to report the impersonation. Nonparody impersonations are a violation of the Twitter rules and might result in permanent account suspension, but parody, commentary, and fan accounts are allowed, provided, among other things, that:

- The username is not the exact name of the subject of the parody, commentary, or fandom. (The account should include a qualifier such as *not*, *fake*, or *fan*.)

- The profile name should not list the exact name of the subject without some other qualifying word, such as *not*, *fake*, or *fan*.

- The bio should include a statement to distinguish it from the real identity, such as "This is a parody," "This is a fan page," or "This is not affiliated with."

- The account should not, through private or public communication with other users, try to deceive or mislead others about the account creator's real identity.[6]

Trademark Infringement Under the Lanham Act

The Lanham (Trademark) Act[7] embodies federal trademark law in the United States. Under Section 32 of the Act (which applies to federally registered marks), one is liable for trademark infringement if he or she, without the consent of the trademark owner, "… use[s] in commerce any reproduction, counterfeit, copy, or colorable imitation of a registered mark in connection with the sale, offering for sale, distribution, or advertising of any goods or services …[in which] such use is likely to cause confusion, or to cause mistake, or to deceive."[8]

Similarly, under Section 43(a) of the Act (which applies equally to registered and unregistered marks), one is liable for trademark infringement if he or she "uses in commerce" another's mark "on or in connection with any goods or services" where such use is likely to cause confusion, mistake, or deception regarding the "affiliation, connection, or association" of that person with the markholder, or as to the "origin, sponsorship, or approval" of that person's "goods, services, or commercial activities."[9]

The key issue in a trademark dispute is whether the unauthorized use of another's mark is likely to cause confusion as to the source, sponsorship or affiliation of the goods or services in question. Generally, courts consider the following factors (often referred to as *the Polaroid factors*[10]), or similar factors, when assessing likelihood of consumer confusion:

- The strength of the plaintiff's mark

- The similarity of the marks at issue

- The degree to which the products or services compete

- The likelihood that the plaintiff will "bridge the gap" and offer a product or service similar to the defendant's in the reasonably near future

- Actual confusion between the products or services

- Good faith on the defendant's part in selecting its name or mark

- The quality of the defendant's products or services (that is, whether the plaintiff's reputation could be jeopardized by virtue of the fact that the defendant's product is of inferior quality)

- The sophistication of the buyers in the relevant market

 Note

Under the Lanham Act, one is liable for trademark infringement if he or she "use[s] in commerce" the mark of another, without the owner's permission. In several jurisdictions,[11] the casual use of another's trademark on a personal social media sites (or elsewhere) does not constitute "use in commerce," absent a showing that the party is using the mark to sell goods or services. In jurisdictions applying this rule, brands may have little recourse other than lodging platform-specific complaint and takedown requests to obtain removal of an infringing social media user name, account name or handle, as court relief will most likely prove unavailing.

In *New York City Triathlon, LLC v. NYC Triathlon Club, Inc.,*[12] the U.S. District Court for the Southern District of New York granted a preliminary injunction prohibiting the seller of triathlon equipment from using three proposed marks: NYC Triathlon Club, NYC Tri Club, and New York City Triathlon Club. These marks were prohibited because they would likely cause consumer confusion with (and therefore be infringing of) New York City Triathlon, LLC's preexisting marks: NEW YORK CITY TRIATHLON, NYC TRIATHLON, and NYC TRI.

The court concluded that New York City Triathlon, LLC was likely to succeed on the merits of its claim under Section 43(a) of the Lanham Act. Based on that decision, the court forbade NYC Triathlon Club, Inc. from using the marks "as a domain name on the Internet, or in any other way that is likely to cause confusion with Plaintiff or its trade name and trademarks."[13]

After learning that NYC Triathlon Club, Inc. had failed to "totally deactivate" its Twitter account, the court renewed its order:

> *"Defendant's actions with respect to its Twitter account violate the express terms of this Court's order, which enjoined Defendant from using any and all of Plaintiffs marks. The fact that Defendant is not accepting additional 'followers' on its 'nyctriclub' Twitter account and has 'protected' its 'tweets' (rendered them private)..., does not alter the fact that Defendant's 'nyctri-club' account is publicly viewable and patently in violation of the terms of the injunction. Defendant is ordered to remove any reference to 'nyctriclub' or any of Plaintiff's Marks or anything similar from all websites, social net-working sites and other forms of electronic media."[14]*

 ## Legal Insight

To avoid appearing as a corporate bully, brands should carefully consider the option of *not* reclaiming their usernames on social media pages, particularly if the page creator is a brand-friendly "evangelist" with many thousand followers. Coca-Cola's success with its Facebook page, which was created by two fans of Coca-Cola (and not the company itself), is a model in social media risk management.

Although Facebook's terms prohibit users from creating a branded Facebook page unless authorized by or associated with the brand, Coca-Cola elected not to close the page, but to keep it open and partner with both page founders, given the extraordinary popularity of the fan page.[15] Coca-Cola's social savvy paid off: The page repeatedly is ranked in the top 20 most popular Facebook pages in the world, and as of the date of this writing has more than 36 million followers.

Conversely, Chick-fil-A, the second-largest fast-food chicken restaurant chain in the United States and the owner of the federally registered trademark EAT MOR CHIKIN, did not fare so well when seeking to protect its intellectual property interests in our current social media climate.

According to an Associated Press article,[16] in October 2011, Chick-fil-A sent Bo Muller-Moore, creator of the EAT MORE KALE t-shirts, a cease and desist letter demanding that he stop using the phrase and transfer his website to Chick-fil-A.

Instead of backing down, Muller-Moore turned to social media and the press to defend his right to use the EAT MORE KALE slogan. In addition to creating a Facebook page (Protect "Eat More Kale") (which has more than 1,000 *likes* and more than 900 *talking abouts*), Mr. Muller-Moore's supporters created a petition on Change.org titled "Chick-fil-A: Stop Bullying Small Business Owners," which has more than 29,000 signatures. (See Figure 8.4.) Given the significant public and viral backlash that can arise from too aggressive trademark enforcement actions, companies should carefully weigh the benefits of such actions against the potentially sizeable negative impact on the company's reputation and consumer goodwill.

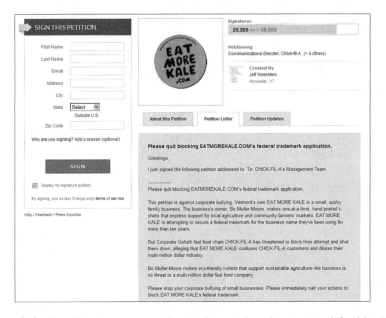

Figure 8.4   *Small business owner takes to the social media street to defend his EAT MORE KALE slogan against larger corporate trademark owner.*

Likewise, in *Black Sheep Television, Ltd. v. The Town of Islip*,[17] the U.S. District Court for the Eastern District of New York granted a preliminary injunction prohibiting Black Sheep Television—an airport information website operator that provides information and services to travelers of Macarthur Airport, formerly known as Islip Airport—from using several of its Twitter accounts that were similar to trademarks owned by the town of Islip. In particular, following failed negotiations between the parties, Black Sheep registered several domain names (for example, macarthurairport.com and islipairport.com) and reserved @FlyLIMA, @IslipAirport, @MacArthurAirprt, and @ISPAirport as Twitter addresses. Although Islip filed a complaint through Twitter's internal trademark infringement complaint mechanism seeking removal of all four imposter accounts, Twitter removed just one. In holding that the Town of Islip was likely to succeed on the merits of its claim that its marks were unlawfully incorporated into Black Sheep's Twitter accounts, the court ordered as follows:

> *"Plaintiff and all agents, representatives or assigns thereof ... are hereby enjoined from any use of the DOMAIN NAMES and the Twitter Accounts during the pendency of this action. These domain names and Twitter Accounts shall remain in the ownership, custody, and control of the Town of Islip throughout the pendency of this litigation."*[18]

 Legal Insight

On November 21, 2011, the German pharmaceutical company Merck KGaA (Merck) brought legal action in the New York State Supreme Court seeking an order requiring Facebook to disclose the circumstances leading to the "apparent takeover of its Facebook page."[19]

According to the legal papers filed in the case, Merck entered into an agreement with Facebook for the exclusive rights to facebook.com/merck in March 2010. However, when Merck checked the site in late 2011, it discovered that it had lost control of the page, and that content on the site now belonged to its U.S. rival, Merck & Co.

Merck claimed that the social network "is an important marketing device [and] the page is of great value." To determine its potential claims in a lawsuit against Merck & Co (for instance, for breach of contract, contractual interference with actual and prospective business relations, and/or civil theft), Merck sought prelitigation disclosure from Facebook "to determine the nature of the misconduct...and to identify the proper defendant or defendants."

This will be an interesting case to follow; it might offer important guidance regarding the legal remedies available for trademark infringement on social networks.

The Anticybersquatting Consumer Protection Act (ACPA)

The Anticybersquatting Consumer Protection Act (ACPA)[20] is a 1999 amendment to the Lanham Act that targets *cybersquatting*. An ACPA violation occurs when a domain name registrant registers, uses, or traffics in a domain name that is identical or confusingly similar to or dilutive of a distinctive or famous[21] trademark, with bad faith intent to profit from the goodwill associated with the trademark.

 Note

"Cybersquatting" occurs when an "individual other than the trademark owner registers a domain name similar or identical to the trademark and 'then attempts to profit from this by either ransoming the domain name back to the trademark holder or by using the domain name to divert business from the trademark holder to the domain name holder.'" [22] Methods of cybersquatting include registration of another's mark (and spelling variations thereof, so-called "typosquatting") as a domain name; registration of another's mark with an extension other than ".com"; and registration of another's mark as part of a domain name.

In determining whether the domain name registrant has a bad faith intent to profit (unlike in the Lanham Act, the ACPA does not require "use in commerce"), a court may consider the following nonexclusive (and nonexhaustive) factors:

- The registrant's trademark or other intellectual property rights, if any, in the domain name.

- Whether the domain name consists of the registrant's legal or common name (for example, Senator John McCain may not monopolize a LinkedIn URL taken by another individual legitimately so named).

- The registrant's prior use, if any, of the domain name in connection with the bona fide offering of goods or services.

- The registrant's bona fide noncommercial or fair use of the mark in a site accessible by the domain name (for example, comparative advertising, comment, criticism, parody, and news reporting).

- The registrant's intent to divert customers from the mark owner's online location to a site accessible under the domain name that could harm the goodwill represented by the mark, either for commercial gain or with the intent to tarnish or disparage the mark, by creating a likelihood of confusion as to the source, sponsorship, affiliation, or endorsement of the site.

- The registrant's offer to transfer, sell, or otherwise assign the domain name to the mark owner or a third party for financial gain, without having used, or having an intent to use, the mark in a legitimate site.

- The registrant's providing material and misleading false contact information when applying for the registration of the domain name.

- The registrant's registration or acquisition of multiple domain names that are identical or confusingly similar to marks of others.

- The extent to which the mark in the domain name registration is distinctive or famous.[23]

 ## Legal Insight

The ACPA does not prevent the fair use of trademarks or any use protected by the First Amendment, including criticism, parody, or gripe sites. *Mayflower Transit, LLC v. Prince*[24] is a good example. The defendant (Dr. Brett Prince) claimed that his personal property was lost in a moving incident involving Mayflower Transit, LLC. Afterward, Prince registered the Internet domain name mayflowervanlinebeware.com and posted a website at this address. The home page is headlined "Beware of Lincoln Storage Warehouse. Beware of Mayflower Van Line," and states, "If you are thinking about moving or had a bad experience moving with Mayflower Van Lines or Lincoln Storage Warehouses then please read on and reply to me at the following email address: MayflowerBeware@Yahoo.com."

A link to another page warned, "Unless you're willing to risk a total loss of your possessions, do not do business with Lincoln Storage Warehouses or Mayflower Van Lines. What happened to me can and will happen to you! Don't be their next victim!"

The court granted summary judgment in favor of Prince after finding that Prince did not have a bad faith intent to profit from Mayflower Transit, when he registered the domain name. The court dismissed Mayflower Transit's ACPA claim, too.

"The totality of circumstances in this case demonstrate that Defendant's motive for registering the disputed domain names and posting his criticism was to express his customer dissatisfaction through the medium of the Internet. Defendant's 'cyber-griping' is a far cry from the 'squatting' activity made illegal by the ACPA, in which a person purchases numerous domain names of prominent companies cheaply with the purpose of selling the domain names at a higher price to those companies. Whereas Defendant's activity may be actionable under other statutory provisions, a question the Court need not decide today, it is clear that these actions do not fall within the ambit of the ACPA."[25]

In *Grooms et al. v. Legge et al.,*[26] James Grooms (together with his girlfriend and their sport apparel company) sued the Legges (husband and wife) and their competing company for trademark infringement and cybersquatting in violation of the ACPA. Grooms created the name Knukle Inc. and some initial drawings, which combined the name Knukle Inc and a symbol representing brass knuckles. Knukle was deliberately misspelled by omitting the letter *c* and turning the second *k* backward. The name and these drawings gave rise to a line of apparel and accessories targeted at fans of extreme sports and mixed martial arts. Grooms reserved the domain name knuckleinc.com (Knukle website), and subsequently filed a federal *intent to use* trademark application for the mark Knukle (with the second *k* turned backward).

According to the allegations in the complaint, after a failed attempt at forming a partnership with the Legges, the plaintiffs learned that the Legges were covertly starting their own company also around a line of apparel targeting fans of extreme sports and mixed martial arts. The Legges allegedly planned to market the apparel with the brand name Knukle Inc (with the second *k* turned forward) (the Knukle Two mark).

Likewise, shortly after the breakdown of the parties' relationship, the plaintiffs discovered a new website had been posted at knukleinc.com, but that they were unable to log on to the website as the site owner. Plaintiffs also noticed that the Knukle Inc. Facebook and MySpace pages began receiving postings calling the plaintiffs imposters and that the pages contained information that could only be known by someone with intimate knowledge of the business relationship between the parties.

Since the dissolution of the business relationship, the Legges promoted their products using the Knukle Two mark and the Knukle website. Other than the orientation of the second *k* in Knukle, the Knukle Two mark is presented on the same-color merchandise, written in the same font, written in the same color, and accompanied by the same designs and symbols as plaintiffs' mark.

On March 11, 2009, plaintiffs filed a complaint in federal court alleging 15 claims for relief, including counts for unfair competition and false designation of origin of goods under Section 43(a) of Lanham Act and for cybersquatting in violation of Section 43(d) of the Lanham Act. More particularly, plaintiffs alleged that the defendants, with bad intent, committed cyberpiracy by registering, trafficking, and using the Knukle website. Plaintiffs further alleged that the bad intent is evidenced by the conversion of the domain name knukleinc.com and use of the Knukle Two mark.

The court granted a preliminary injunction prohibiting the defendants from using knukleinc.com, the Knukle name, the Knukle marks or substantially similar marks (whether on the World Wide Web, Facebook, MySpace, or traditional media channels). The court found that the plaintiffs were likely to succeed on the merits of their trademark infringement and cybersquatting claims. As to the latter claim, the court observed the following:

> *"In the instant case, plaintiffs have shown a likelihood that defendants have committed cybersquatting in violation of the ACPA. The Legges (1) registered a domain name that (2) is identical to the distinctive Knukle trademark, with (3) the bad faith intent to profit from the trademark. As discussed above, the Legges' bad faith is evidenced by their covert control of the website, the use of the infringing Knukle Two mark, and the exclusion of plaintiffs from their own company's website. Defendants have a bad faith intent to profit from the trademark by using the site.*
>
> *The fact the site is registered to Knukle Two is irrelevant. Defendants admit that Grooms and Phelan were never given their shares of Knukle Two; therefore, Knukle Two is wholly owned and operated by the Legges. As such, the Legges could have, and did, use Knukle Two's control of the domain name to prevent plaintiffs from accessing the site."*[27]

Post-Domain Path Names and the ACPA

Are personalized social media subdomains (for example, twitter.com/Pepsi) covered by the ACPA? Surprisingly, the answer (currently, at least) is most likely no, because usernames, which appear in the post-domain path of a URL, are not technically domain names under the ACPA.

 Note

The ACPA defines the term *domain name* as "any alphanumeric designation which is registered with or assigned by any domain name registrar, domain name registry, or other domain name registration authority as part of an electronic address on the Internet."[28] Likewise, a post-domain path is the text after the .com in a URL.

"Pepsi" is therefore the post-domain path in twitter.com/Pepsi, whereas "twitter.com" is the domain name.

In 2003, the U.S. Court of Appeals for the Sixth Circuit stated in *Interactive Products Corp. v. a2z Mobile Office Solutions, Inc.*[29] that "because post-domain paths do not typically signify source, it is unlikely that the presence of another's trademark in a post-domain path of a URL would ever violate trademark law."

Note

In *a2z Mobile Office Solutions, Inc.*, the trademark at issue was LapTraveler and the allegedly infringing address was:

a2zsolutions.com/desks/floor/laptraveler/dkfl-lt.htm

The court held that such use of the trademark was a purely technical non-infringing use, rather than a "trademark use"—that is, a use that identifies the source of a product or service.

Since the Sixth Circuit's *a2z Mobile Office Solutions* opinion, other jurisdictions have considered whether post-domain paths of a URL enjoy trademark protection, but never specifically in the context of those for social media networking sites. In *Knight-McConnell v. Cummins*,[30] for example, a New York federal district court found that defendant's use of the plaintiff's name in the post-domain path of a URL and placement of those URLs using the plaintiff's name in the post-domain paths on chat forums and search engines do not give rise to any source confusion.

It is unlikely that the post-domain path of a URL would be deemed a domain name for purposes of the ACPA. Technically, the post-domain path is not a registered domain with a registrar and is merely, as the *a2z Mobile Office Solutions* court explained, the manner in which website's data is organized within the host computer's files.

Of course, the *a2z Mobile Office Solutions* case applies only in states within the Sixth Circuit (that is, Kentucky, Michigan, Ohio, and Tennessee) and in other jurisdictions where courts have issued similar rulings.

Nevertheless, bringing a successful username-jacking claim under the ACPA as it relates to screen names and post-domain paths on social media networking sites might still prove to be a viable option for the following reasons:

- The increasing association of a company's brand with social media networking site's post-domain paths (that is, the increasing tendency to identify a URL's post-domain path as a signifier of source rather than merely of how the website's data is organized within the host computer's files)

- The fact that sites such as Twitter and Facebook (which capitalize on making post-domain paths valuable, meaningful, and "brand"-identifying) were launched after the enactment of the ACPA.

Absent definitive guidance from other courts in others jurisdictions, whether the registration of usernames on social networking sites can ever be deemed to enjoy ACPA protection remains an open (if only slight) question.

Platform-Specific Trademark Enforcement Mechanisms

Recognizing the value of online brand protection for their customers, the major social sites have adopted various trademark policies. Perhaps the simplest and most cost-effective way to protect one's brand on social networking sites is to directly utilize the site's dispute resolutions mechanisms, and request removal of infringing materials.

Twitter Policies

Twitter's current Trademark Policy states the following:

> "Using a company or business name, logo, or other trademark-protected materials in a manner that may mislead or confuse others with regard to its brand or business affiliation may be considered a trademark policy violation."[31]

Twitter asserts it may take several actions after reviewing reports of violations of its Trademark Policy, including the following:

- If a clear intent to mislead others through the unauthorized use of a trademark is found, Twitter will suspend the account and notify the account holder.

- If it is determined that an account appears to be confusing users, but is not purposefully passing itself off as the trademarked good or service, Twitter will give the account holder an opportunity to clear up any potential confusion. Twitter may also release a username for the trademark holder's active use.

Further, Twitter specifically prohibits "username squatting," warning users that accounts that are "inactive for more than 6 months may also be removed without further notice."[32] Twitter states that it considers the following factors in determining whether username squatting is occurring: (i) the number of accounts created; (ii) whether the accounts were created for the purpose of preventing others from using those account names; (iii) whether the accounts were created for the purpose of selling those accounts (which Twitter proscribes); and (iv) whether feeds of third-party content are being used to update and maintain accounts under the names of those third parties.

LinkedIn Policies

LinkedIn also requires that its users not "[u]pload, post, email, InMail, transmit or otherwise make available or initiate any content that ... [i]nfringes upon patents, trademarks, trade secrets, copyrights or other proprietary rights."[33]

In response to alleged trademark (or other IP) violations, LinkedIn may:

- Remove or disable access to specified content appearing on its website upon receipt of a verified notice asserting that the content infringes IP rights, is inaccurate, or is otherwise unlawful.

- Disable and/or terminate the accounts of users who may infringe or repeatedly infringe the IP rights of others, or who otherwise post inaccurate or unlawful content.

Facebook Policies

For its part, Facebook also reserves the right to remove or reclaim a username if it believes appropriate, "such as when a trademark owner complains about a username that does not closely relate to a user's actual name."[34] Further, Facebook adopted its own intellectual property policy, which includes the following:

> "Facebook is committed to protecting the intellectual property of third parties. On this page, rights holders will find information regarding how to report copyright and other intellectual property infringements by users posting content on our website, and answers to some frequently asked questions regarding our policies. ...
>
> To report an infringement of your copyright or other intellectual property right (for example, trademark) by a Facebook user, please fill out our automated IP infringement form."[35]

The automated IP infringement form is shown in Figure 8.5.

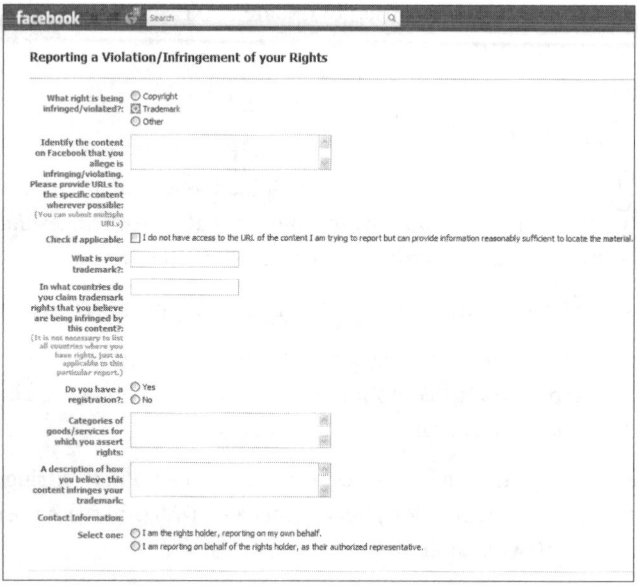

Figure 8.5 *Facebook encourages brands to report claims of trademark infringement by using its automated IP infringement form.*

The exact extent and manner in which Facebook will enforce these terms has yet to be seen. Regarding trademark infringement, for instance, will a common law mark or pending trademark application be sufficient to trigger removal, or must the challenger own a valid federally registered mark? Likewise, will Facebook protect marks registered overseas, or only those marks registered in the United States? Will all permutations of a registered mark be protected (for example, different spellings or the addition of generic terms), or will Facebook protect exact matches only? These questions have not yet been answered.

In light of these uncertainties, relying solely on the brand-protection tools offered by social networks will most likely not prove sufficient. Companies should take additional proactive steps to protect their brands online, including obtaining branded accounts (with reasonable number of username variants) before a would-be infringer.

In addition, should companies find themselves the victims of trademark infringement in a social media networking site, they should consider pursuing claims for trademark infringement and cyberpiracy under Sections 43(a) and 43(d) of the Lanham Act.

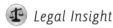 *Legal Insight*

Companies may also be authorized to "seize" domain names that sell counterfeit goods. On September 20, 2011, for example, the luxury brand Chanel brought a complaint[36] against 1,000 "John Doe" defendants who operated websites selling Chanel knock-offs. Chanel claimed that the defendants violated Sections 43(a) and 43(d) of the Lanham Act. The U.S. District Court for the District of Nevada first entered an initial temporary restraining order (TRO)[37]—that is, an emergency order entered against a party without advance notice prohibiting certain conduct—and a preliminary injunction (PI)[38]—that is, an order entered against a party after that party has had an opportunity to be heard—against 400 domain names. Then, on November 14, 2011, the Nevada court granted Chanel's second application for a TRO and PI against an additional 228 domain names.[39]

The court prohibited the defendants from using any Chanel marks or selling any Chanel products and (quite remarkably) directed the top-level domain name registries to change the registrar of record for the domain names to GoDaddy (to ensure that none of the sites can be accessed). The court's order also required Google, Bing, Yahoo!, Facebook, Google+, and Twitter to "de-index and/or remove [the suspect domain names] from any search results pages."[40]

Apart from the technical problems posed by this order—how exactly does one *de-index* domains from Twitter's index, for example—it remains to be seen whether Google and Bing will comply with this order (assuming they are properly subject to the order at all). The extent to which de-indexing and removing potentially infringing user-posted links from the Web and social media sites is an effective (let alone feasible) means for companies to combat trademark is also an open question.

Uniform Domain Name Dispute Resolution

Instead of filing suit in federal court under the ACPA, a trademark owner may pursue a claim under the Uniform Domain Name Dispute Resolution Policy (UDRP).[41] The UDRP is administered by the Internet Corporation for Assigned Names and Numbers (ICANN), which is a nonprofit organization responsible for assigning unique names and numbers used on the Internet, such as domain names. The UDRP, to which all domain name registrants agree to upon registration, allows a trademark owner to challenge domain name registrations in proceedings that are generally quicker and cheaper for trademark owners than an ACPA lawsuit.

Generally speaking, the UDRP allows trademark owners to request arbitration for a quick resolution of a domain-name suit, foregoing the need for (in traditional litigation) civil discovery. The UDRP will award the domain name to the trademark owner if he or she can prove that: (i) the domain name is identical or confusingly similar to the owner's mark; (ii) the current owner of the domain name has no right to or legitimate interest in the domain name; and (iii) the current owner of the domain name has registered the domain name, and is using it in bad faith.

Despite these advantages, the UDRP has several important limitations. Most notably, the only remedies available under the UDRP are cancellation of the domain name or transfer of the domain name registration. Further, trademark owners who find success in an administrative proceeding under the UDRP do not automatically shield themselves from later suit in federal court.

For example, in *AirFX.com v. AirFX, LLC*,[42] the U.S. District Court for the District of Arizona allowed AirFX.com's "reverse domain name hijacking"[43] claim under the ACPA[44] to proceed, despite the prior ruling before the UDRP against it. In this case, AirFX.com purchased the domain name airfx.com intending to use it in a business venture marketing a wind tunnel for skydivers to practice aerial stunts.

 Note

> "Cybersquatters who violate the ACPA are said to hijack a domain name from someone who, because of his trademark ownership, would normally be expected to possess the right to use that domain name. Conversely, if a trademark owner 'overreaches' when exercising his ACPA rights, he 'reverse hijacks' the domain name from the person who registered it."[45]

AirFX, LLC (the defendant company—a motorcycle retailer) owned the federally registered trademark AIRFX for shock absorbers and suspension systems for vehicles. Although AirFX, LLC was successful in its UDRP claim (which ordered the transfer of airfx.com to it), the federal court refused to dismiss plaintiff's reverse hijacking claim on the basis that "any decision made by a panel under the UDRP is no more than an agreed-upon administration that is not given any deference under the ACPA."[46] In other words, a federal court is not bound by, and is free to ignore decisions by the UDRP.

 Note

> The *AirFX* case is an important reminder that although UDRP proceedings are cheaper and faster, such cases could lead to reverse domain name hijacking claims under the ACPA, potentially turning a qualified victory into a certain loss.

Companies that find themselves the victim of trademark infringements on social media sites—or that wish to take proactive steps to avoid such infringements before they occur—have a number of weapons to protect their brand. While the leading social networking sites offer some brand protection remedies, they are limited. It is important that you obtain branded accounts (with a reasonable number of username variants) before a would-be infringer beats you to the punch. Companies who are the victims of username jacking should also consider pursuing claims for trademark infringement, unfair competition, false designation of origin, and cybersquatting. Figure 8.6 summarizes practical steps companies should consider to protect their brands.

Social Media Legal Tips for Trademark Protections from Brandjacking and Cybersquatting

DOs	DON'Ts
■ Register your brand name on all social networks. Proactive registration will not only keep would-be brandjackers and cybersquatters at bay—and thereby block unauthorized uses of your trademark—it will also assist in creating an authentic online presence for your brand.	■ In defensively registering domain names (and social media usernames, account names, and handles), do not neglect to reserve common and predictable misspellings or variations of your brand names. Consider registering "gripe" versions of your brand as well (for example, www.ihate[brand].com or www.[brand]sucks.com).
■ Avail yourself of the platform-specific trademark protection enforcement mechanisms provided by popular social network sites. If your brand is being used in any way that violates the terms of use of Facebook, Twitter, and so on. (for example, the content is abusive, offensive, defamatory, or infringes on your trademark rights), use this as leverage to have the offending content removed.	■ Do not assume that you have the right to automatically recover domain names or social media usernames that use or incorporate your company's name. For example, gripe sites, either as stand-alone websites or as pages within a social media site, are generally protected by the First Amendment, and cannot be forcibly shut down—particularly (and this is key) if the site owner is not engaging in commercial activity.
■ Develop a comprehensive policy of what constitutes an objectionable use of your trademark, and implement a monitoring program to patrol the major social networks for potential misuses of your brand.	■ Do not over-react to every instance of social media misuse of your brand name. Being overzealous can generate more negative attention in "winning" the social media battle, while "losing" the social media war by inciting the backlash of maligners who paint you out to be a corporate bully.
■ In cases of trademark infringement, consider filing an action under the Uniform Domain Name Dispute Resolution Policy (UDRP), which provides a quick and cost-effective means of recovering an infringing domain name.	■ In seeking to enforce your trademark rights, do not assume that the proper party to sue is the social network site. Generally, these sites are immune from liability because they are merely hosting the content, not creating it or receiving a direct financial benefit from it. Further, "generalized" knowledge of infringement—without a showing that the infringement was encouraged—is usually insufficient to impose upon the site owner an affirmative duty to remedy the problem.

Figure 8.6   *Social Media Legal Tips Regarding Trademark Protection.*

Chapter 8 ENDNOTES

1   *La Russa v. Twitter, Inc. and Does* 1-25, Case No. CGC-09-488101, Superior Court of California, County of San Francisco (May 6, 2009); case subsequently removed to federal court on June 5, 2009. The case was settled in June 2009.

2   *Coventry First, LLC v. Does 1-10*, Case No. 2:11-CV-03700-JS (E.D. Penn. Jun. 7, 2011)

3   Twitter, Inc.'s Parody, Commentary, and Fan Accounts Policy, available at https://support.twitter.com/articles/106373-parody-commentary-and-fan-accounts-policy

4   *ONEOK, Inc. v. Twitter, Inc.*, Case No. 4:09-CV-00597-TCK –TLW (N.D. Ok. Sep. 15, 2009)

5   Twitter, Inc.'s About Verified Accounts, available at https://support.twitter.com/groups/31-twitter-basics/topics/111-features/articles/119135-about-verified-accounts

6   Twitter, Inc.'s Parody, Commentary, and Fan Accounts Policy, available at https://support.twitter.com/articles/106373-parody-commentary-and-fan-accounts-policy

7   15 U.S.C. Chapter 22

8   15 USC § 1114(1)(a)

9   Section 43(a) of Lanham Act, codified at 15 U.S.C. §1125(a)

10   *Polaroid Corp. v. Polarad Elecs. Corp.*, 287 F.2d 492, 495 (2d Cir. 1961), *cert. denied*, 368 U.S. 820 (1961)

11   Jurisdictions which apply a limiting interpretation of the "use in commerce" to assess trademark infringement include the Second Circuit (covering Kentucky, Michigan, Ohio and Tennessee) and the Eighth Circuit (covering Arkansas, Iowa, Minnesota, Missouri, Nebraska, North Dakota, and South Dakota).

12   *See* Decision and Order Granting Plaintiff's Motion for a Preliminary Injunction (McMahon, J.) (Document No. 10) (Mar. 9, 2010), in *The New York City Triathlon, LLC v. NYC Triathlon Club, Inc.*, Case No. 1:10-CV-01464-CM-THK (S.D. N.Y. Feb. 22, 2010).

13   *Id.*

14   *See* Decision and Order Granting Plaintiff's Motion to Enforce The Preliminary Injunction and Denying Defendant's Motion to Vacate the Preliminary Injunction (McMahon, J.) (Document No. 44-2) (May 4, 2010), in *The New York City Triathlon, LLC v. NYC Triathlon Club, Inc.*, Case No. 1:10-CV-01464-CM-THK (S.D. N.Y. Feb. 22, 2010).

15   Abbey Klaassen, "How Two Coke Fans Brought the Brand to Facebook Fame," *Advertising Age* (March 16, 2009), available at http://adage.com/article/digital/coke-fans-brought-brand-facebook-fame/135238/

16   http://hosted.ap.org/dynamic/stories/U/US_KALE_VS_CHIKIN?SITE=NYSAR&SECTION=HOME&TEMPLATE=DEFAULT

17   *Black Sheep Television, Ltd. v. The Town of Islip*, Case No. 2:10-CV-04926-LDW-ARL (E.D. N.Y. Oct. 26, 2010)

18   Order Granting Preliminary Injunction (Wexler, J.) (Document No. 22) (Dec. 6, 2010), in *Black Sheep Television, Ltd. v. The Town of Islip*, Case No. 2:10-CV-04926-LDW-ARL (E.D. N.Y. Oct. 26, 2010)

19   *In the Matter of Merck KGaA*, Index No. 11113215, Supreme Court of State of New York (Nov. 21, 2011). A copy of the proposed Order to Show Cause for Pre-Action Disclosure is available at http://iapps.courts.state.ny.us/iscroll/C_PDF?CatID=711057&CID=113215-2011&FName=0.

20 15 U.S.C. § 1125(d) (Section 43(d) of the Lanham Act)

21 A trademark is famous if the owner can prove that the mark "is widely recognized by the general consuming public of the United States as a designation of source of the goods or services of the mark's owner." *See* 15 U.S.C. § 1125(c)(2)(A).

22 *Verizon California Inc. v. Online NIC Inc.*, 2008 WL 5352022 (N.D. Cal. Dec. 19, 2008)

23 15 U.S.C. § 1125(d)(1)(B)(i)(I)-(IX)

24 *Mayflower Transit, LLC v. Prince*, 314 F. Supp. 2d 362 (D.N.J 2004)

25 *Id.* at 369

26 *Grooms et al. v. Legge et al.*, Case No. 3:09-CV-489-IEG-POR (S.D. Cal. Mar, 11, 2009)

27 Order Granting in Part the Preliminary Injunction, (Gonzalez, J.) (Document No. 51) (Apr. 8, 2009), in *Grooms et al. v. Legge et al.*, 09-CV-489-IEG-POR (S.D. Cal. Mar, 11, 2009)

28 15 U.S.C. § 1127

29 *Interactive Products Corp. v. a2z Mobile Office Solutions, Inc. et al.*, 326 F.3d 687 (6th Cir. 2003); Also see *Nagler v. Garcia*, 370 Fed. Appx. 678, 2010 FED App. 0195N (6th Cir. 2010) (Where plaintiff-physician owned trademark of weight-loss system called Diet Result, the Appeals Court held that defendant did not commit trademark infringement by website that did not mention the Diet Results weight-loss program but had a page at the address www.beautyinaflash.com/dietresults. html.)

30 *Knight-McConnell v. Cummins*, 2004 U.S. Dist. LEXIS 14746 (S.D. N.Y.)

31 Twitter, Inc.'s Trademark Policy (last revised 2/14/12), available at http://support.twitter.com/articles/18367-trademark-policy

32 *See* the Twitter Rules, available at https://support.twitter.com/articles/18311-the-twitter-rules#

33 LinkedIn Corporation's User Agreement (last revised 6/16/11), available at http://www.linkedin. com/static?key=user_agreement&trk=hb_ft_userag

34 Facebook's Statement of Rights and Responsibilities (last revised 4/26/11), available at http://www. facebook.com/terms.php?ref=pf

35 Facebook's How to Report Claims of Intellectual Property Infringement page, available at http:// www.facebook.com/legal/copyright.php?howto_report

36 *Chanel, Inc. v. Does 1-1000 et al.*, Case No. 2:11-CV-01508-KJD-PAL (D. Nev. Sept. 20, 2011)

37 Order Granting Plaintiff's *Ex Parte* Application for Entry of Temporary Restraining Order and Preliminary Injunction, (Dawson, J.) (Document No. 10) (Sept. 26, 2011), in *Chanel, Inc. v. Does 1-1000 et al.*, Case No. 2:11-CV-01508-KJD-PAL (D. Nev. Sept. 20, 2011)

38 Order Granting Plaintiff's Application for Entry of Preliminary Injunction, (Dawson, J.) (Document No. 22) (Oct. 11, 2011), in *Chanel, Inc. v. Does 1-1000 et al.*, Case No. 2:11-CV-01508-KJD-PAL (D. Nev. Sept. 20, 2011)

39 Order Granting Plaintiff's Second *Ex Parte* Application for Entry of Temporary Restraining Order and Preliminary Injunction, (Dawson, J.) (Document No. 37) (Nov. 14, 2011), in *Chanel, Inc. v. Does 1-1000 et al.*, Case No. 2:11-CV-01508-KJD-PAL (D. Nev. Sept. 20, 2011)

40 *Id.*

41 A copy of ICANN's Uniform Domain-Name Dispute Resolution Policy is *available at* http://www. icann.org/en/dndr/udrp/policy.htm.

42 *See* Order Denying Defendant's Motion to Dismiss (Martone, J.) (Document No. 19) (Oct. 20, 2011), in *AirFX.com v. AirFX, LLC,* Case No. 2:11-CV-01064-PHX-FJM (D. Ariz. May 27, 2011).

43 *Id.*

44 Subsection 1114(2)(D)(v) of the ACPA provides:

"A domain name registrant whose domain name has been suspended, disabled, or transferred under a policy described under clause (ii)(II) may, upon notice to the mark owner, file a civil action to establish that the registration or use of the domain name by such registrant is not unlawful under this chapter. The court may grant injunctive relief to the domain name registrant, including the reactivation of the domain name or transfer of the domain name to the domain name registrant."

45 Order Denying Defendant's Motion to Dismiss (Martone, J.) (Document No. 19) (Oct. 20, 2011), in *AirFX.com v. AirFX, LLC,* Case No. 2:11-CV-01064-PHX-FJM (D. Ariz. May 27, 2011)

46 Order Denying Defendant's Motion to Dismiss (Martone, J.) (Document No. 19) (Oct. 20, 2011), in *AirFX.com v. AirFX, LLC, supra, citing Barcelona.com v. Excelentisimo Ayuntamiento de Barcelona,* 330 F.3d 617 (4th Cir. 2003)

Balancing Gamification Legal Risks and Business Opportunities

One of the hottest trends in technology today is gamification—that is, the practice of applying the mechanics and dynamics of gaming to non-gaming activities. Although gamification is sometimes dismissed as a simple fad and the tech buzzword du jour, there is a growing number of industry experts who regard gamification as a transformative movement that is shaping the future of business.

Even the world's largest coffee chain is rewarding users with virtual points and virtual badges for visiting their retail stores. Starbucks, in partnership with location-based social network Foursquare, allows its customers to check in at their retail locations on their mobile phones and to earn points and special (barista) badges in the process. Although the points and badges generally do not translate into free coffees, the fun experience is designed to encourage people to visit their stores more often and to buy more drinks, while simultaneously allowing the company to gain metrics by which to track consumer behavior.

Nike has also successfully embraced gamification to attract and retain new customers. In 2010, Nike developed an app called Nike+ which allows runners to track their runs and monitor their results over time. In addition to tracking their steps, calorie burn, distances, and duration, users can compare themselves against their friends, and stay motivated with virtual competitions, mid-run cheers, trophies, medals, "attaboys," and congratulatory messages from sporting icons like Lance Armstrong. Players can also participate in a game of Nike+ Tag. Runners compete against each other, and whoever runs the slowest or the shortest distance is designated as "it." Here, gamification is a win-win: for the user, it encourages exercise and a healthy lifestyle; for the company, it creates customer loyalty and more sales of sneakers, accessories and the $1.99 app itself.

Gamification strategies have garnered considerable (and growing) interest across industries—and for good reason. Indeed, according to a recent Gartner report, by 2015, more than 50 percent of organizations that manage innovation processes will gamify those processes.[1] Further, by 2014, "a gamified service for consumer goods marketing and customer retention will become as important as Facebook, eBay or Amazon, and more than 70 percent of Global 2000 organizations will have at least one gamified application."[2] Some reports also indicate that by 2016, worldwide corporate spending on gamification projects will grow to as much as $2.8 billion, from $100 million in 2011.[3]

The fundamental principles behind why gamification works so well to influence user behavior are hardly a recent phenomenon. Consider frequent flyer points, for example. Applying the dynamics and mechanics of gamification to social media interactions (on web and mobile sites) might very well revolutionize how business is conducted. Like all business applications of new technologies, although this explosion in gamification may be heralded as a good thing, there are nevertheless important legal risks to consider.

> Although this explosion in gamification may be heralded as a good thing, there are nevertheless important legal risks to consider.

By no means intended as an exhaustive study of the topic, this chapter will discuss several unique legal issues encountered when gamification is employed as a marketing technique. In particular, the FTC Act and Endorsement Guides (regarding deceptive advertisement and "expert"-badge endorsements), the legal status (and regulation) of virtual goods and currencies, and federal privacy regulations (regarding collection and use of precise geolocation data collected) are examined. Prudence dictates carefully identifying and weighing potential legal risks and striking a balance between them and the gains which gamification can win for your business.

Unfair and Deceptive Marketing Practices

Like all marketing campaigns, those employing gamification techniques must avoid running afoul of Section 5 of the FTC Act, which prohibits deceptive acts and practices in advertising.[4] To be found *deceptive*, three elements must be shown:

- There must be a representation, omission, or practice that is likely to mislead the consumer.

- The act or practice must be evaluated from the perspective of a reasonable consumer (which, in the case of communications targeted to children, means from the standpoint of an ordinary child or teenager).

- The representation, omission, or practice must be *material*—that is, likely to affect the consumer's purchasing decision.[5]

The recent Complaint and Request for FTC investigation brought against PepsiCo and Frito-Lay by a consumer advocacy group illustrates the unique dangers involved when gamification techniques are employed in a company's marketing initiatives.[6]

Beginning in 2008, PepsiCo's subsidiary Frito-Lay, through its alias Snack Strong Productions (SSP), developed innovative marketing campaigns to sell more Doritos chips, including through its Hotel 626 and Asylum 626 online promotional games. In Hotel 626, players were trapped inside a haunted hotel, and could escape only by successfully completing 10 challenges, "each of which involves its own creepy, unique task or puzzle."[7] Players were encouraged to use their webcams, microphones, and mobile phones to make their escape. To increase the scare factor, the hotel was only open at dark, from 6 p.m. to 6 a.m. Players were allowed to explore the hotel in full motion 3D graphics, similar to first-person shooter games. Players had to maneuver through creepy hallways, dodge a serial killer's lair, and even sing a demon baby to sleep to reach safety.

Remarkably, without showing a single corn chip or naming Doritos beyond the first screen, Hotel 626 had a major affect on sales, with more than two million bags sold in just 3 weeks after its launch in 2008.[8] The success of Hotel 626 led to an even more terrifying campaign the following year, called Asylum 626 (see Figure 9.1)

Like its predecessor, Asylum 626 was only open at dark, between the hours of 6 p.m. and 6 a.m. This time, players "awaken to find themselves strapped to a bed in an insane asylum, held hostage at the mercy of a mad doctor."[9] To escape from the asylum, players had to "dodge lobotomy tools, electroshock therapy and crazed patients."[10]

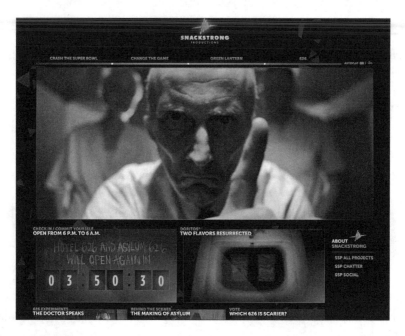

Figure 9.1   *The mad doctor examines you in the insane asylum.*

Asylum 626 also employed head-tracking technology, which allowed viewers to control the action using their webcams (by literally moving their heads to avoid an attack or waiving their hands to dodge a chainsaw, for example). The player's webcam was used to project his or her image into the game. For example, players may see a reflection of their face in some water and the murderer standing behind them.

Players of Asylum 626 were also encouraged to allow access to their Facebook and Twitter accounts. The game generated tweets and Facebook posts designed to appear as if they come directly from the player, asking the player's followers and friends to participate. The player's Facebook friends were invited to save the player by screaming into their microphones or hitting as many keys on their keyboards as possible to distract the assailant.[11] Players were also presented with photos of two of their Facebook friends and forced to "sacrifice one of these people to the murderer."[12] Facebook updates were also sent "to let the world know your choice."[13]

The game abruptly stopped just as it reached its climactic final scene. To continue, players were told that they must buy a bag of Doritos Black Pepper Jack or Smoking Cheddar BBQ (the two flavors "brought back from the dead") and use the infrared marker on the bag to unlock the ending.[14] If players did not make the purchase, they were unable to complete the game.

It is reported that in the first four months following the release of Asylum 626, Frito-Lay had 850,000 visitors to the Asylum 626 website, received 18,000 Twitter mentions, and sold approximately five million bags of Doritos.[15]

Despite the tremendous success of these SSP campaigns, Pepsi Co and Frito-Lay became the target of an FTC complaint for unfair and deceptive marketing practices based on a report that found teens uniquely susceptible to the techniques employed by SSP, such as the following:

- *"Augmented reality, online gaming, virtual environments, and other immersive techniques* that can induce 'flow,' reduce conscious attention to marketing techniques, and foster impulsive behaviors"

- *"Social media techniques* that include surveillance of users' online behaviors without notification, as well as viral brand promotion"

- *"Data collection and behavioral profiling* designed to deliver personalized marketing to individuals without sufficient user knowledge or control"

- *"Location targeting and mobile marketing,* techniques that follow young peoples' movements and are able to link point of influence to point of purchase"

- *"Neuromarketing,* which employs neuroscience methods to develop digital marketing techniques designed to trigger subconscious, emotional arousal."[16]

The complaint alleges that Pepsi Company's Frito-Lay's SSP promotions are deceptive acts or practices in violation of the Section 5 of the FTC Act in at least three ways:

- Disguising its marketing campaigns as entertaining video games and other "immersive" experiences, thus making it more difficult for teens to recognize such content as advertising

- Claiming to protect teens' privacy while collecting and using various forms of personal information without meaningful notice and consent

- Using viral marketing techniques that violate the FTC Endorsement Guidelines

It is important to note that the underlying complaint is not a lawsuit, but a request for investigation (albeit the first of its kind filed with the FTC regarding digital marketing to teens). Whether the FTC will find Frito-Lay's techniques deceptive is still an open question. Nevertheless, companies should take note to avoid the following:

- Disguising advertisements as entertainment, including using fake media and immersive marketing (and other forms of augmented reality) to promote campaigns, particularly those targeting children

- Engaging in viral marketing where recommendations and other communications appear to be from friends when they are not (for example, Facebook postings made without the explicit knowledge or consent of the sender by definition do not honestly reflect the views of the game player, and should therefore be avoided)

- Requesting contact information without adequately disclosing that it will be used for marketing purposes, or otherwise acting inconsistently with your company's privacy policy.

✉ *Note*

Whenever marketing to children is involved, companies should also take care to observe COPPA (as discussed in Chapter 7, "The Law of Social Advertising")—or risk significant penalties. In *United States v. Playdom, Inc.,*[17] for example, the operators of 20 online virtual worlds agreed to pay $3 million as part of settlement that they illegally collected and disclosed children's information, in violation of COPPA.

The consolidated class-action suit against Apple, *In re Apple In-App Purchase Litigation,*[18] offers additional cautionary guidance when employing gamification techniques directed toward children. In this case, the class-action plaintiffs sued Apple for selling *In-App Purchases* (that is, virtual supplies, ammunition, fruits and vegetables, cash, and other fake "game currency") within the game to advance or speed up game play, without the parents' knowledge or consent. In the app Smurfs' Village, for example, players are encouraged to buy Smurfberries to expedite construction of the village. Smurfberries are sold in units of 50 (for $4.99) and 1,000 (for $59), generating (according to the complaint) approximately $4 million per month in sales. One 8-year-old reportedly racked up $1,400 in in-app purchased Smurfberries.

(In light of numerous public complaints and an FTC investigation, Smurfs' Village has apparently updated its download screen to provide an in-app purchase warning —see Figure 9.2.)

Figure 9.2 *Smurfs' Village app warns that it charges "real money for additional in-app content" and provides instructions regarding how to "lock out" this ability on your device.*

Whether Apple's alleged bait-and-switch tactics will result in liability has yet to be established. (As of this writing, the cases are still pending.) Nonetheless, whenever virtual currencies are offered for sale, companies should take care to make prominent disclosures, both at the time of purchase and upon download of the "free" app, and should require affirmative consent (via password reentry, for example) for all individual sales transactions.

FTC Guidelines on Endorsements

As discussed in Chapter 2 ("Online Endorsements and Testimonials: What Companies and Their Employees Can and Cannot Tweet, Blog, or Say"), the 2009 Federal Trade Commission (FTC) Endorsement Guides[19] cover consumer testimonials, such as reviews or recommendations endorsing a product, on any social media site. Under the FTC Endorsement Guides, the endorser needs to disclose the connection between the endorser and the advertiser, if the endorser is given anything of value for the endorsement. In other words, promotional strategies inducing third-parties to say positive things (via free goods, points, badges, and so on) should be disclosed by the endorser and through the companies' promotional policies and literature.

For example, if a blogger gets a free video game in exchange for evaluating and reviewing the game, he must clearly and conspicuously disclose that he received the game free of charge.[20] Likewise, if someone receives redeemable points each time he or she tells friends about a product, this fact needs to be clearly and conspicuously disclosed.[21]

 Note

In one recent case,[22] the FTC charged a PR firm with a violation of the FTC Act after its employees took to the iTunes store and other social media sites to promote video games developed by companies it represented. The employees' posts, such as "Amazing new game" and "Really Cool Game," failed to disclose that the posters were employed by the PR firm. According to the FTC, such tactics constituted unfair or deceptive acts or practices and unfair methods of competition in violation of the FTC Act.

There are additional considerations to be aware of in the case of *experts*. Social media strategies increasingly award "expert" badges as an incentive for consumers to frequently write positive reviews of a company's products and service. However, if an advertisement portrays an endorser as an expert, the endorser's qualifications must in fact give the endorser the expertise that he or she is represented as possessing.[23] Leaderboards, badges, and expert labels all implicate truth-in-advertisement issues (and FTC enforcement actions) to the extent that such labels imply an expert status that the user does not actually possess with respect to the endorsed product.

Legal Status of Virtual Goods

Gamification relies heavily upon "virtual goods," which generally refers to both "virtual items" and "virtual currencies."

Like all "virtual goods," virtual items are intangible objects purchased for use in online communities and games, mobile applications, and social networks. Virtual items can take on many forms, including: points, tokens, badges, rewards, mayorships, discounts, credits, golden tickets, avatars, and even "Smurfberries."

Virtual currency is used for a variety of reasons, including as a mechanism for exchange (in the case of virtual worlds), for purchase of in-game virtual goods that enhance game play (in the case of gaming), and for the purchase of points that enhance status and prestige (for social networking sites).

As a business model, virtual goods enjoy several distinct advantages:

- **Direct Monetization**—Revenue comes directly from users, and not from ads, customer data, or other indirect sources.

- **Profitability**—As the costs to make virtual goods are low, the profit margins associated with the sale of virtual goods are relatively high.

- **Engagement**—Users who purchase virtual goods are invested. They have a reason to return to your site, and to encourage others to visit your site as well. This creates customer loyalty and brand virality.

In light of these benefits, it is little wonder that the sale of virtual goods is a highly lucrative industry. Indeed, PlaySpan, the Visa-owned Monetization-as-a-Service provider released a report in early 2012 that found, among other things, that consumer spending on virtual goods has almost doubled in two years, from $1.8 billion in 2009 to $2.3 billion in 2011.[24]

Despite the ubiquity of virtual goods, their exact legal status is not precisely defined. (As usual, the law lags behind the technological times.) The key debate is whether virtual goods are 'goods' (that is, property) or whether they are services (like entertainment) or something else. If virtual goods are property, then who owns them? Are they to be taxed? Are they subject to revenue-recognition reporting obligations? Can they be transferred? Can they be redeemed for the equivalent real monetary value in real cash? Can they be sold to third-parties?

If virtual goods are services, however, then presumably contract law—that is, th operator's Terms of Service (TOS) or End-User License Agreement (EULA)—controls the relationship between the parties, and not property law.

While no court has yet provided a definitive answer to these questions (let alone one that can serve as precedent for jurisdictions outside from where it sits), there have been a rising number of cases in which such questions are implicated, from which guidance can be sought.

 Legal Insight

A spotlight is put on the precarious legal status of "virtual goods" whenever a game using virtual goods announces that it is being discontinued, as users, who spent considerable money in purchasing these items, are being effectively told such goods will be of no use (value) anymore. Consider the example of ZipZapPlay, which discontinued its popular Facebook game "Baking Life" in early 2012 (see Figure 9.3).

Baking Life, which allowed players to run a virtual bakery and make virtual "dough" ("money") in the process, reportedly once attracted 6.7 million users per month, but closed shop in January 2012, despite having close to 760,000 average monthly customers.[25]

And what was to happen after closing day to any virtual goods and virtual currency (Zip Cash) that players had accumulated in the game? That was to be lost. (Although ZipZapPlay may accept the currency for use in its other games, it does not appear that it is legally required to do so.)

Baking Life's Terms of Services[26] provides that:

- All virtual currency and virtual items are the property of ZipZapPlay

- All virtual currency and virtual items are for the user's personal and non-commercial use

- All virtual currency and virtual items are for use in the Baking Life app only and they are not transferable between or among different ZipZapPlay games and applications

- All purchases of virtual items and virtual currency are final and non-refundable

- All virtual currency and virtual items are not transferable or redeemable for any sum of money or monetary value from ZipZapPlay or any third party

- The user has no right or title to or interest in any virtual currency or virtual items earned or purchased by him or her

In the event that virtual goods are deemed not to be property (such that the TOS controls), players buying virtual goods in games that are later discontinued may simply be out of luck (and legal recourse).

For example, in 2006, Marc Bragg brought a lawsuit[27] against Linden Labs, the developer of Second Life (the popular, massively multiplayer online role-playing game) (MMOG) for terminating his Second Life account, and seizing all of his in-game assets, including virtual land and other items (valued at between $4,000 and $6,000) and approximately $2,000 in real-world money on account. Linden Labs disabled Bragg's account when it discovered that he had allegedly purchased virtual land at lower than market prices through a loophole in an auction system, in violation of Linden Labs' Terms of Service. (The case ultimately settled.)

Figure 9.3   *Baking Life closes shop. Players' "cash" no longer accepted at this "store."*

On April 15, 2010, Linden Labs found itself again the target of a lawsuit—*Evans et al. v. Linden Research, Inc., et al.*[28]—with the issue of virtual goods in play. According to the complaint, the defendants made false representations as part of a national campaign to induce individuals to visit the Second Life website and purchase virtual property. In particular, users were repeatedly told that they retained/obtained ownership rights to the land they purchased and retained all intellectual property right for any virtual items or content they created. Despite these representations, the defendants unilaterally changed the terms of its service agreement to state that these land and property owners no longer owned what they had created, bought, and paid for, but instead merely had a limited license to use them. Further, the plaintiffs' accounts were terminated, and their virtual property was taken from them without compensation by the defendants.

 Note

Although a Second Life participant's goods are *virtual*, they are valuable property in the real world, which can be sold, licensed, or transferred both directly online and through third-party sites (such as eBay.com). The world-wide market for virtual properties, both virtual land and goods, is estimated in the billions.[29] Indeed, MMOG *Entropia Universe* entered the Guinness Book of World Records in 2009 for the most expensive virtual world objects ever sold—a virtual space station (called Crystal Palace), for which the "owner" paid $330,000 real U.S. dollars. (See Figure 9.4.) Fast forward a few years later, and the record for the most expensive virtual property ever bought now belongs to SEE Virtual Worlds, which reportedly paid $6 million U.S. in order to acquire the virtual property *Planet Calypso* within *Entropia Universe*.

Figure 9.4   *This dedicated player paid 3,300,000 PEDs—or $330,000 real U.S. dollars—to own a virtual Crystal Palace.*

As of this writing, *Evans et al. v. Linden Research, Inc., et al.* is still pending in a federal district court in California. While it's possible that the court may decide the case on different grounds (or that the case may settle), a court decision firmly addressing the legal status of virtual goods would have a profound impact on the gaming and gamification industry. Rather than relying upon their Terms of Service and End-User License Agreements to regulate their relationship with their users, businesses offering virtual goods may be required to honor greater property rights that users may have in these goods (particularly if they make representations elsewhere regarding the "rights" users have in these goods). Until courts provide a definitive resolution of this issue, businesses must operate with a certain degree of legal uncertainty. To hedge their bets, however, businesses that sell or interact with virtual goods should avoid making any representations that in-game goods are "property" that "belong" to their users.

The Credit CARD Act of 2009

As noted earlier, virtual currency is a gaming and gamification staple, and comes in the form of points, coins, redeemable coupons, store credit, and so forth. Because these forms of virtual currencies often operate like gift certificates (in that they are issued to be redeemed at a later date), they may be subject to both state and federal gift card regulations.

On the federal law front, the Credit Card Accountability Responsibility and Disclosure Act of 2009 (Credit CARD Act of 2009)[30] protects consumers from unfair credit card billing practices. This Act also establishes guidelines for gift certificates, store gift cards, and general-use prepaid cards, which are collectively defined to include cards, electronic promises, payment codes and other devices, and include virtual currencies.[31]

Title 4 of the Credit CARD Act (which amends the Electronic Funds Transfer Act [EFTA]) prohibits retailers from:

- Setting expiration dates less than 5 years after the card, code, or device is sold or issued.[32]

- Charging dormancy, inactivity, and service fees unless the card, code or device has not been used for at least 12 months.[33] If fees are charged after this period, retailers cannot assess more than one fee per month under any circumstances.[34] Clear and conspicuous disclosures are required before purchase if card, code, or device is assessed fees or if they expire.[35]

NOTABLE EXCLUSIONS

The Credit CARD Act of 2009 includes the following exclusions for general-use prepaid cards, gift certificates, and store gift cards:

- Used solely for telephone services

- Reloadable and not marketed or labeled as a gift card

- A loyalty, award or promotional card (if required disclosures are made)

- Not marketed to the general public

- Issued in paper form only

- Redeemable solely for admission at events or venues or to obtain goods and services in conjunction with admission to such events or venues.[36]

The majority of states have also enacted their own laws applicable to gift cards.[37] Such laws either restrict the circumstances under which dormancy, inactivity, or service fees may be charged or restrict the circumstances under which the card or funds underlying the card may expire. Other states simply require the disclosure of fees or expiration dates.

Perhaps as a precursor to an impending wave of gamification-based lawsuits, the first CARD Act litigation *(Ferreira v. Groupon Inc., Nordstrom, Inc.*[38]*)* was filed on January 21, 2011, against Groupon, a web-based company that offers discounted deals to consumers if they agree to purchase a specified number of *groupons* for a particular *Daily Deal* (the product or service that is being offered for sale that day).

This class-action lawsuit includes all consumers nationwide who purchased or acquired gift certificates (groupons) for products and services with expiration dates of less than 5 years from the date of purchase. The defendant retail class comprises all persons or entities that contract and/or participate with Groupon to promote their products and/or services using Groupon gift certificates with expiration dates. According to the complaint, groupons are gift certificates as defined under the CARD Act, and selling them with expiration dates is prohibited under the Act.

 Note

> Even apparently small matters can have large consequences. In *Ferreira v. Groupon,* the individually named plaintiff allegedly paid $25 to Groupon on November 21, 2010, in exchange for a $50 Groupon gift certificate redeemable at Nordstrom. The gift certificate expired on December 31, 2010, before Mr. Ferreira could redeem it.

Other Little-Known Laws Relating to Virtual Currencies

Virtual currencies are potentially subject to a wide variety of laws that prudent businesses transacting in virtual goods would be wise to consider.

For example, in certain circumstances, the offering of virtual currencies may trigger state money transmitter laws. These laws, typically enforced by a state's department of financial institutions, generally regulate businesses that provide money transfer services or payment instruments, such as those offered by Western Union or PayPal.

Most money transmitter laws require that the money transmitter maintain a state license, post a surety bond (ranging from $25,000 to more than $1 million), and maintain a minimum net worth (ranging from $5,000 to $100,000).

In the case of virtual currencies, these laws may be most applicable when the virtual currency can be redeemed for real cash through third parties or transferred between users. Failure to comply with money transmitter laws can result in both civil and criminal penalties.

Further, many states have applied *unclaimed property* or *escheat laws* (that is, laws which require merchants to pay the value of any unused gift cards to the state if the card owner dies without heirs) to funds remaining on gift cards. Some states also require that consumers have the option of receiving cash back when the underlying balance falls below a certain amount. Whenever virtual currency is involved, therefore, these specific state law variables will need to be factored in, as well.

Finally, conversion between in-game and real-world currency may constitute *virtual winnings*, subject to federal and state gambling laws. In circumstances where real-world transactions for in-game assets are not permitted, but there is an unofficial secondary market, care must be taken to ensure that the rewards given do not have monetary value, perhaps by demonstrating enforcement of a company's terms of service prohibiting secondary markets.

Location-Based Services

By leveraging social media technologies (such as tweeting and blogging) with geolocation data and game dynamics/mechanics, business can promote their products like never before. Given the technological advances over the past few years, behavioral targeting is expected to explode. *Behavioral targeting* is defined as the leveraging of social history data (where you are and what you are doing at any given time).

Despite the significant business value of leveraging real-time consumer data, companies need to be mindful of privacy issues regarding recording, storing, handling, and transferring geolocation data without the owner's consent or knowledge.

Indeed, a wave of class-action lawsuits have been filed against Apple and many makers of popular mobile apps for allegedly unlawfully tracking users and sending their geolocation data history to advertisers.

For example, in *In re iPhone/iPad Application Consumer Privacy Litigation*,[39] the class action plaintiffs allege that Apple's unique device IDs (UDIDs)—the globally unique number assigned to each user's iPhone, iPod touch, or iPad—capture users' location and usage patterns (such as when and how long apps are used). The suit alleges that the UDID also captures other identifying information (such as the users' real name or user ID and the time-stamped IP address and GPS coordinates). The suit further claims that such information is being shared with third-party ad networks without the users' knowledge or consent.

According to the complaint, most users are unaware of the UDIDs on their iPhones and other Apple devices and cannot disable the UDID or prevent UDID information from being transferred. In addition, the complaint alleges that some app makers are selling additional information to ad networks, including user location, age, gender, income, sexual orientation, ethnicity, and political affiliation, without the users' prior knowledge or consent. The plaintiffs sought an injunction against future unauthorized tracking, as well as damages under the Computer Fraud and Abuse Act,[40] the Electronic Communications Privacy Act of 1986,[41] and state consumer protection laws.

On September 20, 2011, the case was dismissed[42] (without prejudice to re-file) because the plaintiffs were found to lack Article III standing—that is, the legal right to bring a claim based on a concrete (actual, not hypothetical) and particularized (personal and individual) injury.[43] Finding that the plaintiffs' failed to demonstrate how the defendants' alleged conduct harmed them, the court rejected the plaintiffs' argument that personal data has economic value that is somehow lost or diminished when shared for advertising or analytics purposes.

 Note

Following the district court's ruling in *In re iPhone/iPad Application Consumer Privacy Litigation*, several other courts similarly ruled that the unauthorized collection of personal information is not by itself sufficient to confer Article III standing. For example, in *Del Vecchio v. Amazon.com Inc.*,[44] a federal district court in Washington rejected plaintiffs' claim that Amazon's harvesting of user data without their consent (which allegedly deprived them of "the opportunity to exchange their valuable information"), constituted Article III standing. The court found this theory to be "entirely speculative" because, "[w]hile it may be theoretically possible that Plaintiffs' information could lose value as a result of its collection and use by Defendant, Plaintiffs do not plead any facts from which the Court can reasonably infer that such devaluation occurred in this case."[45]

Similarly, in *Low v. LinkedIn Corp.*,[46] a California district court held that allegations that LinkedIn permitted third parties to track plaintiffs' online browsing history "without the compensation to which [plaintiff] was due" were "too abstract and hypothetical to support Article III standing."[47]

On November 22, 2011, in a bid to cure these deficiencies, the plaintiffs filed an amended complaint, alleging the following harm (and presumed standing):

- The alleged collection of data "consumed portions" of the "memory on their devices," and the iPhones' bandwidth and battery life were also diminished as a result of Apple storing their location information without permission.

- Plaintiffs would have paid less for an iPhone had they known of its true nature.

- Plaintiffs "lost and have not been compensated for the value" of their data.

- The data had inherent value that the plaintiffs were entitled to exploit.

On January 10, 2012, the defendants filed another motion to dismiss, which (as of the time of this writing) is still pending before the court. Whether plaintiffs' reformulation of harm will be sufficient to confer standing remains to be seen.

Regardless of the outcome, the case is still highly instructive. First, it reminds plaintiffs of their need to show specific injuries arising from specific acts caused by specific defendants; it is not enough to simply allege harm to consumers at large. Further, *In re iPhone/iPad Application Consumer Privacy Litigation* serves as a clarion call to companies that their data collection and privacy practices are under increasingly aggressive legal scrutiny.

Designing a Precise Geolocation Data Security Plan

Section 5 of the FTC Act grants the FTC broad enforcement authority to protect consumers from unfair trade practices, including in how companies handle consumers' personal data. Companies handling consumers' geolocation data are not exempt from the FTC's reach, and should therefore adopt and enforce a comprehensive security plan to protect such data and to notify consumers when such data is lost or stolen.

Given that the tracking, storage, and sharing of precise geolocation information is becoming increasingly subject to legal and regulatory challenge, companies should establish compliance frameworks regarding how they will handle precise geolocation (PGL) data. At a minimum, the comprehensive PGL data security plan should include the following provisions:

- **Program implementation and oversight:** Companies should designate one or more senior-level employees to maintain and enforce a comprehensive PGL data security plan. The company's plan should be in writing.

- **Notice and choice:** Companies should clearly and conspicuously provide consumers a choice as to whether they want their PGL data collected. With respect to social media services, if consumer information will be conveyed to a third-party app developer, the notice-and-choice mechanism should appear at the time the consumer is deciding whether to use the application and, in any event, before the application obtains the consumer's PGL information. Companies involved in information collection and sharing on mobile devices (for example, carriers, operating system vendors, applications, and advertisers) should provide meaningful choice mechanisms for consumers and clearly and conspicuously inform consumers that their PGL data is being shared with advertisers or other third parties.

- **Security policies:** Companies should create policies governing whether and how employees keep, access, and transport records containing PGL data. Companies should also impose disciplinary measures for violations of its comprehensive PGL data security plan.

- **Limited access:** Companies should impose reasonable restrictions upon physical and electronic access to records containing PGL information. Terminated employees' physical and electronic access to records containing PGL data should be immediately blocked, including deactivating their passwords and usernames.

- **Disposal procedures:** Companies should retain personal information no longer than reasonably necessary. Companies should have in place disposal procedures to properly delete or destroy PGL data after it is no longer necessary (from a legal and business perspective) to maintain.

- **Monitoring and updating:** Companies should regularly monitor and update the PGL data security plan to ensure its proper operation and effectiveness, particularly in light of ever changing security threats and technology.

- **Security breaches:** Companies should document responsive actions taken in connection with any incident involving a security breach. The plan should address what happens if PGL data is lost, stolen, or misused, and should detail who is to be alerted and what steps are to be taken to mitigate further damage.

- **Employee training:** Companies should educate and train their employees on the proper use of and the importance of PGL data information security. Employee access to PGL data of the employee's customers should be limited to *on a need to know* basis.

The laws governing gamification are still relatively in their infancy (at least as applied to this new technology). Nonetheless, there are practical steps business can take to mitigate their legal exposure. To balance the business gains of gamification against the corresponding business risks, companies should observe the best practices summarized in Figure 9.5.

Legal Tips for Social Media Gamification

DOs	DON'Ts
■ If your company offers users a chance to earn or obtain virtual goods (points, coins, redeemable coupons, stored credit, and so on), familiarize yourself with the Credit Card Accountability, Responsibility, and Disclosure (CARD) Act. This Act generally prohibits dormancy, inactivity, and service fees and requires a minimum expiration date of 5 years from the date virtual goods were issued.	■ Do not forget that leaderboards, badges, and expert labels all implicate truth-in-advertisement issues (and FTC enforcement actions) to the extent that such labels imply an expert status that the user does not actually have with respect to the endorsed product. If an advertisement portrays an endorser as an expert, the endorser's qualifications must in fact give the endorser the expertise that he or she is represented as possessing.
■ Conspicuously disclose any "payments" given to third-party reviewers, including free goods, points, badges, and so on. Disclosures should be made by the endorser and within the companies' promotional policies and literature.	■ Do not use gamification tactics where recommendations and other communications appear to be from friends when they are not (for example, Facebook postings made without the explicit knowledge or consent of sender by definition do not honestly reflect the views of the game player, and should therefore be avoided).
■ When requesting contact information, be sure to adequately disclose that it will be used for marketing purposes and that you otherwise are acting consistently with your company's privacy policy.	■ If virtual currency in the form of a card, code, or other device is assessed fees or expires, do not fail to make requisite disclosures prior to purchase, on the card and with the card, in a clear and conspicuous manner.
■ As a company transacting in virtual goods, be sure that your end-user license agreement (EULA) and terms of service (TOS) explicitly state that you own all virtual goods in your game or promotion and that you can deny users access to these goods at any time and for any reason in your sole and absolute discretion. Be sure to limit all claims that users can assert against you in connection with the offering of virtual goods.	■ Do not make any representation that users have any rights or title to virtual goods earned, purchased or created by him/her, or the accounts for which they pay, including the right to buy, sell, gift, or trade any such goods. At a minimum, the EULA and TOS should specify that all virtual currency and virtual items are for the user's personal and non-commercial use, are not transferable or redeemable for any sum of money, are final and non-refundable, and can't be sold for "real" money.

Figure 9.5 *Legal Tips for Social Media Gamification.*

Chapter 9 ENDNOTES

1 http://www.gartner.com/it/page.jsp?id=1629214

2 *Id.*

3 *See* Gamification Vendor Survey Results - Fall 2011(M2 Research), available at http://www.m2re-search.com/.

4 15 U.S.C. §45

5 *Cliffdale Associates, Inc.*, 103 F.T.C. 110, 170–71 (1984)

6 Complaint and Request for Investigation of PepsiCo's and Frito-Lay's Deceptive Practices in Marketing Doritos to Adolescents (filed on Oct. 19, 2011), available at http://case-studies.digitalads. org/wp-content/uploads/2011/10/complaint.pdf

7 *Hotel 626: The Online Haunted House*, Facebook, http://www.facebook.com/pages/Hotel-626-The-Online-Haunted-House/179823455397906?sk=info

8 Kevin Ritchie, "Doritos Continues Interactive Horror Franchise with Asylum 626," *Boards Magazine* (Sept. 22, 2009), available at http://www.boardsmag.com/articles/online/20090922/asy-lum626.html

9 *Id.*

10 "Doritos / Hotel 626," *Contagious*, available at http://www.contagiousmagazine.com/2009/09/dori-tos_5.php

11 Kevin Ritchie, "Doritos Continues Interactive Horror Franchise with Asylum 626," *Boards Magazine* (Sept. 22, 2009), available at http://www.boardsmag.com/articles/online/20090922/asy-lum626.html

12 The BuzzBubble Interviews Jeff Goodby, available at http://case-studies.digitalads.org/ftc-complaint/

13 Asylum 626 Case Study Video, available at http://case-studies.digitalads.org/ftc-complaint/

14 Kevin Ritchie, "Doritos Continues Interactive Horror Franchise with Asylum 626," *Boards Magazine* (Sept. 22, 2009), available at http://www.boardsmag.com/articles/online/20090922/asy-lum626.html

15 Asylum 626 Case Study Video, available at http://case-studies.digitalads.org/ftc-complaint/

16 Complaint and Request for Investigation of PepsiCo's and Frito-Lay's Deceptive Practices in Marketing Doritos to Adolescents (filed on Oct. 19, 2011), available at http://case-studies.digitalads. org/wp-content/uploads/2011/10/complaint.pdf

17 *United States v. Playdom, Inc.*, Case No. 8:11-CV-00724-AG-AN (C.D. Cal., filed May 11, 2011). You can find a copy of the consent decree and order at http://www.ftc.gov/os/caselist/1023036/1105 12playdomconsentorder.pdf.

18 *In Re Apple In-App Purchase Litigation*, Case No. 5:11-CV-1758 JF (N.D. Cal. Jun. 16, 2011)

19 16 C.F.R. § 255 *et seq.*, *Guides Concerning the Use of Endorsements and Testimonials in Advertising*

20 16 C.F.R. § 255.5 (Example 7)

21 16 C.F.R. § 255.5 (Example 9)

22 *In the Matter of Reverb Communications, Inc. et al.*, FTC File No. 092 3199 (Nov. 26, 2010). A copy of complaint is available at http://www.ftc.gov/os/caselist/0923199/101126reverbcmpt.pdf.

23 16 C.F.R. § 255.3

24 *See* PlaySpan's Virtual Goods Trends Report (Feb. 29, 2012), available at http://www.slideshare.net/robblewis/playspan-magid-virtual-goods-report

25 http://www.eurogamer.net/articles/2012-01-20-popcap-to-shut-down-baking-life

26 http://www.zipzapplay.com/terms.html

27 *Bragg v. Linden Research, Inc. et al.*, Case No. 2:06-CV-04925-ER (E.D. Penn. 2006), removed from Pennsylvania state court (Civil Action No. 06-08711) (Ct. Com. Pl. Chester County Pa. Oct. 4, 2006) in October 2006

28 *Evans et al v. Linden Research, Inc., et al.*, Case No. 2:10-CV-1679-ER (E.D. Penn. Apr. 15, 2010); case subsequently transferred to U.S. District Court, Northern District of California, Case No. 4:11-CV-01078-DMR (N.D. Cal. Mar. 8, 2011)

29 http://mashable.com/2011/10/14/social-gaming-economics-infographic/

30 The Credit Card Accountability Responsibility and Disclosure Act of 2009, Public Law 111-24, 123 Stat. 1734 (2009)

31 15 U.S.C. § 1693l–1(a)(2)(A)-(C)

32 15 U.S.C. § 1693l–1(c)

33 15 U.S.C. § 1693l–1(b)

34 15 U.S.C. § 1693l–1(b)(2)(C)

35 15 U.S.C. §§ 1693l–1(b)(2)(B) and 1693l–1(c)(2)

36 15 U.S.C. § 1693l–1(a)(2)(D)

37 For a representative list of state gift card consumer protection laws, see http://www.consumersunion.org/pub/core_financial_services/003889.html.

38 *Ferreira v. Groupon Inc., Nordstrom, Inc.*, Case No. 3:11-CV-0132-DMS-RBB (S.D. Cal. Jan. 21, 2011)

39 *In re iPhone/iPad Application Consumer Privacy Litigation*, Case No. 5:11-MD-02250-LHK (N.D. Cal. Aug. 25, 2011) (consolidated cases)

40 18 U.S.C. § 1030, which makes it unlawful to intentionally accesses a computer used for interstate commerce or communication without authorization, or in excess of authorization, and thereby obtain information

41 18 U.S.C. § 2520, which provides a civil cause of action to "any person whose wire, oral, or electronic communications is intercepted, disclosed, or intentional used" in violation of the ECPA

42 Order Granting Defendants' Motions to Dismiss for Lack of Article III Standing with Leave to Amend (Document No. 8) (Sept. 20, 2011) in *In Re iPhone/iPad Application Consumer Privacy Litigation*, Case No. 5:11-MD-02250-LHK (N.D. Cal. Aug. 25, 2011).

43 A plaintiff must meet a number of requirements to have his/her case heard in federal court, including Article III of the United States Constitution which provides, among other matters, that "The Judicial Power shall extend to all Cases …[and] to Controversies…." To satisfy Article III, a plaintiff "must show that (1) it has suffered an 'injury in fact' that is (a) concrete and particularized and (b) actual or imminent, not conjectural or hypothetical; (2) the injury is fairly traceable to the challenged action of the defendant; and (3) it is likely, as opposed to merely speculative, that the injury will be redressed by a favorable decision." *Friends of the Earth, Inc. v. Laidlaw Envtl. Sys. (TOC), Inc.*, 528 U.S. 167, 180-81 (2000).

44 *Del Vecchio et al. v. Amazon.com Inc.*, Case No. 2:11-CV-00366-RSL (W.D. Wash. Mar. 2, 2011)

45 *See* Order Granting Defendant's Motion to Dismiss (Document No. 58) (Dec. 1, 2011), in *Del Vecchio et al. v. Amazon.com Inc.*, Case No. 2:11-CV-00366-RSL (W.D. Wash. Mar. 2, 2011).

46 *Low v. LinkedIn Corp.*, Case No. 5:11-CV-01468-LHK (N.D. Mar. 25, 2011) (N.D. Cal. Nov. 11, 2011)

47 *See* Order Granting Defendant's Motion to Dismiss (Document No. 28) (Nov. 11, 2011), in *Low v. LinkedIn Corp.*, Case No. 5:11-CV-01468-LHK (N.D. Mar. 25, 2011)

Social Media's Effect on Privacy and Security Compliance

The emergence of online social networks, and the new technologies which support them, carries with it new challenges and threats to consumer privacy and data security. In addition to our families, friends, acquaintances, and colleagues, as well as businesses and marketers, numerous other parties are interested in the information we share within social networks. Identity thieves, scammers, and fraudsters are also seeking to exploit social networks to acquire data about consumers. The social networks themselves are feverishly collecting an ever-growing number of data points about users (including their age, gender, hobbies, interests, spending patterns, location, and so forth) not only to improve and personalize the user experience, but also to monetize the data through the sale of ads, and other means.

Unfortunately, the enhanced ability to collect and store consumer data has dramatically increased the risks that data will be shared more broadly than understood or intended by consumers (such as with third party advertisers or affiliates that are many layers removed from consumers), or used for purposes that were not disclosed—or even contemplated—at the time of collection.

While many businesses enjoy the promotional advantages of social media, they fail to properly ensure they have good compliance programs in place. Recent Federal Trade Commission (FTC) settlements with Facebook, Twitter, and Google—as discussed in this chapter—highlight the risk of using social media without properly structured and implemented privacy and security compliance guidelines.

Because smaller companies are not immune from the FTC's enforcement reach, these cases serve as an important reminder about the risks inherent whenever companies collect consumer information, particularly when that information is private (for example, date of birth, sexual orientation, financial or medical history) or designated by the consumer as such (for example, contacts, friends list, buying practices, reading lists). In light of the ever-increasing scrutiny by the FTC of consumer data privacy and data protection issues, companies should take steps to ensure that their privacy and security policies, statements, and practices are truthful, nondeceptive, factually supportable, and consistent with evolving legal standards and industry best practices.

(Companies collecting information from children younger than 13 years old are also reminded of their obligations to comply with COPPA, as discussed in Chapter 7, "The Law of Social Advertising.")

This chapter highlights the security and privacy risks inherent in the use of social media by examining recent FTC regulatory action brought against Facebook, Twitter, and Google. Readers will gain insights learned from their reported missteps to assist them in avoiding liability and regulatory scrutiny.

 Note

In December 2010, the FTC released a draft report—entitled *"Protecting Consumer Privacy in an Era of Rapid Change"*[1]—which proposed a new framework for the online and offline collection and use of consumer data consistent with the following three principles: (1) **privacy by design**—that is, companies should promote consumer privacy throughout their organizations and at every stage of the development of their products and services (for example, by collecting only the data needed for a specific business purpose and retaining such data only as long as necessary to fulfill that purpose), (2) **simplified consumer choice**—that is, companies should present choices to consumers at the point of data collection, and may forego choice altogether for "commonly accepted" uses of consumer information (such as product/service fulfillment, first-party marketing, fraud prevention, or internal operations), and (3) **greater transparency**—that is, companies should increase the transparency of their practices with respect to the collection, use and sharing of consumer information (for example, by providing consumers with clearer, shorter, and more standardized privacy statements describing a company's data practices, in easy-to-understand language). The FTC released its final report on March 26, 2012[2]. As much of the FTC's recent past (and expected future) enforcement activity regarding a company's data security and privacy practices is being measured against these principles, companies would be wise to follow them.

Privacy Compliance

The Google Buzz launch debacle is a perfect example of the serious consequences that can occur when a company neglects to abide by its own privacy policy. Within days after releasing its social networking service in February 2010, Google faced strong public criticism, a complaint[3] filed with the FTC, and a consumer class-action lawsuit alleging violations of the Electronic Communications Privacy Act (ECPA), the Stored Communications Act (SCA), the Computer Fraud and Abuse Act (CFAA), and other privacy violations inconsistent with Google's privacy policy.[4]

Google Buzz was a platform that enabled users to share updates, comments, photos, videos, and other information through posts (or *buzzes*) made either publicly or privately to individuals or groups of users. Google used the information of consumers who signed up for Gmail, including first and last name and email contacts, to populate the social network. According to the allegations in the complaint, without prior notice or the opportunity to consent, Google Buzz was automatically added to all Gmail users, and the program automatically converted into "followers" the contacts with whom users emailed and "chatted" the most. By default, the users' information and followers were also made public, including their photos. As noted in the complaint, the automatic public generation of email lists could reveal the names of a user's psychiatrist, attorney, romantic partner, children, job recruiters, or other personal information.

On May 31, 2011, U.S. District Court Judge James Ware granted approval of an $8.5 million class-action settlement to be divided among the plaintiffs' attorneys ($2.125 million) and various privacy-related advocacy groups, nonprofits, and education organizations.

Likewise, on October 24, 2011, the FTC finalized its settlement with Google.[5] The FTC found that Google used deceptive tactics and violated its own privacy policy by using information provided for Gmail for another purpose (social networking) without obtaining consumers' permission in advance. Although Google led Gmail users to believe that they could choose whether they wanted to join the network, the options for declining or leaving the social network were ineffective. Even Gmail users who thought they turned off Google Buzz remained in the social network.

According to the terms of the FTC settlement, Google is prohibited from making further privacy-related representations inconsistent with its privacy policy and is required to obtain express affirmative user consent before sharing information with a third party in any manner that differs from its practices as it existed when the user's information was first collected. The settlement further requires Google to implement a comprehensive privacy program and to undergo independent privacy audits every 2 years for the next 20 years.

In 2010, Facebook also found itself the target of an FTC investigation for failing to abide by its privacy promises. According to the complaint,[6] Facebook engaged in the following unfair and deceptive acts or practices:

- In December 2009, Facebook changed its website so certain information that users may have previously designated as private (such as their friends list, gender, or city of residence) was made public. However, Facebook failed to warn users of the change or to obtain their opt-in consent before implementing the new privacy settings.

- Facebook claimed that third-party apps that users installed would have access only to user information that they needed to operate. However, the apps could access nearly all the users' personal data, including data the apps did not need.

- Facebook claimed that users could restrict sharing of data to limited audiences (for example, with friends only). However, selecting "Friends Only" did not prevent their information from being shared with third-party applications their friends used.

- Although Facebook promised users that it would not share their personal information with advertisers, it did not honor this promise.

- Facebook claimed that when users deactivated or deleted their accounts, their photos and videos would be inaccessible. However, Facebook allowed access to such content, even after users had deactivated or deleted their accounts.

On November, 29, 2011, Facebook reached a settlement with the FTC. The proposed settlement[7] bars Facebook from misleading consumers about how the company uses their personal information, requires that the company get consumers' approval before it changes the way it shares their data, and requires that it obtain periodic assessments of its privacy practices by independent, third-party auditors for the next 20 years.

Specifically, under the proposed settlement, Facebook is:

- Precluded from making misrepresentations about the privacy or security of consumers' personal information (including the extent to which consumers can control the privacy of their personal information);

- Required to obtain consumers' affirmative express consent (opt-in) before enacting changes that override their privacy preferences;

- Required to, prior to sharing a user's nonpublic user information with any third party, which materially exceeds the restrictions imposed by a user's privacy setting(s), (a) "clearly and prominently disclose to the user, separate and apart from any "privacy policy," "data use policy," "statement of rights and responsibilities" page, or other similar document: (1) the categories of nonpublic user information that will be disclosed to such third parties, (2) the identity or specific categories of such third parties, and (3) that such sharing exceeds the restrictions imposed by the privacy setting(s) in effect for the user"; and (b) "obtain the user's affirmative express consent";

- Required to prevent anyone from accessing a user's information more than 30 days after the user has deleted such information or terminated his or her account;

- Required to establish and maintain a comprehensive privacy program designed to address privacy risks related to the development and management of new and existing products and services, and to protect the privacy and confidentiality of consumers' information; and

- Required, within 180 days, and every 2 years thereafter for the next 20 years, to obtain independent, third-party audits certifying that it has a privacy program in place that meets or exceeds the requirements of the FTC's order, and to ensure that the privacy of consumers' information is protected.

What lessons can companies learn from the *Facebook* settlement?

- First, companies handling personally identifiable information and other consumer data should adopt a comprehensive privacy program that is reasonably designed to protect the privacy and security of such information, including controls and procedures, such as monitoring and auditing, to identify and prevent predictable risks.

- Second, like any other advertising claim, what companies represent about how they handle consumer information has to be truthful, not deceptive, and objectively supportable.

- Third, whenever companies represent that consumer data will be kept private, they should obtain opt-in consent from users before implementing new privacy settings affecting how this data is used. (User consent may be obtained when the user returns to the business's website, re-logs in to the business's mobile app, or otherwise next interacts with the business.)

- Fourth, important changes in a company's privacy practices (how they share data with third parties, for example) should be disclosed clearly (that is, with minimal "geek-speak and legal mumbo-jumbo"[8]) and conspicuously, and not merely in their privacy policies or other legal boilerplate.

- Finally, at least annually, companies should audit their privacy practices and should consider, particularly if large volumes of personally identifiable and other consumer information are regularly collected, voluntarily submitting to periodic independent, third-party audits certifying that they have legally adequate privacy programs in place.

Security Compliance

In addition to holding companies liable for their failures to abide by their privacy policies, the FTC will hold companies accountable for failures in honoring their representations regarding their security practices.

On March 11, 2011, in the agency's first such case against a social networking service, the FTC finalized a proposed settlement with Twitter, which resolved charges that Twitter deceived consumers and put their privacy at risk by failing to safeguard their personal information.[9] Specifically, the FTC claimed that Twitter, contrary to the statements contained in its privacy policy, did not provide reasonable and appropriate security to prevent unauthorized access to consumers' personal information and did not honor the consumers' privacy choices in designating certain tweets as nonpublic. Hackers exploited these failures and obtained administrative control of the Twitter system, which led to two high-profile hacker attacks in 2009. (See side note.) These intruders were able to gain unauthorized access to nonpublic tweets and user information, reset any user's password, and send unauthorized tweets from any user account.

 Note

In January 2009, a hacker used an automated password-guessing tool to gain unauthorized administrative control of Twitter. At the time, Twitter's system did not have a safeguard in place to automatically lock users from accessing the site if they failed to enter the correct password after a certain number of attempts. After "guessing" the correct site password (happiness), the hacker was able to send out phony tweets from any Twitter account, including those belonging to the official feed for FOX News and then-President-elect Barack Obama (offering his more than 150,000 followers a chance to win $500 in free gasoline).

In April 2009, another hacker was able to gain administrative access to a Twitter employee's email account, where the employee's Twitter administrative password was stored in plain text. Once in the administrative account, the hacker reset at least one Twitter user's password and could access nonpublic user information and tweets for any Twitter user.

Twitter's privacy policy stated, "Twitter is very concerned about safeguarding the confidentiality of your personally identifiable information. We employ administrative, physical, and electronic measures designed to protect your information from unauthorized access." According to the FTC complaint, Twitter failed to prevent unauthorized administrative control of its system (and therefore violated its privacy policy) by, among other matters, failing to:

- Require that administrative passwords be hard to guess, and establish policies that: "(i) prohibit the use of common dictionary words as administrative passwords; and (ii) require that such passwords be unique"—that is, different from any password that the employee uses for other programs, websites, and networks;

- Prohibit storage of administrative passwords in plain text within employees' personal email accounts;

- Suspend or disable administrative passwords after a reasonable number of failed login attempts;

- "[P]rovide an administrative login web page that is made known only to authorized persons and is separate from the login web page for other users;"

- Enforce periodic changes of administrative passwords (setting them to expire every 90 days, for example);

- "[R]estrict each person's access to administrative controls according to the needs of that person's job;" and

- "[I]mpose other reasonable restrictions on administrative access, such as by restricting access to specified IP addresses."[10]

Under the terms of the settlement, Twitter must implement a comprehensive information security program that is reasonably designed to protect the privacy and security of nonpublic consumer information, and is prohibited from misrepresenting the extent to which it protects such information for 20 years. An independent auditor must conduct assessments every other year for 10 years to determine whether Twitter's information security program adequately protects consumer information as required by the settlement. In addition, Twitter is required to file a report describing its compliance with the settlement and alert the FTC to any change in the corporation that may affect its compliance obligations. Each violation of the FTC settlement order may result in a civil penalty of up to $16,000.

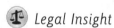 Legal Insight

In the class-action case of *Claridge v. RockYou*,[11] plaintiffs alleged that social network application developer RockYou failed to secure and safeguard its users' personally identifiable information (PII) (including their email addresses and passwords, as well as their login credentials for social networking sites such as Facebook and MySpace), resulting in a breach affecting more than 32 million users. In particular, according to the allegations in the complaint, RockYou stored its users PII in an unencrypted database (in *clear* or *plain* text) with poor network security, despite the representations in its privacy policy that it "uses commercially reasonable physical, managerial, and technical safeguards to preserve the integrity and security of your personal information." On April 11, 2011, a federal district court denied the defendant's motion to dismiss, and allowed plaintiffs' negligence and breach of contract claim to proceed. The court held that the loss of personal information alone was sufficient grounds for the claim, even if there are no *actual* damages as traditionally understood (for example, unauthorized charges on a credit or debit card resulting from the identity theft). Rather, a user's PII "constitutes valuable property that is exchanged not only for defendant's products and services, but also in exchange for defendant's promise to employ commercially reasonable methods to safeguard the PII that is exchanged. As a result, defendant's role in allegedly contributing to the breach of plaintiff's PII caused plaintiff to lose the 'value' of their PII, in the form of their breached personal data."[12] The decision is important because it contrasts with the overwhelming majority of other cases which have generally refused to confer Article III standing—that is, the legal right to bring a claim based on a concrete (actual, not hypothetical) and particularized (personal and individual) injury—upon consumers whose online personal information has been disclosed and whose only *injury* is the loss of the data itself.[13]

On December 15, 2011, the parties in *Claridge v. RockYou* submitted a settlement[14] for court approval. Under the terms of the proposed settlement, RockYou agreed: (i) to undergo two independent audits of its security policies for 3 years to ensure that consumers' personal information is stored in a secure and commercially reasonable manner; (ii) to correct any deficiencies in its policies to the extent such audits reveal any credible security threats; (iii) to pay the lead plaintiff $2,000 (as an "incentive award" for bringing the claim); and (iv) to pay plaintiff's attorney's fees of $290,000. It is important to note that the proposed settlement does not void the district court's April 2011 decision—future litigants are free to rely upon it as precedent (or persuasive authority) for the proposition that the loss of personal information alone is sufficient to confer standing.

The Twitter, Facebook, and Google FTC settlements highlight the security and privacy risks associated with social media. Companies that engage in social networking and deal with any form of personal information should proceed with caution because, as can be seen, privacy and security have become lightning rod topics for both the FTC and consumer advocacy groups. While consumers who use social networking sites may choose to share some information with others, they still have a right to expect that their personal information will be kept private and secure. At a minimum, as part of their privacy and security compliance guidelines, companies should require the following:

- Passwords must be unique and different from what their employees, who have administrative control of the companies' system, use to access third-party programs and networks.

- All administrative passwords must be changed periodically.

- All passwords in personal email accounts must be stored encrypted rather than in plain text.

Bottom line: If you represent that you will keep your users' information private and secure, you better make good on that promise. As the FTC is demanding of Facebook, Google, and Twitter, companies should audit their privacy and security practices at least annually and ensure that they are consistent not only with applicable law, but also with the policies and statements they have communicated to consumers.

Although the law oftentimes has a difficult time keeping pace with the rapid growth of technologies and business models, this is not entirely the case as it relates to companies that collect and use consumers' information in new ways. Here, the law (in the form of the FTC) is keeping close stride. The FTC's zealous enforcement and regulatory activity seeking to protect consumers from new and emerging forms of data security and privacy risks should serve as a wake-up call to all businesses to take these risks seriously. With the right combination of due diligence and strategic risk management (see Figure 10.1), companies collecting and using consumer data can hopefully avoid liability and regulatory scrutiny.

Legal Tips for Social Media Data Security & Privacy Compliance

DOs	DON'Ts
■ Conduct an audit of each user data point your company is collecting through social media and evaluate the legal risks associated with collecting, storing, and protecting such data. Be sure to include the appropriate information technology and digital marketing executives in that review process.	■ Do not install third-party applications on your website or social media page without first conducting a due diligence regarding the application's privacy and security—that is, whether it collects or shares consumer data, what data is transmitted, and to whom.
■ Carefully review your Terms of Use, Privacy Policies, End-User License Agreements, and promotional materials to ensure that the representations made therein accurately reflect your company's practices as it relates to the collection, use, sharing, privacy and security of consumer information.	■ Do not misrepresent the scope or frequency of your data collection practices, the number/nature of third parties with whom such information is shared (and the categories of information so shared), or for how long such information is retained.
■ Be sure your company has an up-to-date legally-compliant data breach incident response plan. Audit your privacy practices at least annually to ensure that they are consistent with applicable law and with the policies and statements you have communicated to consumers.	■ Do not rely upon legalese. Privacy Policies should be concise, clear, and easily understood. Companies should highlight—in plain-English—the important terms of their privacy policies at the beginning of the policy and direct users to the remainder of the document for more comprehensive explanations.
■ Obtain consumers' express affirmative consent before enacting retroactive changes that override users' privacy preferences—for example, by changing their privacy setting defaults so that data that had been private when it was initially provided later becomes public or subject to use by third-party applications.	■ Do not hide your information collection and sharing practices. Be sure to prominently disclose whether information is shared and how to opt-out, including a direct link to the opt-out mechanism. Within close proximity to the opt-out mechanism, be sure to provide consumers with information about your data collection practices and the current status of the user's choice (opted-out or not opted-out).
■ Obtain appropriate contractual protections from your social media business partners (such as media agencies, web publishers, advertising networks, and third-party application providers) requiring them to provide warranties and indemnities related to the unauthorized transmission, use, or tracking of your users' personal information.	■ If consumer information will be conveyed automatically (through a default setting) to a third-party application developer, do not rely solely upon the privacy policy to disclose this fact. Rather, this fact should be disclosed clearly and conspicuously at the time the consumer becomes a member of your service.

Figure 10.1 *Legal Tips for Social Media Data Security and Privacy Compliance.*

Chapter 10 ENDNOTES

1   *See* FTC's Preliminary Staff Report *Protecting Consumer Privacy in an Era of Rapid Change: A Framework Businesses and Policymakers* (Dec. 1, 2010), available at http://www.ftc.gov/os/2010/12/101201privacyreport.pdf.

2   *See* FTC's Staff Report Protecting Consumer Privacy in an Era of Rapid Change: A Framework Businesses and Policymakers (Mar. 26, 2012), available at http://ftc.gov/os/2012/03/120326privacyreport.pdf

Unlike in its 2010 draft report (wherein the FTC's recommendations applied to all commercial entities that collect or use consumer data that can be linked to a specific consumer, computer, or other device), the FTC concludes in its final report that its privacy framework should not apply to "companies that collect only non-sensitive data from fewer than 5,000 consumers a year, provided they do not share the data with third parties."

Moreover, whereas the preliminary report noted that choice shouldn't be necessary for certain "commonly accepted practices," the final Report concludes that choice needn't be provided for data practices which are "consistent with the context of the transaction or the company's relationship with the consumer, or where required or specifically authorized by law." The FTC noted that many of the five "commonly accepted practices" identified in the preliminary report would generally meet this revised standard, although there may be exceptions.

3   *In the Matter of Google Inc.*, Complaint, Request for Investigation, Injunction, and Other Relief (Feb. 16, 2010), available at http://epic.org/privacy/ftc/googlebuzz/GoogleBuzz_Complaint.pdf

4   *In Re Google Buzz Privacy Litigation*, Case No. 5:10-CV-00672-JW (N.D. Cal. Feb. 17, 2010)

5   *In the Matter of Google Inc.*, FTC File No. 102 3136 (Oct. 24, 2011). A copy of the Decision and Final Order is available at http://www.ftc.gov/os/caselist/1023136/111024googlebuzzdo.pdf.

6   *In the Matter of Facebook, Inc.*, FTC File No. 092 3184 (Nov. 29, 2011). A copy of the draft complaint is available at http://www.ftc.gov/os/caselist/0923184/111129facebookcmpt.pdf.

7   *In the Matter of Facebook, Inc.*, FTC File No. 092 3184 (Nov. 29, 2011). A copy of the agreement containing consent order is available at http://www.ftc.gov/os/caselist/0923184/111129facebookagree.pdf.

8   *See* FTC staff attorney Leslie Fair's 12/2/11 FTC blog post "Lessons from the Facebook Settlement (even if you are not Facebook)," available at http://business.ftc.gov/blog/2011/12/lessons-facebook-settlement-even-if-youre-not-facebook.

9   *In the Matter of Twitter, Inc.*, FTC File No. 092-3093 (Mar. 11, 2011). A copy of the decision and order is available at http://www.ftc.gov/os/caselist/0923093/110311twitterdo.pdf.

10   *In the Matter of Twitter, Inc.*, FTC File No. 092-3093 (Mar. 11, 2011). A copy of the complaint is available at http://www.ftc.gov/os/caselist/0923093/110311twittercmpt.pdf.

11   *Claridge v. RockYou, Inc.*, Case No. 4:09-CV-6032-PJH (N.D. Cal. Dec. 28, 2009)

12   *Order Granting in Part and Denying in Part Motion to Dismiss* (Docket No. 47) (Apr. 11, 2011), *Claridge v. RockYou, Inc.*, Case No. 4:09-CV-6032-PJH (N.D. Cal. Dec. 28, 2009)

13 A plaintiff must establish a number of requirements to have his/her case heard in ederal court, including Article III of the United States Constitution which provides, among other matters, that "The Judicial Power shall extend to all Cases …[and] to Controversies…." To satisfy Article III, a plaintiff "must show that (1) it has suffered an 'injury in fact' that is (a) concrete and particularized and (b) actual or imminent, not conjectural or hypothetical; (2) the injury is fairly traceable to the challenged action of the defendant; and (3) it is likely, as opposed to merely speculative, that the injury will be redressed by a favorable decision." *Friends of the Earth, Inc. v. Laidlaw Envtl. Sys. (TOC), Inc.*, 528 U.S. 167, 180-81 (2000)

14 *Plaintiff's Motion for Approval of Class Action Settlement* (Docket No. 55) (Dec. 15, 2011), *Claridge v. RockYou, Inc.*, Case No. 4:09-CV-6032-PJH (N.D. Cal.) (Dec. 28, 2009)

11

Legal Guidelines for Developing Social Media Policies and Governance Models

With the rapid business adoption of social media, a growing need exists for companies to establish corporate social media policies and governance models to guide and monitor employee and corporate social media activity. This chapter details a number of important legal issues businesses should consider when drafting (or updating) their social media policies and governance programs.

Businesses must tailor policies and programs not only to serve their unique strategic goals, but also to comply with the laws governing corporate and employee business use and monitoring of social networking activity. Businesses should have a general understanding of the laws and regulations implicated in the social media space so that their policies are not written overly broad and their governance does not overstep legal boundaries. These potential legal pitfalls are only increasing as we observe the adoption of social media for an expanding number of business applications which include not only marketing, public relations, and sales, but also research and development, product design, customer service, human resources, and others.

Developing a corporate social media policy, regardless of your company's size, makes good business and legal sense. In addition to minimizing a company's legal exposure, a social media policy also serves as an internal branding and communications guideline and empowers team members with the information they need in order to comfortably (and responsibly) use social media.

Developing a corporate social media policy, regardless of your company's size, makes good business and legal sense.

Given the prevalence of social media in the workplace, it is becoming increasingly incumbent upon employers to establish a social medial policy to permit the effective monitoring of employee use of social media and guidelines for that use. Corporate social media policies should contain a hybrid mix of social media objectives, values, guidelines and best practices, rules on what is considered appropriate and inappropriate use of social media, and the governance procedures a company follows when the rules are broken (either by employees or by the enterprise). It is important to emphasize that each social media policy should be tailored to the specific needs, values, and objectives of the organization, and should be consistent with the company's existing policies, strategic initiatives, and business objectives.

Vital Corporate Social Media Policy Provisions

No one-size-fits-all approach works, so at a minimum the social media policy should contain the following provisions:

- **Social Media Goals:** A corporate social media policy should begin with its *charter* (a statement of desired goals which your company is working to achieve through the use of social networks and tools). These goals serve not only as a list of business objectives, but also as a guideline in establishing your key performance indicators for accountable social media programs.

- **Consistency:** A corporate social media policy should embody the core values of the company itself, and should therefore be drafted in alignment with the company's internal policies, including those contained in an employee handbook or company code of conduct. This section should include guidance on what types of behavior employees are expected to abide by in both their personal and professional social media engagement. A list of examples of unacceptable behavior, statements, and activities is helpful to delineate between conduct that embodies the values of the social media policy and those that do not.

- **Permission and Parameters:** The policy should state whether the use of social media is permitted, and provide parameters for such use in the workplace (for example, business use only, limited personal use, quotas for timed access). The company should also provide a list of approved social networks sites made available to its employees for usage (delineating between approved personal and professional use while at work), and block (or limit) access to sites not on the list.

- **Monitoring:** The policy should advise its employees that the company may monitor employee postings within the workplace and, subject to certain limitations, outside of the workplace as well. The policy should state that all use of the Internet via the company's computer systems, networks, and related equipment is nonprivate, and by using the company's computer systems, networks and related equipment, the employees consent to have the employer access, review, monitor, record, and restrict all such use. Note, however, that many states have enacted off-duty conduct laws that prohibit employers from basing employment decisions on legal activities of employees outside of work time. Employers should familiarize themselves with these laws in each jurisdiction where its employees carry out company business.

 Note

The legality of employer monitoring of employee online communications generally hinges on the *reasonable expectation of privacy* that the employee has in his/her electronic communications. This standard is interpreted objectively; that is, what is objectively reasonable given the operational realities of the workplace, such as policies disclosing that computers and social postings are subject to monitoring, and a history of enforcing such a policy even-handedly (for example, monitoring all employee's Facebook pages, not only just select employees). To dispel any reasonable expectation of privacy that employees may otherwise have in their social media communications, employers should implement (and enforce) policies stating that all electronic communications on company computers, via company networks, are monitored, as are all employee public postings however posted.

- **Spokespersons:** The policy should specify who within the organization has authority to represent the company as an official spokesperson across all media. Official spokespersons are employees authorized to participate in interviews with bloggers, analysts, journalists, and so on. The policy should be careful to explicitly state, however, that it does not prevent employees from speaking to the media about their own employment concerns.

- **Employee Participation:** Social media practitioners within a company are not necessarily limited solely to spokepersons or the marketing and publicity team. Each employee should understand clearly what his or her level of participation and role is within social networks. This section should include a statement which alerts employees to the fact that even though they may not be official company spokespersons, they will be perceived as extensions of the company, and that the content published within their social media networks can (even if inadvertently) not only adversely impact an employer's social media presence, but also expose the employer to legal violations. Employees should be reminded to avoid making defamatory or discriminatory statements about their employers, colleagues, customers, and competitors; and to refrain from all postings of a sexual, harassing, offensive, or violent nature.

- **Confidential/Proprietary Information:** The policy should require employees to comply with all company policies concerning confidential information and trade secrets, and remind employees that even "private" messages between individuals may be accessed by third parties. The policy should forbid employees from disclosing any proprietary information (including unreleased product, sales, and market share information, financial forecasts, customer lists, client lists, research and development initiatives, and so on) on any social media site. In the event confidential, proprietary or trade secret information is disclosed, employers should take prompt action to limit the propagation of the information and to safeguard additional information from being released. These steps help ensure that the company is not subsequently found to have impliedly waived the protection afforded to such information by failing to reasonably protect it.

✉ *Note*

The inadvertent release of a company's proprietary information by its employees on social media sites is a real risk, as Hewlett-Packard Co. learned all too well in 2011, after its Chief Technologist and interim Vice President of Engineering, allegedly disclosed details of his company's plans for its new cloud services business on his public LinkedIn profile.[1]

Likewise, a company may also lose its trade secret protection in confidential customer lists or clients lists if such information is posted on social network sites. While no court has yet so ruled, permitting your employees to publicly disclose their (otherwise private) contacts on LinkedIn and Facebook may result in a loss of protection of such information, as such information was not properly designated (or maintained) as being private.

- **Use Privacy Settings:** The policy should require its employees to learn the privacy settings of approved social media platforms and to update their privacy settings so that their company-related profiles, groups, and postings are protected.

- **Nondisparagement and Nondiscrimination:** The policy should prohibit the use of racial or ethnic slurs, personal insults, pornography, obscenity, or derogatory, discriminatory and harassing postings or materials. The policy should make clear that employees are prohibited from using online social networks to harass, disparage, libel, or discriminate against others in the workplace, or the company's competitors, vendors, customers, and so forth. Further, the policy should stress that any online communication (whether work related or not) may contribute to an unlawful hostile work environment and that all employees have an affirmative duty to inform management of any improper online conduct of which they may become aware.

- **Protected Activity:** The policy should make explicit that it does not prohibit employees from discussing the terms and conditions of their employment (including employee criticisms of employers or supervisors). This does not mean, however, that employers cannot take action against employees for social media posts concerning the company and its management if:

  - The employee is disparaging the company or management, and the statements clearly do not concern work conditions, benefits, wages, and other terms and conditions of employment;

  - The employee is discussing privileged and confidential client communications or proprietary company information; or

  - The employee is harassing, threatening, or making racist or other discriminatory statements directed at a co-worker.

- **Personal Versus Official Use:** The policy should forbid employees from using the company's name, trademarks, logos, or symbols when posting online, or making statements attributable to the company, without the company's prior authorization. The policy should state that employees are not permitted to use the employer's trademarks, logos or symbols on their own personal page (LinkedIn page, Facebook page, Twitter handle, and so forth) and that they are precluded from using the company's name in any URL. Care should be taken, however, to remind employees that this and other policy provisions do not relate to activity otherwise protected by the National Labor Relations Act (NLRA) (see Chapter 4, "Monitoring, Regulating, and Disciplining Employees Using Social Media ").

- **Register Social Media Accounts in Company's Name:** To the fullest extent possible, companies should register social media accounts in their own names or through a senior marketing manager if the account needs to be in the name of a person. The policy should prohibit employees from conducting business through social media using individual accounts held in their own names.

- **Establish Ownership of Social Media Accounts:** All company business should be done only with company owned social media accounts, and employees should be required to use company-provided account logins and passwords. Further, companies should take proactive steps to ensure that they (and not their employees) "own" their social media accounts (and, perhaps more importantly, their followers) when the employment relationship is terminated. Ownership rights should be clearly set forth in a written agreement prior to the establishment of any employer-sponsored social media account.

 Note

With more and more businesses actively encouraging their employees to use social media as a marketing tool, litigation over the ownership of social media accounts is undoubtedly likely to increase. In one case,[2] a tech website (PhoneDog) sued an ex-employee for his Twitter account (@PhoneDog_Noah), valuing his approximately 17,000 followers at $2.50 each. The company alleged that it provided its employees on a need-to-know basis confidential information, including passwords to all @PhoneDog_NAME Twitter accounts used by PhoneDog's employees. The company further alleged that the followers are its business trade secrets; and that Kravitz' actions were the equivalent of stealing a customer list. On November 8, 2011, in denying (in part) the former employee's motion to dismiss, the District Court for the Northern District of California allowed PhoneDog's claim for misappropriation of trade secrets and conversion (that is, civil theft) to proceed.[3] Although the actual value of a Twitter follower will have to be decided by a jury, the case reminds employers to take preemptive steps to mitigate the risk of misappropriation, both by way of the social media policy and individual employment contracts delineating that whatever the employee "builds" on company time or with company resources belongs to the employer.

Eagle v. Morgan[4] is another example of an employer-employee social media account ownership dispute, which could have been easily avoided had there been a contract in place. In this case, the employer, a financial services and training company, claimed it owned its former chief executive's LinkedIn account because (i) its policy required its employees to create and maintain LinkedIn accounts (using a pre-approved template), (ii) its employees used the accounts to promote the employer's business, (iii) the employer developed and maintained all connections and much of the content on its employees' accounts, and (iv) the employer otherwise had substantial involvement in the creation, operation, and monitoring of the accounts. Although the terminated employee alleged that the LinkedIn account belonged to her as a matter of law (as the account contained her profile information, including honors and awards, recommendations, and connections), a federal court in Pennsylvania disagreed, and concluded that the employer's policy and level of participation regarding its employees' LinkedIn accounts was sufficient evidence to state a valid claim of misappropriation, leaving the question of ownership to a jury.[5] How a jury will ultimately decide is unknown. But to avoid disputes over social media account ownership, employers are reminded to get it in writing!

- **Disclosures/Disclaimers:** The policy should require employees to be transparent in their social media communications, to disclose their true identity, and to never use aliases or make anonymous posts. A disclaimer stating that "the views expressed herein are that of the individual and not of the company" should also be required on all postings, blogs, and the like whenever appropriate.

- **Endorsements:** The policy should require employees to disclose their name and employment relationship with the company whenever the employee makes favorable statements regarding the company, or the company's products and services. Employees should also be required to disclose whether they are making such statements on their own behalf or on behalf of the company. The company might want to limit or preclude altogether any employee endorsement in any online forum. Further, the company should have a separate policy for third-party bloggers, outside media agencies, and other independent contractors, whom should be required to disclose any material connections they have with the company in their endorsements (for example, that they were paid or received free products in connection with their endorsement). In all circumstances, companies should have procedures in place to monitor the online postings of its employees, bloggers, vendors, and others as it relates to product endorsements (or otherwise).

- **Respect Copyrights and Intellectual Property Rights of Others:** The policy should forbid employees from infringing the copyrights, trademarks, and other intellectual property rights of third parties. The policy should remind employees that any form of original expression fixed in a tangible medium (including music, movies, graphics, text, photographs, and artwork) is subject to copyright, even if there is no copyright notice. To ensure that the copyright, trademark, and other intellectual property rights of others are respected, companies should monitor content that is posted to the organization's social media sites, whether by employees or users of the site.

- **Disciplinary Action:** The policy should clearly state what the consequences are for violations of the social media policy, and that employees may face disciplinary action, up to and including termination of employment. (Reminder: As discussed in Chapter 4, "Monitoring, Regulating, and Disciplining Employees Using Social Media," the National Labor Relations Act (NLRA) prohibits disciplinary action if the employee is using a social media platform to initiate, induce, or prepare for group action regarding wages, benefits, performance, staffing levels, scheduling issues, or other terms and conditions of employment. The social media policy should be drafted so as not to run afoul of the NLRA or of federal and state whistleblower or retaliation statutes.)

- **Security:** Social media in the workplace continues to represent a serious risk, particularly in the form of malware and data theft. Organizations should inform their employees of these risks and adopt the necessary security controls to mitigate or reduce them, such as antivirus/antimalware, endpoint security, and secure web gateways with real-time content analysis that analyzes online postings contemporaneously with their creation and consumption. Employees should be encouraged not to click on unknown links appearing on social media sites, particularly those whose signature block is unrecognized or which have a suspicious payload.

✉ Note

No company is immune from security threats, even the beloved *Sesame Street*. In October, 2011, *Sesame Street*'s YouTube channel was hacked and reprogrammed with pornographic videos, requiring it to briefly go offline.[6] Online security vulnerabilities can have much more devastating consequences to a company, in terms of congressional investigations and enforcement actions, brand dilution, consumer erosion, and lost revenue.

- **Employee Training:** A social media policy is not enough. Education, resources, and training for employee social media practitioners are essential, and the actual social media policy document should merely be a supplement and a reference during mandatory employee training. Companies may want to appoint a compliance officer for monitoring and accepting complaints regarding employee use of social media.

> A social media policy is not enough. Education, resources, and training for employee social media practitioners are essential.

- **Acknowledgment/Signature:** The social media policy should be signed by each employee to acknowledge that the employee has read and understood it and agrees to abide by its terms. Moreover, employees should initial the section disclosing that the company has the right to monitor all company equipment and employee postings and that it has the employee's authorization to do so.

Social media undoubtedly represents both a great opportunity and tremendous challenge for business. With this new digital era of unprecedented connectivity, communication, and collaboration come significant legal risks that responsible companies must identify and properly navigate. What's more, the laws triggered by social media and networking continue to evolve in the wake of rapid technological innovation. Businesses need to be extra vigilant in light of this ever-changing legal landscape.

Recommended Social Media Marketing Policies

Social media policies and governance models are not silver bullets. For marketing practitioners, whether they are on the client side, or the agency side, there is also merit to establishing a clearly written Social Marketing Policy to serve as a framework for best-practices and guidelines for the drafting of social media campaigns, especially as it relates to the creation of social media content and targeting.

At a minimum, social media marketing policies should include the following provisions:

- **Social Media Content-Creation Guidelines:** By definition, social media engagement strategies are content driven, whether the content takes on the form of text, links, images, audio, video, podcasts, games/quizzes, eBooks, or rich media. It is incumbent upon organizations using social media programs to include a policy provision outlining best practice guidelines for the creation of the content. The content guidelines should address substantive, stylistic, and tonal approaches to the development of content. For example, you might want to include guidance outlining a preference for social content to be educational, info-training, or informational rather than hard-hitting advertorial or promotional. You might also want to include recommendations on the frequency of publication within each social platform, on the recommended timeline for response to user messages within each platform, and so on.

- **Targeted Social Media Audience:** An effective social media policy outlines precisely the audience segments your social media efforts are aimed at, your target audiences, how they align to your company's business objectives, what social platforms each audiences utilizes, and what the recommended types of engagement are for each.. For social media initiatives designed for, or that would reasonably attract children under 13 years of age, the requirements of the Children's Online Privacy Protection Act (COPPA) need to be observed (see Chapter 7, "The Law of Social Advertising").

A social media policy should serve to protect the considerable investment companies make in their brand and reputation, while promoting its online presence in a legally compliant way. A well-drafted and consistently enforced social media policy (see Figure 11.1), together with ongoing employee training, is perhaps the greatest protection an employer can have to avoid liability from the use of social media.

Legal Tips for Writing Social Media Policies and Designing Governance Models

DOs	DON'Ts
■ Maintain an up-to-date social media policy and governance program and regularly educate your employees on what is, and is not, permissible social media use.	■ Do not hide your company's Social Media Policy in a stack of new hire paperwork or allow it to become outdated. New media, along with online technologies and platforms, is evolving rapidly; businesses need to keep pace.
■ Draft your Social Media Policy as a team with input and advice from all key business stakeholders, including your CEO, CIO, IT Director, Director of Human Resources, Director of Marketing, Customer Service Director, and anyone who manages teams who will be using social media for business.	■ Don't rely solely on your corporate Social Media Policy to educate your staff on the important issues, risks, and best-practices associated with social media. Establish a proactive educational training program designed to preempt legal disputes and regulatory scrutiny.
■ Prohibit the use of social media to post or display comments about coworkers, supervisors, or the employer that are vulgar, obscene, threatening, intimidating, harassing, or a violation of the employer's workplace policies against discrimination or harassment on account of age, race, religion, sex, ethnicity, nationality, disability, or any other protected class.	■ Do not adopt social media policies, which include broad prohibitions against damaging the employer's reputation, embarrassing the employer, or which otherwise broadly prohibit employees from discussing the company, its management, employees, or competitors, or from making any disparaging remarks or engaging in any inappropriate discussions, without providing limiting language explicitly stating that such prohibitions do not apply to "concerted activity" under National Labor Relations Act (NLRA).
■ Prohibit employees from representing in any way that they are speaking on the company's behalf without prior written authorization to do so. Prohibit employees from using the company's name or logo when engaging or depicting in social media any conduct which violates the company's policies or is unlawful, but be sure to exclude from this prohibition activity protected by the NLRA.	■ Do not implement rules that require employees to avoid identifying themselves as employees of the employer unless discussing the terms and conditions of employment in an "appropriate" manner, without defining "appropriate"—either through specific examples of what is covered or through limiting language that would exclude NLRA-protected activity.
■ Include a disclaimer that the policy will not be construed or applied to limit employees' rights under the NLRA or applicable law, even for discussions the employer may consider unprofessional or inappropriate.	■ Do not rely exclusively upon a disclaimer to comply fully with the NLRA, as provisions elsewhere in your policy may be ambiguous and reasonably interpreted as restricting the exercise of NLRA rights.

■ Remind employees that they cannot disclose the employer's (or its customers') confidential, proprietary, or non-public information, or trade secrets, on any social networking site, but provide examples of the types of information it you deem confidential, proprietary, and non-public (for example, personal health information about customers or patients) and clarify that the policy does not prohibit Section 7 NLRA activity (such as discussing wages with family members, for example).	■ Do not assume your company owns the social media accounts employees are using on behalf of your business. Ensure your Social Media Policy explicitly states the employer owns and controls all social media accounts, and that employees are not permitted to use those accounts, nor the information contained within them, for their personal benefit.
■ Draft your social media policies from the perspective of what conduct a "reasonable" employee would construe as being limited. Policies restricting employee posts should avoid overly broad language, ambiguous and vague words, and undefined terms.	■ Avoid policies that include overly broad and undefined prohibitions against "offensive conduct," "rude and discourteous behavior;" or "inappropriate discussions," wherever such prohibitions do not include limiting language to remove potential ambiguities regarding whether Section 7 activity is prohibited.
■ Enforce your social media policies uniformly, particularly as they relate to employee discipline for social networking activity.	■ Do not overlook the risks of data security breaches arising from employee use of social media. Cultivate a corporate social media culture wherein employees respect the need to maintain strict compliance with your company's or clients' confidential, proprietary, or non-public information, or trade secrets.

Figure 11.1   *Social media policy drafting legal tips*

Chapter 11 ENDNOTES

1   http://www.channelregister.co.uk/2011/05/03/hp_vp_leaks_company_cloud_plans/

2   *PhoneDog, LLC v. Noah Kravitz*, Case No. 3:11-CV-03474-MEJ (N.D. Cal. Jul. 15, 2011)

3   See Order on Defendant's Motion to Dismiss (Document No. 28) (Nov. 8, 2011), in *PhoneDog, LLC v. Noah Kravitz*, Case No. 3:11-CV-03474-MEJ (N.D. Cal. Jul. 15, 2011).

4   *Eagle v. Morgan et al.*, Case No. 2:11-CV-4303-RB (E.D. Pa.) (Jul. 1, 2011)

5   See Memorandum/Order on Plaintiff's Motion to Dismiss Counterclaims (Document No. 43) (Dec. 22, 2011), in *Eagle v. Morgan et al.*, Case No. 2:11-CV-4303-RB (E.D. Pa.) (Jul. 1, 2011).

6   http://articles.cnn.com/2011-10-16/tech/tech_sesame-street-hacking_1_youtube-users-video-web-site-youtube-s-community-guidelines?_s=PM:TECH

12

Looking Ahead at Social Media Business Opportunities, Expectations, and Challenges

The past few years witnessed a flurry of lawsuits stemming from social media activity. Legal challenges are bound to increase as the rate of social media adoption in businesses continues to rise.

Indeed, the next few years promises to be very fruitful in the social media legal field, as courts (and legislatures) wrestle with issues such as publicity rights, privacy, data security, online tracking, behavioral advertising and geolocation marketing, mobile payments, and ownership rights of social media accounts and followers.

Businesses will need to be vigilant—and respond swiftly—to new legal challenges arising from social media, as the law governing this space continues to unfold almost on a daily basis.

In looking forward to mitigate risk, one should also look back to learn from the mistakes that have been made along the way by others. Table 12.1 outlines 10 noteworthy social media business entanglements, and the lessons businesses should glean from them.

Table 12.1   10 Social Media Lessons

1. Your Twitter Hashtag Can Be Used Against You	In 2012, *McDonald's* commenced a 24-hour Twitter campaign to promote its use of fresh produce under the hashtag, #MeetTheFarmers. The PR initiative proceeded well enough, but when McDonald's changed the hashtag to #McDStories, the fast-food chain found itself a scratching post for dissatisfied customers of all sorts, with complaints ranging from finding fingernails in BigMacs to chipping teeth and being food poisoned.
2. Train Your Employees on Anti-Discrimination (and Other Company) Policies	In 2012, a customer of *Papa John's* restaurant in New York posted a copy of her receipt wherein the cashier referred to her as "lady chinky eyes." Although *Papa John's* quickly issued an apology via Twitter, the derogatory and racially insulting comment outraged many of the restaurant's followers (as it rightfully should).
3. Monitor Your Social Media Postings (and Those from Whom You Authorize to Post)	In 2011, *Chrysler Automotive's* Twitter feed accidently posted the following message regarding the company's hometown, "I find it ironic that Detroit is known as the #motorcity and yet no one here knows how to [f***ing] drive." Worse, the tweet was authored by an employee of the marketing firm hired by Chrysler to grow its social media presence.
4. Be Careful What You Tweet	In 2011, a tweet from clothing designer *Kenneth Cole's* official Twitter page was posted: "Millions are in uproar in #Cairo. Rumor is they heard our new spring collection is now available online." Given the tremendous amount of media attention to the protests in Cairo as part of the "Arab Spring," the fashion designer's hijacking of the Twitter hashtag to promote its products was met with public outrage.
5. Remind Your Employees and Agents That What They Say Online Can Impact Your Brand	In 2011, comedian Gilbert Gottfried, the voice behind the famous *Aflac* duck, posted several tweets joking about the Japan earthquake and tsunami tragedy. The insurance company quickly terminated Gottfried.

6. Adopt A Strong Code of Professionalism and Ethics	In 2011, *FedEx*, the global parcel and freight handler, learned the hard way that their employees are being watched by the world when a video posted on YouTube captured a *FedEx* delivery person tossing a computer monitor over a fence. The thought of one's packages being mishandled by reckless delivery workers is hard to erase in the minds of consumers. As of the date of this publication, the video has grabbed more than 4.5 million views.
7. Don't Silence Criticism With Questionable DMCA Take-Down Requests	In 2010, *Greenpeace* and *Nestlé* had a veritable social media "kat" fight. In a video posted on YouTube, the environmental protection group challenged Nestlé's use of palm oil in Nestlé's KitKat candy bar, implying that Nestlé's acquisition of palm oil contributed to rainforest deforestation and threatened endangered species like the Orangutan. In response, Nestlé had the video removed from YouTube, claiming "copyright" infringement. In the ensuing social media public uproar, Nestlé eventually backed down and announced a "zero deforestation" policy.
8. Do Not Pay For or Use False Endorsements	In 2009, *Belkin* became the subject of a media firestorm when it was discovered that *Belkin* paid reviewers ($0.65 per review) to write positive reviews for its products on Amazon.com, whether they used the products or not. To make matters worse, *Belkin* also asked people to find negative reviews of its products and mark them as not helpful.
9. Always Be Prepared With A Social Media Crisis Management Plan	In 2009, *Domino's* also suffered a social media crisis when videos posted on YouTube showed an employee sticking his uncovered hands in food prep stations, sticking cheese up his nose, and passing gas on a sandwich. The prank video reportedly gained more than one million viewers within a few days
10. Secure Your Social Media Handles Before Someone Else Does	In 2009, *EasyJet* found itself behind the Twitter eight-ball because it failed to secure the Twitter handle '@easyjetservice' before a dissatisfied passenger did, who aired his grievances online about the budget airline. *EasyJet* ultimately secured its own Twitter account under the name '@easyJetCare.'

As demonstrated by the cases in Table 12.1, like all technology, social media has practical benefits, limitations and unexpected dangers. While social media provides unprecedented levels of quick and relatively inexpensive means for businesses to communicate directly with their customers and prospects, it simultaneously carries substantial risks (including less control over the company's message and brand and potential liability for the social networking actions of its employees and customers).

Although social media might appear too risky for many companies protective of their brand and market positioning, it need not be so with a fuller appreciation of the laws in this space. Customer engagement occurs with or without a company's blessing, and cloistering oneself away from social media's reach is no longer a viable option. It is better to be leading the conversation than responding to it (perhaps too late).

The law governing social media is significantly outpaced by rapid changes in technology. Inevitably, as the social media landscape evolves, so too will the law, as it continues to play catch-up to technological innovations. While the business usage of social media carries with it tremendous advantages, it also carries risk of legal exposure that businesses would do well to keep updated on and take prudent steps to mitigate. Reading this book is hopefully a forward step in that direction.

Stay connected:

To keep track of further social media legal developments, you are encouraged to follow me on Twitter (@rmchalelaw) and Facebook (facebook.com/rmlaw).

Appendix A

Table of Legal Authorities

Federal Statutes and Regulations

- 15 U.S.C. §§ 41-58 (*as amended*), The Federal Trade Commission Act of 1914

- 15 U.S.C. § 1125(a), Section 43(a) of Lanham Act

- 15 U.S.C. § 1125(d), Anticybersquatting Consumer Protection Act ("ACPA")

- 15 U.S.C. § 1681 *et seq.*, Fair Credit Reporting Act ("FCRA")

- 15 U.S.C. §1693 *et seq.*, Electronic Funds Transfer Act ("EFTA") (as amended by the Credit Card Accountability Responsibility and Disclosure ("CARD") Act of 2009, Public Law 111-24, 123 Stat. 1734.)

- 15 U.S.C. § 6501 *et seq.*, Children's Online Privacy Protection Act ("COPPA") of 1998

- 15 U.S.C. § 7701 *et seq.*, Controlling the Assault of Non-Solicited Pornography and Marketing ("CAN-SPAM") Act of 2003

- 16 C.F.R. Part 255, FTC's Revised Guides Concerning Use of Endorsements and Testimonials in Advertising

- 16 C.F.R. Part 312, Children's Online Privacy Protection Rule

- 17 U.S.C. §101 *et seq.*, the Copyright Act

- 17 U.S.C. § 512, Online Copyright Infringement Liability Limitation Act ("OCILLA") (passed as a part of the 1998 Digital Millennium Copyright Act ("DMCA") (Public Law No. 105-304)

- 18 U.S.C. § 1030, Computer Fraud and Abuse Act

- 18 U.S.C. § 2701 *et seq.*, Electronic Communications Privacy Act (including the Stored Wire and Electronic Communications and Transactional Records Access, or the Stored Communications Act ("SCA")

- 29 U.S.C. § 151–169 (*as amended*), National Labor Relations Act (Public Law 74-198, 49 Stat. 449)

- 31 U.S.C. §§ 5361-5366, the Unlawful Internet Gambling Enforcement Act of 2006

- 47 U.S.C. § 230, Communications Decency Act ("CDA") of 1996 (Public Law No. 104-104)

Case Law

- *A&M Records, Inc. v. Napster, Inc.*, 239 F.3d 1004 (9th Cir. 2001)

- *AirFX.com v. AirFX, LLC,* Case No. 2:11-CV-01064-PHX-FJM (D. Ariz. May 27, 2011)

- *American Medical Response of Connecticut, Inc.*, Case No. 34-CA-12576 (Region 34, NLRB) (Oct. 27, 2010)

- *Barcelona.com v. Excelentisimo Ayuntamiento de Barcelona,* 330 F.3d 617 (4th Cir. 2003)

- *Barnes v. CUS Nashville, LLC,* Case No. 3:09-CV-00764 (M.D. Tenn. June 3, 2010)

- *Bragg v. Linden Research, Inc. et al.*, Case No. 2:06-CV-04925-ER (E.D. Penn. 2006)

- *Caraballo v. City of New York,* 2011 N.Y. Misc. LEXIS 1038 (N.Y. Sup. Richmond County, Mar. 4, 2011)

- *Carafano v. Metrosplash.com, Inc.*, 339 F.3d 1119 (9th Cir. 2003)

- *Chanel, Inc. v. Does 1-1000 et al.*, Case No. 2:11-CV-01508-KJD-PAL (D.Nev. Sept. 20, 2011)

- *Chang et al. v. Virgin Mobile USA, LLC et al.*, Case No. 3:07-CV-01767-D (N.D. Tex., Oct. 19, 2007)

- *Chang et al. v. Virgin Mobile USA, LLC et al.*, 5:08-MC-80095-JW (N.D. Tex., May 8, 2008)

- *Chicago Lawyers' Comm. for Civil Rights Under the Law, Inc. v. Craigslist, Inc.*, 461 F. Supp. 2d 681 (N.D. Ill. 2006)

- *City of Ontario et al. v. Quon et al.*, 130 S. Ct. 2619 (2010)

- *City of Ontario et al. v. Quon et al.*, 529 F. 3d 892 (9th Cir. 2008)

- *Claridge v. RockYou, Inc.*, Case No. 4:09-CV-6032-PJH (N.D. Cal. Dec. 28, 2009)

- *Cliffdale Associates, Inc.*, 103 F.T.C. 110 (1984)

- *Columbia Insurance Company v. Seescandy.com*, 185 F.R.D. 573 (N.D. Cal. 1999)

- *Commonwealth v. Williams*, 456 Mass. 857 N.E.2d 1162 (Mass. 2010)

- *Coventry First, LLC v. Does 1-10*, Case No. 2:11-CV-03700-JS (E.D. Penn. Jun. 7, 2011)

- *Crispin v. Audigier, Inc.*, 717 F.Supp.2d 965 (C.D. Calif. May 26, 2010)

- *Delfino et al. v. Agilent Technologies, Inc.*, 145 Cal. App. 4th 790 (Calif. Ct. App., 6th App. District 2006), *cert. denied*, 52 U.S. 817 (2007)

- *Del Vecchio et al. v. Amazon.com Inc.*, Case No. 2:11-CV-00366-RSL (W.D. Wash. Mar. 2, 2011)

- *Doctor's Associates, Inc. v. QIP Holder LLC, et al.*, Case No. 3:06-CV-1710 (D. Conn. Oct. 27, 2006)

- *Doe v. Friendfinder Network, Inc. et al.*, 540 F.Supp.2d 288 (D.N.H. 2008)

- *Doe v. 2TheMart.Com, Inc.*, 140 F.Supp.2d 1088 (W.D. Wash. 2001)

- *Doe v. XYZ Corp.*, 382 N.J. Super. 122 (App. Div. 2005)

- *Doe II, a Minor, etc., et al., v. MySpace Incorporated*, 175 Cal. App. 4th 561 (2009)

- *EEOC v. Simply Storage Mgmt., LLC*, 270 F.R.D. 430 (S.D. Ind. 2010)

- *Ellison v. Robertson*, 357 F.3d 1072 (9th Cir. 2004)

- *Endicott Interconnect Technologies, Inc. v. NLRB*, 453 F.3d 532 (D.C. Cir. 2006)

- *Evans et al. v. Linden Research, Inc., et al.*, Case No. 2:10-CV-1679-ER (E.D. Penn. Apr. 15, 2010); *case subsequently transferred to* N.D. Cal., Case No. 4:11-CV-01078-DMR (N.D. Cal. Mar. 8, 2011)

- *Facebook, Inc. v. MaxBounty, Inc.,* Case No. 5:10-CV-04712-JF (N.D. Cal. Mar. 28, 2011)

- *Fair Housing Council v. Roommates.com, LLC,* 521 F.3d 1157 (9th Cir. 2008) (*en banc*)

- *Ferreira v. Groupon Inc., Nordstrom, Inc.,* Case No. 3:11-CV-0132-DMS-RBB (S.D. Cal. Jan. 21, 2011)

- *Five Star Transportation, Inc.,* 349 NLRB 42 (2007), *enforced,* 522 F.3d 46 (1st Cir. 2008)

- *Friends of the Earth, Inc. v. Laidlaw Envtl. Sys. (TOC), Inc.,* 528 U.S. 167 (2000)

- *Gentry v. eBay, Inc.,* 99 Cal. App. 4th 816 (2002)

- *Griffin v. Maryland,* 19 A.3d 415 (Md. Apr. 28, 2011)

- *Griffin v. Maryland,* 995 A.2d 791 (Md. Ct. Spec. App. 2010)

- *Grooms et al. v. Legge et al.,* Case No. 3:09-CV-489-IEG-POR (S.D. Cal. Mar. 11, 2009)

- *Herbert et al. v. Endemol USA Inc. et al.,* Case No. 2:07-CV-03537-JHN-VBK (C.D. Cal. May 31, 2007)

- *Hispanics United Of Buffalo, Inc. v. Ortiz,* NLRB Case No. 3-CA-27872 (Sept. 2, 2011)

- *In the Matter of Google Inc.,* FTC File No. 102 3136 (Oct. 24, 2011)

- *In the Matter of Legacy Learning Systems, Inc., et al.,* FTC File No. 102 3055 (Jun. 10, 2011)

- *In the Matter of Reverb Communications, Inc. et al.,* FTC File No. 092 3199 (Nov. 26, 2010)

- *In the Matter of Twitter, Inc.,* FTC File No. 092-3093 (Mar. 11, 2011)

- *In re Apple In-App Purchase Litigation,* Case No. 5:11-CV-1758-JF (N.D. Cal. Jun. 16, 2011)

- *In re Google Buzz Privacy Litigation,* Case No. 5:10-CV-00672-JW (N.D. Cal. Feb. 17, 2010)

- *In re iPhone/iPad Application Consumer Privacy Litigation,* Case No. 5:11-MD-02250-LHK (N.D. Cal. Aug. 25, 2011)

- *Independent Newspapers, Inc. v. Brodie,* 966 A.2d 432 (Md. 2009)

- *Interactive Products Corp. v. a2z Mobile Office Solutions, Inc. et al.*, 326 F.3d 687 (6th Cir. 2003)

- *Johnson v. K Mart Corp.*, 723 N.E.2d 1192 (Ill. App. 2000)

- *JT's Porch Saloon*, NLRB Div. of Advice No. 13-CA-46689 (Jul. 7, 2011)

- *Katiroll Co. v. Kati Roll and Platters, Inc.*, Case No. 3:10-CV-03620 (D.N.J. Jul. 19, 2010)

- *Knight-McConnell v. Cummins*, Case No. 1:03-CV-05035-NRB (S.D. N.Y. Jul. 7, 2003)

- *Konop v. Hawaiian Airlines, Inc.*, 302 F.3d 868 (Ct. App., 9th Cir. 2002)

- *Lalo v. Apple, Inc., et al.*, Case No. 5:10-CV-05878-LHK (N.D. Cal. Dec. 23, 2010), *transferred and consolidated with four related cases, In re iPhone/iPad Application Consumer Privacy Litigation*, 5:11-MD-02250-LHK, (N.D. Cal. Aug. 25, 2011)

- *La Russa v. Twitter, Inc. and Does 1-25*, Case No. CGC-09-488101, Superior Court of California, County of San Francisco (May 6, 2009)

- *Lenz v. Universal Music Corp. et al.*, 572 F. Supp. 2d 1150 (N.D. Cal. 2008)

- *Levitt et al., v. Yelp! Inc.*, Case No. 3:10-CV-01321-EMC (N.D. Cal. Mar. 29, 2010)

- *Low v. LinkedIn Corp.*, Case No. 5:11-CV-01468-LHK (N.D. Cal. Nov. 11, 2011)

- *Maremont v. Susan Fredman Design Group, Ltd. et al.*, Case No. 1:10-CV-07811 (N.D. Il. Dec. 9, 2010)

- *Martin House*, NLRB Div. of Advice No. 34-CA-12950 (Jul. 19, 2011)

- *Mayflower Transit, L.L.C. v. Prince*, 314 F. Supp. 2d 362 (D.N.J. 2004)

- *Meyers Industries (Meyers I)*, 268 NLRB 493 (1984), *revd. sub nom Prill v. NLRB*, 755 F.2d 941 (D.C. Cir. 1985), *cert. denied* 474 U.S. 948 (1985), *on remand Meyers Industries (Meyers II)*, 281 NLRB 882 (1986), *affd. sub nom Prill v. NLRB*, 835 F.2d 1481 (D.C. Cir. 1987), *cert. denied* 487 U.S. 1205 (1988)

- *MGM Studios Inc. v. Grokster, Ltd.*, 545 U.S. 913 (2005)

- *Moreno v. Hartford Sentinel, Inc.*, 91 Cal. App. 4th 1125 (2009)

- *Morrow v. State*, 511 P.2d 127 (Alaska 1973)

- *MySpace v. The Globe.Com, Inc.*, CV 06-3391-RGK (JCx) (C.D. Cal. Feb. 27, 2007)

- *MySpace v. Wallace*, 498 F.Supp.2d 1293, 1300 (C.D. Cal. 2007)

- *Nagler v. Garcia*, 370 Fed. Appx. 678, 2010 FED App. 0195N (6th Cir. 2010)

- *The New York City Triathlon, LLC v. NYC Triathlon Club, Inc.*, Case No. 1:10-CV-01464-CM-THK (S.D. N.Y. Feb. 22, 2010)

- *NLRB v. Knauz BMW*, Case No. 13-CA-045452 (Jul. 21, 2011)

- *Northern Star Industries, Inc., v. Douglas Dynamics, LLC*, Case No. 2:11-CV-1103-RTR (E.D. Wis. Dec. 5, 2011)

- *Ocean Spray Cranberries, Inc. v. Decas Cranberry Prods., Inc.*, Case No. 1:10-CV-11288-RWZ (D. Mass. Aug. 2, 2010)

- *Offenback v. LM Bowman, Inc. et al.*, Case No. 1:10-CV-1789, (M.D. Pa. Jun. 22, 2011)

- *ONEOK, Inc. v. Twitter, Inc.*, Case No. 4:09-CV-00597-TCK–TLW (N.D. Ok. Sep. 15, 2009)

- *Patterson v. Turner Construction Co.*, 931 N.Y.S.2d 311 (N.Y. App. Div. 2011)

- *People v. Lenihan*, 911 N.Y.S.2d 588 (N.Y. Sup. Queens Cty. 2010)

- *PhoneDog, LLC v. Noah Kravitz*, Case No. 3:11-CV-03474-MEJ (N.D. Cal. Jul. 15, 2011)

- *Pietrylo v. Hillstone Rest. Group*, Case No. 2:06-CV-05754-FSH-PS (D. N.J. Nov. 30, 2006)

- *Polaroid Corp. v. Polarad Elecs. Corp.*, 287 F.2d 492, 495 (2d Cir. 1961), *cert. denied*, 368 U.S. 820 (1961)

- *Reno v. ACLU*, 521 U.S. 844, 117 S.Ct. 2329 (1997)

- *Robins v. Spokeo, Inc.*, Case No. 2:10-CV-5306-ODW (AGR) (C.D. Cal. Jul. 20, 2010)

- *Romano v. Steelcase*, 907 N.Y.S.2d 650 (N.Y. Sup. Ct., Suffolk Co. 2010)

- *Schneider v. Amazon.com, Inc.*, 108 Wn. App. 454, 31 P.3d 37 (2001)

- *Sony Music Entertainment Inc. v. Does 1-40*, 326 F.Supp.2d 556 (S.D. NY 2004)

- *State v. Eleck*, 130 Conn. App. 632 (Conn. App. Ct. 2011)

- *Stengart v. Loving Care Agency, Inc.*, 990 A.2d 650 (N.J. 2010)

- *UMG Recordings, Inc., et al. v. Veoh Networks, Inc.*, Case No. 10-55732 (9th Cir. Dec. 20, 2011)

- *U.S. v. Godwin (d/b/a skidekids.com)*, Case No. 1:11-CV-03846-JOF (N.D. Ga. Nov. 8, 2011)

- *U.S. v. Industrious Kid, Inc.*, Case No. 3:08-CV-00639 (N.D. Cal. Jan. 28, 2008)

- *U.S. v. Playdom, Inc. et al.*, Case No. 8:11-CV-00724-AG-AN (C.D. Cal. May 11, 2011)

- *U.S. v. Sony BMG Music Entertainment*, Case No. 1:08-CV-10730 (S.D.N.Y. Dec. 10, 2008)

- *U.S. v. W3 Innovations LLC et al.*, Case No. 5:11-CV-03958 (N.D. Cal., Aug. 12, 2011)

- *U.S. v. Xanga.com, Inc. et al.*, Case No. 1:06-CV-06853-SHS (S.D.N.Y., Sept. 7, 2006)

- *Verizon California Inc. v. OnlineNIC, Inc.*, Case No. 3:08-CV-02832 (N.D. Cal. Jun. 6, 2008)

- *Wal-Mart*, NLRB Div. of Advice No. 17-CA-25030 (Jul. 19, 2011)

- *Yath v. Fairview Clinics, N. P.*, 767 N.W.2d 34 (Minn. App. Ct.) (2009)

- *Zeran v. America Online, Inc.*, 129 F.3d 327, 330 (4th Cir. 1997)

Miscellaneous

- Facebook's Promotions Guidelines, *available at* http://www.facebook.com/promotions_guidelines.php

- Facebook's Statement of Rights and Responsibilities, *available at* http://www.facebook.com/terms.php?ref=pf

- LinkedIn's User Agreement, *available at* http://www.linkedin.com/static?key=user_agreement

- Guidelines for Contests on Twitter, *available at* http://support.twitter.com/entries/68877-guidelines-for-contests-on-twitter

- Google+ Pages Contest and Promotion Policies, *available at* http://www.google.com/intl/en/+/policy/pagescontestpolicy.html

- Twitter, Inc.'s Parody, Commentary, and Fan Accounts Policy, *available at* https://support.twitter.com/articles/106373-parody-commentary-and-fan-accounts-policy

- Twitter Rules, *available at* https://support.twitter.com/articles/18311-the-twitter-rules#

Appendix B

The Federal Trade Commission Act of 1914

(15 U.S.C. §§ 41–58) *(as amended)*

 Note
{§§ 41 to 44 intentionally omitted}

---

§ 45. Unfair methods of competition unlawful; prevention by Commission

(a)   Declaration of unlawfulness; power to prohibit unfair practices; inapplicability to foreign trade

(1)   Unfair methods of competition in or affecting commerce, and unfair or deceptive acts or practices in or affecting commerce, are hereby declared unlawful.

 Note
{§§ 45(2) to 45(3)(B) intentionally omitted}

---

(4)

(A)   For purposes of subsection (a), the term "unfair or deceptive acts or practices" includes such acts or practices involving foreign commerce that—

(i)   cause or are likely to cause reasonably foreseeable injury within the United States; or

(ii)   involve material conduct occurring within the United States.

(B)   All remedies available to the Commission with respect to unfair and deceptive acts or practices shall be available for acts and practices described in this paragraph, including restitution to domestic or foreign victims.

 Note
{§§ 45(b) to 45(l) intentionally omitted}

(m)   Civil actions for recovery of penalties for knowing violations of rules and cease and desist orders respecting unfair or deceptive acts or practices; jurisdiction; maximum amount of penalties; continuing violations; de novo determinations; compromise or settlement procedure

(1)

(A)   The Commission may commence a civil action to recover a civil penalty in a district court of the United States against any person, partnership, or corporation which violates any rule under this chapter respecting unfair or deceptive acts or practices (other than an interpretive rule or a rule violation of which the Commission has provided is not an unfair or deceptive act or practice in violation of subsection (a)(1) of this section) with actual knowledge or knowledge fairly implied on the basis of objective circumstances that such act is unfair or deceptive and is prohibited by such rule. In such action, such person, partnership, or corporation shall be liable for a civil penalty of not more than $10,000 for each violation.

(B)   If the Commission determines in a proceeding under subsection (b) of this section that any act or practice is unfair or deceptive, and issues a final cease and desist order, other than a consent order, with respect to such act or practice, then the Commission may commence a civil action to obtain a civil penalty in a district court of the United States against any person, partnership, or corporation which engages in such act or practice—

(1)   after such cease and desist order becomes final (whether or not such person, partnership, or corporation was subject to such cease and desist order), and

(2)   with actual knowledge that such act or practice is unfair or deceptive and is unlawful under subsection (a)(1) of this section.

In such action, such person, partnership, or corporation shall be liable for a civil penalty of not more than $10,000 for each violation.

(C)   In the case of a violation through continuing failure to comply with a rule or with subsection (a) (1) of this section, each day of continuance of such failure shall be treated as a separate violation, for purposes of subparagraphs (A) and (B). In determining the amount of such a civil penalty, the court shall take into account the degree of culpability, any history of prior such conduct, ability to pay, effect on ability to continue to do business, and such other matters as justice may require.

(2)   If the cease and desist order establishing that the act or practice is unfair or deceptive was not issued against the defendant in a civil penalty action under paragraph (1)(B) the issues of fact in such action against such defendant shall be tried de novo. Upon request of any party to such an action against such defendant, the court shall also review the determination of law made by the Commission in the proceeding under subsection (b) of this section that the act or practice which was the subject of such proceeding constituted an unfair or deceptive act or practice in violation of subsection (a) of this section.

(3)   The Commission may compromise or settle any action for a civil penalty if such compromise or settlement is accompanied by a public statement of its reasons and is approved by the court.

 Note

{§§ 45(n) to 55 intentionally omitted}

Appendix C

The Lanham Act—Section 43(a)

(15 U.S.C. § § 1114(1) and 1125(a))

§ 1125. **False designations of origin, false descriptions, and dilution forbidden**

(a)   Civil action

(1)   Any person who, on or in connection with any goods or services, or any container for goods, uses in commerce any word, term, name, symbol, or device, or any combination thereof, or any false designation of origin, false or misleading description of fact, or false or misleading representation of fact, which—

(A)   is likely to cause confusion, or to cause mistake, or to deceive as to the affiliation, connection, or association of such person with another person, or as to the origin, sponsorship, or approval of his or her goods, services, or commercial activities by another person, or

(B)   in commercial advertising or promotion, misrepresents the nature, characteristics, qualities, or geographic origin of his or her or another person's goods, services, or commercial activities, shall be liable in a civil action by any person who believes that he or she is or is likely to be damaged by such act.

 Note
{§§ 1125(a)(2) to 1125(a)(3) intentionally omitted}

Appendix D

The Anticybersquatting Consumer Protection Act (ACPA)

(15 U.S.C. § 1125(d) - Section 43(d) of Lanham Act)

§ 1125. False designations of origin, false descriptions, and dilution forbidden

 Note

{§§ 1125(a) to 1125(c) intentionally omitted}

(d)   **Cyberpiracy prevention**

(1)

(A)   A person shall be liable in a civil action by the owner of a mark, including a personal name which is protected as a mark under this section, if, without regard to the goods or services of the parties, that person—

(i)   has a bad faith intent to profit from that mark, including a personal name which is protected as a mark under this section; and

(ii)   registers, traffics in, or uses a domain name that—

(I)   in the case of a mark that is distinctive at the time of registration of the domain name, is identical or confusingly similar to that mark;

(II)   in the case of a famous mark that is famous at the time of registration of the domain name, is identical or confusingly similar to or dilutive of that mark; or

(III)   is a trademark, word, or name protected by reason of section 706 of title 18 or section 220506 of title 36.

(B)

(i)   In determining whether a person has a bad faith intent described under subparagraph (A), a court may consider factors such as, but not limited to—

(I)   the trademark or other intellectual property rights of the person, if any, in the domain name;

(II)   the extent to which the domain name consists of the legal name of the person or a name that is otherwise commonly used to identify that person;

(III)   the person's prior use, if any, of the domain name in connection with the bona fide offering of any goods or services;

(IV)   the person's bona fide noncommercial or fair use of the mark in a site accessible under the domain name;

(V)   the person's intent to divert consumers from the mark owner's online location to a site accessible under the domain name that could harm the goodwill represented by the mark, either for commercial gain or with the intent to tarnish or disparage the mark, by creating a likelihood of confusion as to the source, sponsorship, affiliation, or endorsement of the site;

(VI)   the person's offer to transfer, sell, or otherwise assign the domain name to the mark owner or any third party for financial gain without having used, or having an intent to use, the domain name in the bona fide offering of any goods or services, or the person's prior conduct indicating a pattern of such conduct;

(VII)   the person's provision of material and misleading false contact information when applying for the registration of the domain name, the person's intentional failure to maintain accurate contact information, or the person's prior conduct indicating a pattern of such conduct;

(VIII)   the person's registration or acquisition of multiple domain names which the person knows are identical or confusingly similar to marks of others that are distinctive at the time of registration of such domain names, or dilutive of famous marks of others that are famous at the time of registration of such domain names, without regard to the goods or services of the parties; and

(IX)   the extent to which the mark incorporated in the person's domain name registration is or is not distinctive and famous within the meaning of subsection (c).

(ii)   Bad faith intent described under subparagraph (A) shall not be found in any case in which the court determines that the person believed and had reasonable grounds to believe that the use of the domain name was a fair use or otherwise lawful.

(C)   In any civil action involving the registration, trafficking, or use of a domain name under this paragraph, a court may order the forfeiture or cancellation of the domain name or the transfer of the domain name to the owner of the mark.

(D)   A person shall be liable for using a domain name under subparagraph (A) only if that person is the domain name registrant or that registrant's authorized licensee.

(E)   As used in this paragraph, the term "traffics in" refers to transactions that include, but are not limited to, sales, purchases, loans, pledges, licenses, exchanges of currency, and any other transfer for consideration or receipt in exchange for consideration.

 ## Note

{§§ 1125(d)(2) to 1125(d)(4) intentionally omitted}

Appendix E

Fair Credit Reporting Act (FCRA)

15 U.S.C. § 1681 *et seq.*)

 Note
{§ 1681 intentionally omitted}

§ 1681a. Definitions; rules of construction

(a)   Definitions and rules of construction set forth in this section are applicable for the purposes of this subchapter.

(b)   The term "person" means any individual, partnership, corporation, trust, estate, cooperative, association, government or governmental subdivision or agency, or other entity.

(c)   The term "consumer" means an individual.

(d)   Consumer Report.—

(1)   In general.— The term "consumer report" means any written, oral, or other communication of any information by a consumer reporting agency bearing on a consumer's credit worthiness, credit standing, credit capacity, character, general reputation, personal characteristics, or mode of living which is used or expected to be used or collected in whole or in part for the purpose of serving as a factor in establishing the consumer's eligibility for—

(A)   credit or insurance to be used primarily for personal, family, or household purposes;

(B)   employment purposes; or

(C)   any other purpose authorized under section 1681b of this title.

(2)   Exclusions.— Except as provided in paragraph (3), the term "consumer report" does not include—

(A)   subject to section 1681s–3 of this title, any—

(i)   report containing information solely as to transactions or experiences between the consumer and the person making the report;

(ii)   communication of that information among persons related by common ownership or affiliated by corporate control; or

(iii)   communication of other information among persons related by common ownership or affiliated by corporate control, if it is clearly and conspicuously disclosed to the consumer that the information may be communicated among such persons and the consumer is given the opportunity, before the time that the information is initially communicated, to direct that such information not be communicated among such persons;

(B)   any authorization or approval of a specific extension of credit directly or indirectly by the issuer of a credit card or similar device;

(C)   any report in which a person who has been requested by a third party to make a specific extension of credit directly or indirectly to a consumer conveys his or her decision with respect to such request, if the third party advises the consumer of the name and address of the person to whom the request was made, and such person makes the disclosures to the consumer required under section 1681m of this title; or

(D)   a communication described in subsection (o) or (x) of this section.

 Note

{§ 1681a(d)(3) intentionally omitted}

(e)   The term "investigative consumer report" means a consumer report or portion thereof in which information on a consumer's character, general reputation, personal characteristics, or mode of living is obtained through personal interviews with neighbors, friends, or associates of the consumer reported on or with others with whom he is acquainted or who may have knowledge concerning any such items of information. However, such information shall not include specific factual information on a consumer's credit record obtained directly from a creditor of the consumer or from a consumer reporting agency when such information was obtained directly from a creditor of the consumer or from the consumer.

(f)   The term "consumer reporting agency" means any person which, for monetary fees, dues, or on a cooperative nonprofit basis, regularly engages in whole or in part in the practice of assembling or evaluating consumer credit information or other information on consumers for the purpose of furnishing consumer reports to third parties, and which uses any means or facility of interstate commerce for the purpose of preparing or furnishing consumer reports.

 Note

{§ 1681a(g) intentionally omitted}

(h)   The term "employment purposes" when used in connection with a consumer report means a report used for the purpose of evaluating a consumer for employment, promotion, reassignment or retention as an employee.

 Note

{§§ 1681a(i) to 1681a(x) intentionally omitted}

§ 1681b. Permissible purposes of consumer reports

(a)   **In general**

Subject to subsection (c) of this section, any consumer reporting agency may furnish a consumer report under the following circumstances and no other:

(1)   In response to the order of a court having jurisdiction to issue such an order, or a subpoena issued in connection with proceedings before a Federal grand jury.

(2)   In accordance with the written instructions of the consumer to whom it relates.

(3)   To a person which it has reason to believe—

(A)   intends to use the information in connection with a credit transaction involving the consumer on whom the information is to be furnished and involving the extension of credit to, or review or collection of an account of, the consumer; or

(B)   intends to use the information for employment purposes; or

 Note

{§§ 1681b(a)(3)(C) to 1681b(a)(6) intentionally omitted}

(b)   Conditions for furnishing and using consumer reports for employment purposes

(1)   **Certification from user**

A consumer reporting agency may furnish a consumer report for employment purposes only if—

(A)   the person who obtains such report from the agency certifies to the agency that—

(i)   the person has complied with paragraph (2) with respect to the consumer report, and the person will comply with paragraph (3) with respect to the consumer report if paragraph (3) becomes applicable; and

(ii)   information from the consumer report will not be used in violation of any applicable Federal or State equal employment opportunity law or regulation; and

(B)   the consumer reporting agency provides with the report, or has previously provided, a summary of the consumer's rights under this subchapter, as prescribed by the Federal Trade Commission under section 1681g(c)(3) of this title.

(2)   **Disclosure to consumer**

(A)   **In general**

Except as provided in subparagraph (B), a person may not procure a consumer report, or cause a consumer report to be procured, for employment purposes with respect to any consumer, unless—

(i)   a clear and conspicuous disclosure has been made in writing to the consumer at any time before the report is procured or caused to be procured, in a document that consists solely of the disclosure, that a consumer report may be obtained for employment purposes; and

(ii)   the consumer has authorized in writing (which authorization may be made on the document referred to in clause (i)) the procurement of the report by that person.

(B)   **Application by mail, telephone, computer, or other similar means**

If a consumer described in subparagraph (C) applies for employment by mail, telephone, computer, or other similar means, at any time before a consumer report is procured or caused to be procured in connection with that application—

(i)   the person who procures the consumer report on the consumer for employment purposes shall provide to the consumer, by oral, written, or electronic means, notice that a consumer report may be obtained for employment purposes, and a summary of the consumer's rights under section 1681m(a)(3) of this title; and

(ii)   the consumer shall have consented, orally, in writing, or electronically to the procurement of the report by that person.

 Note

{§ 1681b(b)(2)(C) intentionally omitted}

(3)   Conditions on use for adverse actions

(A)   In general

Except as provided in subparagraph (B), in using a consumer report for employment purposes, before taking any adverse action based in whole or in part on the report, the person intending to take such adverse action shall provide to the consumer to whom the report relates—

(i)   a copy of the report; and

(ii)   a description in writing of the rights of the consumer under this subchapter, as prescribed by the Federal Trade Commission under section 1681g(c)(3) of this title.

 Note

{§§ 1681b(b)(3)(B) to 1681m intentionally omitted}

§ 1681n. Civil liability for willful noncompliance

(a)   In general

Any person who willfully fails to comply with any requirement imposed under this subchapter with respect to any consumer is liable to that consumer in an amount equal to the sum of—

(1)

(A)   any actual damages sustained by the consumer as a result of the failure or damages of not less than $100 and not more than $1,000; or

(B)   in the case of liability of a natural person for obtaining a consumer report under false pretenses or knowingly without a permissible purpose, actual damages sustained by the consumer as a result of the failure or $1,000, whichever is greater;

(2)   such amount of punitive damages as the court may allow; and

(3)   in the case of any successful action to enforce any liability under this section, the costs of the action together with reasonable attorney's fees as determined by the court.

(b)   Civil liability for knowing noncompliance

Any person who obtains a consumer report from a consumer reporting agency under false pretenses or knowingly without a permissible purpose shall be liable to the consumer reporting agency for actual damages sustained by the consumer reporting agency or $1,000, whichever is greater.

(c)   Attorney's fees

Upon a finding by the court that an unsuccessful pleading, motion, or other paper filed in connection with an action under this section was filed in bad faith or for purposes of harassment, the court shall award to the prevailing party attorney's fees reasonable in relation to the work expended in responding to the pleading, motion, or other paper.

(d)   Clarification of willful noncompliance

For the purposes of this section, any person who printed an expiration date on any receipt provided to a consumer cardholder at a point of sale or transaction between December 4, 2004, and June 3, 2008, but otherwise complied with the requirements of section 1681c(g) of this title for such receipt shall not be in willful noncompliance with section 1681c(g) of this title by reason of printing such expiration date on the receipt.

§ 1681o. Civil liability for negligent noncompliance

(a)   In general

Any person who is negligent in failing to comply with any requirement imposed under this subchapter with respect to any consumer is liable to that consumer in an amount equal to the sum of—

(1)   any actual damages sustained by the consumer as a result of the failure; and

(2)   in the case of any successful action to enforce any liability under this section, the costs of the action together with reasonable attorney's fees as determined by the court.

(b)   **Attorney's fees**

On a finding by the court that an unsuccessful pleading, motion, or other paper filed in connection with an action under this section was filed in bad faith or for purposes of harassment, the court shall award to the prevailing party attorney's fees reasonable in relation to the work expended in responding to the pleading, motion, or other paper.

 Note

{§ 1681p intentionally omitted}

---

§ 1681q. Obtaining information under false pretenses

Any person who knowingly and willfully obtains information on a consumer from a consumer reporting agency under false pretenses shall be fined under title 18, imprisoned for not more than 2 years, or both.

 Note

{§§ 1681r to 1681x intentionally omitted}

Appendix F

Electronic Funds Transfer Act (EFTA)

(15 U.S.C. §1693 *et seq.*)

(as amended by the Credit Card Accountability Responsibility and Disclosure (CARD) Act of 2009, Public Law 111-24, 123 Stat. 1734)

 Note

{§§ 1693(a) to 1693l intentionally omitted}

§ 1693l–1. General-use prepaid cards, gift certificates, and store gift cards

(a)   **Definitions**

In this section, the following definitions shall apply:

(1)   **Dormancy fee; inactivity charge or fee**

The terms "dormancy fee" and "inactivity charge or fee" mean a fee, charge, or penalty for non-use or inactivity of a gift certificate, store gift card, or general-use prepaid card.

(2)   **General-use prepaid card, gift certificate, and store gift card**

(A)   **General-use prepaid card**

The term "general-use prepaid card" means a card or other payment code or device issued by any person that is—

(i)   redeemable at multiple, unaffiliated merchants or service providers, or automated teller machines;

(ii)   issued in a requested amount, whether or not that amount may, at the option of the issuer, be increased in value or reloaded if requested by the holder;

(iii)   purchased or loaded on a prepaid basis; and

(iv)   honored, upon presentation, by merchants for goods or services, or at automated teller machines.

(B)   **Gift certificate**

The term "gift certificate" means an electronic promise that is—

(i)   redeemable at a single merchant or an affiliated group of merchants that share the same name, mark, or logo;

(ii)   issued in a specified amount that may not be increased or reloaded;

(iii)   purchased on a prepaid basis in exchange for payment; and

(iv)   honored upon presentation by such single merchant or affiliated group of merchants for goods or services.

(C)   **Store gift card**

The term "store gift card" means an electronic promise, plastic card, or other payment code or device that is—

(i)   redeemable at a single merchant or an affiliated group of merchants that share the same name, mark, or logo;

(ii)   issued in a specified amount, whether or not that amount may be increased in value or reloaded at the request of the holder;

(iii)   purchased on a prepaid basis in exchange for payment; and

(iv)   honored upon presentation by such single merchant or affiliated group of merchants for goods or services.

(D)   **Exclusions**

The terms "general-use prepaid card", "gift certificate", and "store gift card" do not include an electronic promise, plastic card, or payment code or device that is—

(i)   used solely for telephone services;

(ii)   reloadable and not marketed or labeled as a gift card or gift certificate;

(iii)   a loyalty, award, or promotional gift card, as defined by the Board;

(iv)   not marketed to the general public;

(v)   issued in paper form only (including for tickets and events); or

(vi)   redeemable solely for admission to events or venues at a particular location or group of affiliated locations, which may also include services or goods obtainable—

(I)   at the event or venue after admission; or

(II)   in conjunction with admission to such events or venues, at specific locations affiliated with and in geographic proximity to the event or venue.

(3)   **Service fee**

(A)   **In general**

The term "service fee" means a periodic fee, charge, or penalty for holding or use of a gift certificate, store gift card, or general-use prepaid card.

(B)   **Exclusion**

With respect to a general-use prepaid card, the term "service fee" does not include a one-time initial issuance fee.

(b)   **Prohibition on imposition of fees or charges**

(1)   **In general**

Except as provided under paragraphs (2) through (4), it shall be unlawful for any person to impose a dormancy fee, an inactivity charge or fee, or a service fee with respect to a gift certificate, store gift card, or general-use prepaid card.

(2)   **Exceptions**

A dormancy fee, inactivity charge or fee, or service fee may be charged with respect to a gift certificate, store gift card, or general-use prepaid card, if—

(A)   there has been no activity with respect to the certificate or card in the 12-month period ending on the date on which the charge or fee is imposed;

(B)   the disclosure requirements of paragraph (3) have been met;

(C)   not more than one fee may be charged in any given month; and

(D)   any additional requirements that the Board may establish through rulemaking under subsection (d) have been met.

(3)   **Disclosure requirements**

The disclosure requirements of this paragraph are met if—

(A)   the gift certificate, store gift card, or general-use prepaid card clearly and conspicuously states—

(i)   that a dormancy fee, inactivity charge or fee, or service fee may be charged;

(ii)   the amount of such fee or charge;

(iii)   how often such fee or charge may be assessed; and

(iv)   that such fee or charge may be assessed for inactivity; and

(B)   the issuer or vendor of such certificate or card informs the purchaser of such charge or fee before such certificate or card is purchased, regardless of whether the certificate or card is purchased in person, over the Internet, or by telephone.

(4)   **Exclusion**

The prohibition under paragraph (1) shall not apply to any gift certificate—

(A)   that is distributed pursuant to an award, loyalty, or promotional program, as defined by the Board; and

(B)   with respect to which, there is no money or other value exchanged.

(c)   **Prohibition on sale of gift cards with expiration dates**

(1)   **In general**

Except as provided under paragraph (2), it shall be unlawful for any person to sell or issue a gift certificate, store gift card, or general-use prepaid card that is subject to an expiration date.

(2)   **Exceptions**

A gift certificate, store gift card, or general-use prepaid card may contain an expiration date if—

(A)   the expiration date is not earlier than 5 years after the date on which the gift certificate was issued, or the date on which card funds were last loaded to a store gift card or general-use prepaid card; and

(B)   the terms of expiration are clearly and conspicuously stated.

 Note

{§ 1693l(d) intentionally omitted}

---

§ 1693m.   **Civil liability**

(a)   **Individual or class action for damages; amount of award**

Except as otherwise provided by this section and section 1693h of this title, any person who fails to comply with any provision of this subchapter with respect to any consumer, except for an error resolved in accordance with section 1693f of this title, is liable to such consumer in an amount equal to the sum of—

(1)   any actual damage sustained by such consumer as a result of such failure;

(2)

(A)   in the case of an individual action, an amount not less than $100 nor greater than $1,000; or

(B)   in the case of a class action, such amount as the court may allow, except that

(i)   as to each member of the class no minimum recovery shall be applicable, and

(ii)   the total recovery under this subparagraph in any class action or series of class actions arising out of the same failure to comply by the same person shall not be more than the lesser of $500,000 or 1 per centum of the net worth of the defendant; and

(3)   in the case of any successful action to enforce the foregoing liability, the costs of the action, together with a reasonable attorney's fee as determined by the court.

 Note

{§§ 1693m(b) to 1693m(g) intentionally omitted}

§ 1693n. Criminal liability

(a)   **Violations respecting giving of false or inaccurate information, failure to provide information, and failure to comply with provisions of this subchapter**

Whoever knowingly and willfully—

(1)   gives false or inaccurate information or fails to provide information which he is required to disclose by this subchapter or any regulation issued thereunder; or

(2)   otherwise fails to comply with any provision of this subchapter;

shall be fined not more than $5,000 or imprisoned not more than one year, or both.

 Note

{§§ 1693n(b) to 1693r intentionally omitted}

Appendix G

Children's Online Privacy Protection Rule

(Title 16 C.F.R. 312)

Sec. 312.1 Scope of regulations in this part.

This part implements the Children's Online Privacy Protection Act of 1998 (15 U.S.C. 6501 *et seq.*), which prohibits unfair or deceptive acts or practices in connection with the collection, use, and/or disclosure of personal information from and about children on the Internet. The effective date of this part is April 21, 2000.

Sec. 312.2 Definitions.

Child means an individual under the age of 13.

Collects or *collection* means the gathering of any personal information from a child by any means, including but not limited to:

(a)   Requesting that children submit personal information online;

(b)   Enabling children to make personal information publicly available through a chat room, message board, or other means, except where the operator deletes all individually identifiable information from postings by children before they are made public, and also deletes such information from the operator's records; or

(c)   The passive tracking or use of any identifying code linked to an individual, such as a cookie.

Commission means the Federal Trade Commission.

Delete means to remove personal information such that it is not maintained in retrievable form and cannot be retrieved in the normal course of business.

Disclosure means, with respect to personal information:

(a)   The release of personal information collected from a child

in identifiable form by an operator for any purpose, except where an operator provides such information to a person who provides support for the internal operations of the website or online service and who does not disclose or use that information for any other purpose. For purposes of this definition:

(1)   *Release of personal information* means the sharing, selling, renting, or any other means of providing personal information to any third party, and

(2)   *Support for the internal operations of the website or online service* means those activities necessary to maintain the technical functioning of the website or online service, or to fulfill a request of a child as permitted by Sec. 312.5(c)(2) and (3); or

(b)   Making personal information collected from a child by an operator publicly available in identifiable form, by any means, including by a public posting through the Internet, or through a personal home page posted on a website or online service; a pen pal service; an electronic mail service; a message board; or a chat room.

Internet means collectively the myriad of computer and telecommunications facilities, including equipment and operating software, which comprise the interconnected world-wide network of networks that employ the Transmission Control Protocol/Internet Protocol, or any predecessor or successor protocols to such protocol, to communicate information of all kinds by wire, radio, or other methods of transmission.

Online contact information means an e-mail address or any other substantially similar identifier that permits direct contact with a person online.

Operator means any person who operates a website located on the Internet or an online service and who collects or maintains personal information from or about the users of or visitors to such website or online service, or on whose behalf such information is collected or maintained, where such website or online service is operated for commercial purposes, including any person offering products or services for sale through that website or online service, involving commerce:

(a)   Among the several States or with 1 or more foreign nations;

(b)   In any territory of the United States or in the District of Columbia, or between any such territory and

(1)   Another such territory, or

(2)   Any State or foreign nation; or

(c)   Between the District of Columbia and any State, territory, or foreign nation. This definition does not include any nonprofit entity that would otherwise be exempt from coverage under Section 5 of the Federal Trade Commission Act (15 U.S.C. 45).

Parent includes a legal guardian.

Person means any individual, partnership, corporation, trust, estate, cooperative, association, or other entity.

Personal information means individually identifiable information about an individual collected online, including:

(a)   A first and last name;

(b)   A home or other physical address including street name and name of a city or town;

(c)   An e-mail address or other online contact information, including but not limited to an instant messaging user identifier, or a screen name that reveals an individual's e-mail address;

(d)   A telephone number;

(e)   A Social Security number;

(f)   A persistent identifier, such as a customer number held in a cookie or a processor serial number, where such identifier is associated with individually identifiable information; or a combination of a last name or photograph of the individual with other information such that the combination permits physical or online contacting; or

(g)   Information concerning the child or the parents of that child that the operator collects online from the child and combines with an identifier described in this definition.

Third party means any person who is not:

(a)   An operator with respect to the collection or maintenance of personal information on the website or online service; or

(b)   A person who provides support for the internal operations of the website or online service and who does not use or disclose information protected under this part for any other purpose.

Obtaining verifiable consent means making any reasonable effort (taking into consideration available technology) to ensure that before personal information is collected from a child, a parent of the child:

(a)   Receives notice of the operator's personal information collection, use, and disclosure practices; and

(b)   Authorizes any collection, use, and/or disclosure of the personal information.

Website or online service directed to children means a commercial website or online service, or portion thereof, that is targeted to children. Provided, however, that a commercial website or online service, or a portion thereof, shall not be deemed directed to children solely because it refers or links to a commercial website or online service directed to children by using information location tools, including a directory, index, reference, pointer, or hypertext link. In determining whether a commercial website or online service, or a portion thereof, is targeted to children, the Commission will consider its subject matter, visual or audio content, age of models, language or other characteristics of the website or online service, as well as whether advertising promoting or appearing on the website or online service is directed to children. The Commission will also consider competent and reliable empirical evidence regarding audience composition; evidence regarding the intended audience; and whether a site uses animated characters and/or child-oriented activities and incentives.

 Note

{§ 312.39 intentionally omitted}

Sec. 312.4 Notice.

(a)   *General principles of notice.* All notices under Secs. 312.3(a) and 312.5 must be clearly and understandably written, be complete, and must contain no unrelated, confusing, or contradictory materials.

(b)   *Notice on the website or online service.* Under Sec. 312.3(a), an operator of a website or online service directed to children must post a link to a notice of its information practices with regard to children on the home page of its website or online service and at each area on the website or online service where personal information is collected from children. An operator of a general audience website or online service that has a separate children's area or site must post a link to a notice of its information practices with regard to children on the home page of the children's area.

(1)   *Placement of the notice.* (i) The link to the notice must be clearly labeled as a notice of the website or online service's information practices with regard to children;

(ii)   The link to the notice must be placed in a clear and prominent place and manner on the home page of the website or online service; and

(iii)   The link to the notice must be placed in a clear and prominent place and manner at each area on the website or online service where children directly provide, or are asked to provide, personal information, and in close proximity to the requests for information in each such area.

(2)   *Content of the notice.* To be complete, the notice of the website or online service's information practices must state the following:

(i)   The name, address, telephone number, and e-mail address of all operators collecting or maintaining personal information from children through the website or online service.

    Provided that: the operators of a website or online service may list the name, address, phone number, and e-mail address of one operator who will respond to all inquiries from parents concerning the operators' privacy policies and use of children's information, as long as the names of all the operators collecting or maintaining personal information from children through the website or online service are also listed in the notice;

(ii)   The types of personal information collected from children and whether the personal information is collected directly or passively;

(iii)   How such personal information is or may be used by the operator(s), including but not limited to fulfillment of a requested transaction, recordkeeping, marketing back to the child, or making it publicly available through a chat room or by other means;

(iv)   Whether personal information is disclosed to third parties, and if so, the types of business in which such third parties are engaged, and the general purposes for which such information is used; whether those third parties have agreed to maintain the confidentiality, security, and integrity of the personal information they obtain from the operator; and that the parent has the option to consent to the collection and use of their child's personal information without consenting to the disclosure of that information to third parties;

(v)   That the operator is prohibited from conditioning a child's participation in an activity on the child's disclosing more personal information than is reasonably necessary to participate in such activity; and

(vi)   That the parent can review and have deleted the child's personal information, and refuse to permit further collection or use of the child's information, and state the procedures for doing so.

 Note

{§ 312.4(c) intentionally omitted}

Sec. 312.5 Parental consent.

(a)   *General requirements.*

(1)   An operator is required to obtain verifiable parental consent before any collection, use, and/or disclosure of personal information from children, including consent to any material change in the collection, use, and/or disclosure practices to which the parent has previously consented.

(2)   An operator must give the parent the option to consent to the collection and use of the child's personal information without consenting to disclosure of his or her personal information to third parties.

(b)   *Mechanisms for verifiable parental consent.*

(1)   An operator must make reasonable efforts to obtain verifiable parental consent, taking into consideration available technology. Any method to obtain verifiable parental consent must be reasonably calculated, in light of available technology, to ensure that the person providing consent is the child's parent.

(2)   Methods to obtain verifiable parental consent that satisfy the requirements of this paragraph include: providing a consent form to be signed by the parent and returned to the operator by postal mail or facsimile; requiring a parent to use a credit card in connection with a transaction; having a parent call a toll-free telephone number staffed by trained personnel; using a digital certificate that uses public key technology; and using e-mail accompanied by a PIN or password obtained through one of the verification methods listed in this paragraph. Provided that: For the period until April 21, 2005 [extended indefinitely], methods to obtain verifiable parental consent for uses of information other than the "disclosures" defined by Sec. 312.2 may also include use of e-mail coupled with additional steps to provide assurances that the person providing the consent is the parent. Such additional steps include: sending a confirmatory e-mail to the parent follow-

ing receipt of consent; or obtaining a postal address or telephone number from the parent and confirming the parent's consent by letter or telephone call. Operators who use such methods must provide notice that the parent can revoke any consent given in response to the earlier e-mail.

(c)   *Exceptions to prior parental consent.* Verifiable parental consent is required prior to any collection, use and/or disclosure of personal information from a child except as set forth in this paragraph.

The exceptions to prior parental consent are as follows:

(1)   Where the operator collects the name or online contact information of a parent or child to be used for the sole purpose of obtaining parental consent or providing notice under Sec. 312.4. If the operator has not obtained parental consent after a reasonable time from the date of the information collection, the operator must delete such information from its records;

(2)   Where the operator collects online contact information from a child for the sole purpose of responding directly on a one-time basis to a specific request from the child, and where such information is not used to recontact the child and is deleted by the operator from its records;

(3)   Where the operator collects online contact information from a child to be used to respond directly more than once to a specific request from the child, and where such information is not used for any other purpose. In such cases, the operator must make reasonable efforts, taking into consideration available technology, to ensure that a parent receives notice and has the opportunity to request that the operator make no further use of the information, as described in Sec. 312.4(c), immediately after the initial response and before making any additional response to the child. Mechanisms to provide such notice include, but are not limited to, sending the notice by postal mail or sending the notice to the parent's e-mail address, but do not include asking a child to print a notice form or sending an e-mail to the child;

(4)   Where the operator collects a child's name and online contact information to the extent reasonably necessary to protect the safety of a child participant on the website or online service, and the operator uses reasonable efforts to provide a parent notice as described in Sec. 312.4(c), where such information is:

(i)   Used for the sole purpose of protecting the child's safety;

(ii)   Not used to recontact the child or for any other purpose;

(iii)   Not disclosed on the website or online service; and

(5)   Where the operator collects a child's name and online contact information and such information is not used for any other purpose, to the extent reasonably necessary:

(i)   To protect the security or integrity of its website or online service;

(ii)   To take precautions against liability;

(iii)   To respond to judicial process; or

(iv)   To the extent permitted under other provisions of law, to provide information to law enforcement agencies or for an investigation on a matter related to public safety.

Sec. 312.6 Right of parent to review personal information provided by a child.

(a)   Upon request of a parent whose child has provided personal information to a website or online service, the operator of that website or online service is required to provide to that parent the following:

(1)   A description of the specific types or categories of personal information collected from children by the operator, such as name, address, telephone number, e-mail address, hobbies, and extracurricular activities;

(2)   The opportunity at any time to refuse to permit the operator's further use or future online collection of personal information from that child, and to direct the operator to delete the child's personal information; and

(3)   Notwithstanding any other provision of law, a means of reviewing any personal information collected from the child. The means employed by the operator to carry out this provision must:

(i)   Ensure that the requestor is a parent of that child, taking into account available technology; and

(ii)   Not be unduly burdensome to the parent.

(b)   Neither an operator nor the operator's agent shall be held liable under any Federal or State law for any disclosure made in good faith and following reasonable procedures in responding to a request for disclosure of personal information under this section.

(c)   Subject to the limitations set forth in Sec. 312.7, an operator may terminate any service provided to a child whose parent has refused, under paragraph (a)(2) of this section, to permit the operator's further use or collection of personal information from his or her child or has directed the operator to delete the child's personal information.

Sec. 312.7 Prohibition against conditioning a child's participation on collection of personal information.

An operator is prohibited from conditioning a child's participation in a game, the offering of a prize, or another activity on the child's disclosing more personal information than is reasonably necessary to participate in such activity.

Sec. 312.8 Confidentiality, security, and integrity of personal information collected from children.

The operator must establish and maintain reasonable procedures to protect the confidentiality, security, and integrity of personal information collected from children.

 Note

{§§ 312.9 to 312.12 intentionally omitted}

Appendix H

FTC's Revised Guides Concerning Use of Endorsements and Testimonials in Advertising

(16 C.F.R. Part 255)

§ 255.0 Purpose and definitions.

 Note
{§ 255.0(a) intentionally omitted}

(b) For purposes of this part, an endorsement means any advertising message (including verbal statements, demonstrations, or depictions of the name, signature, likeness or other identifying personal characteristics of an individual or the name or seal of an organization) that consumers are likely to believe reflects the opinions, beliefs, findings, or experiences of a party other than the sponsoring advertiser, even if the views expressed by that party are identical to those of the sponsoring advertiser. The party whose opinions, beliefs, findings, or experience the message appears to reflect will be called the endorser and may be an individual, group, or institution.

 Note
{§§ 255.0(c) to 255.0(d) intentionally omitted}

(e) For purposes of this part, an expert is an individual, group, or institution possessing, as a result of experience, study, or training, knowledge of a particular subject, which knowledge is superior to what ordinary individuals generally acquire.

Note

{Examples 1 to 8 intentionally omitted}

§ 255.1 General considerations.

(a) Endorsements must reflect the honest opinions, findings, beliefs, or experience of the endorser. Furthermore, an endorsement may not convey any express or implied representation that would be deceptive if made directly by the advertiser.

(b) The endorsement message need not be phrased in the exact words of the endorser, unless the advertisement affirmatively so represents. However, the endorsement may not be presented out of context or reworded so as to distort in any way the endorser's opinion or experience with the product. An advertiser may use an endorsement of an expert or celebrity only so long as it has good reason to believe that the endorser continues to subscribe to the views presented. An advertiser may satisfy this obligation by securing the endorser's views at reasonable intervals where reasonableness will be determined by such factors as new information on the performance or effectiveness of the product, a material alteration in the product, changes in the performance of competitors' products, and the advertiser's contract commitments.

(c) When the advertisement represents that the endorser uses the endorsed product, the endorser must have been a bona fide user of it at the time the endorsement was given. Additionally, the advertiser may continue to run the advertisement only so long as it has good reason to believe that the endorser remains a bona fide user of the product.

(d) Advertisers are subject to liability for false or unsubstantiated statements made through endorsements, or for failing to disclose material connections between themselves and their endorsers. Endorsers also may be liable for statements made in the course of their endorsements.

 Note

{Examples 1 to 4 intentionally omitted}

§ 255.2 Consumer endorsements.

(a) An advertisement employing endorsements by one or more consumers about the performance of an advertised product or service will be interpreted as representing that the product or service is effective for the purpose depicted in the advertisement. Therefore, the advertiser must possess and rely upon adequate substantiation, including, when appropriate, competent and reliable scientific evidence, to support such claims made through endorsements in the same manner the advertiser would be required to do if it had made the representation directly, i.e. , without using endorsements. Consumer endorsements themselves are not competent and reliable scientific evidence.

(b) An advertisement containing an endorsement relating the experience of one or more consumers on a central or key attribute of the product or service also will likely be interpreted as representing that the endorser's experience is representative of what consumers will generally achieve with the advertised product or service in actual, albeit variable, conditions of use. Therefore, an advertiser should possess and rely upon adequate substantiation for this representation. If the advertiser does not have substantiation that the endorser's experience is representative of what consumers will generally achieve, the advertisement should clearly and conspicuously disclose the generally expected performance in the depicted circumstances, and the advertiser must possess and rely on adequate substantiation for that representation.[*]

[*]The Commission tested the communication of advertisements containing testimonials that clearly and prominently disclosed either "Results not typical" or the stronger "These testimonials are based on the experiences of a few people and you are not likely to have similar results."Neither disclosure adequately reduced the communication that the experiences depicted are generally representative. Based upon this research, the Commission believes that similar disclaimers regarding

the limited applicability of an endorser's experience to what consumers may generally expect to achieve are unlikely to be effective.

Nonetheless, the Commission cannot rule out the possibility that a strong disclaimer of typicality could be effective in the context of a particular advertisement. Although the Commission would have the burden of proof in a law enforcement action, the Commission notes that an advertiser possessing reliable empirical testing demonstrating that the net impression of its advertisement with such a disclaimer is non-deceptive will avoid the risk of the initiation of such an action in the first instance.

(c)   Advertisements presenting endorsements by what are represented, directly or by implication, to be "actual consumers" should utilize actual consumers in both the audio and video, or clearly and conspicuously disclose that the persons in such advertisements are not actual consumers of the advertised product.

 Note

{Examples 1 to 7 intentionally omitted}

§ 255.3 Expert endorsements.

(a)   Whenever an advertisement represents, directly or by implication, that the endorser is an expert with respect to the endorsement message, then the endorser's qualifications must in fact give the endorser the expertise that he or she is represented as possessing with respect to the endorsement.

(b)   Although the expert may, in endorsing a product, take into account factors not within his or her expertise (e.g., matters of taste or price), the endorsement must be supported by an actual exercise of that expertise in evaluating product features or characteristics with respect to which he or she is expert and which are relevant to an ordinary consumer's use of or experience with the product and are available to the ordinary consumer. This evaluation must have included an examination or testing of the product at least as extensive as someone with the same degree of expertise would normally need to conduct in order to support the conclusions presented in the endorsement. To the extent that the advertisement implies that the endorsement was based upon a comparison, such comparison must have been included in the expert's evaluation; and as a result of such comparison, the expert must have concluded that, with respect to those features on which he or she is expert and which are relevant and available to an ordinary consumer, the endorsed product is at least equal overall to the competitors' products. Moreover, where the net impression created by the endorsement is that the advertised product is superior to other products with respect to any such feature or features, then the expert must in fact have found such superiority.

 Note

{Examples 1 to 6 intentionally omitted}

§ 255.4 Endorsements by organizations.

Endorsements by organizations, especially expert ones, are viewed as representing the judgment of a group whose collective experience exceeds that of any individual member, and whose judgments are generally free of the sort of subjective factors that vary from individual to individual. Therefore, an organization's endorsement must be reached by a process sufficient to ensure that the endorsement fairly reflects the collective judgment of the organization. Moreover, if an organization is represented as being expert, then, in conjunction with a proper exercise of its expertise in evaluating the product under §255.3 (expert endorsements), it must utilize an expert or experts recognized as such by the organization or standards previously adopted by the organization and suitable for judging the relevant merits of such products.

Note

{Example intentionally omitted}

§ 255.5 Disclosure of material connections.

When there exists a connection between the endorser and the seller of the advertised product that might materially affect the weight or credibility of the endorsement (i.e., the connection is not reasonably expected by the audience), such connection must be fully disclosed. For example, when an endorser who appears in a television commercial is neither represented in the advertisement as an expert nor is known to a significant portion of the viewing public, then the advertiser should clearly and conspicuously disclose either the payment or promise of compensation prior to and in exchange for the endorsement or the fact that the endorser knew or had reason to know or to believe that if the endorsement favored the advertised product some benefit, such as an appearance on television, would be extended to the endorser. Additional guidance, including guidance concerning endorsements made through other media, is provided by the examples below.

 Note

{Examples 1 to 9 intentionally omitted}

Appendix I

Controlling the Assault of Non-Solicited Pornography and Marketing (CAN-SPAM) Act of 2003

(15 U.S.C. § 7701 *et seq.*)

 Note

{§ 7701 intentionally omitted}

---

§ 7702. Definitions

In this chapter:

(1)   Affirmative consent

The term "affirmative consent", when used with respect to a commercial electronic mail message, means that—

(A)   the recipient expressly consented to receive the message, either in response to a clear and conspicuous request for such consent or at the recipient's own initiative; and

(B)   if the message is from a party other than the party to which the recipient communicated such consent, the recipient was given clear and conspicuous notice at the time the consent was communicated that the recipient's electronic mail address could be transferred to such other party for the purpose of initiating commercial electronic mail messages.

(2)   Commercial electronic mail message

(A)   In general

The term "commercial electronic mail message" means any electronic mail message the primary purpose of which is the commercial advertisement or promotion of a commercial product or service (including content on an Internet website operated for a commercial purpose).

(B)   Transactional or relationship messages

The term "commercial electronic mail message" does not include a transactional or relationship message.

 Note

{§§ 7702(C) to 7702(D)(12) intentionally omitted}

(13)   Protected computer

The term "protected computer" has the meaning given that term in section 1030(e)(2)(B) of title 18.

 Note

{§§ 7702(D)(14) to 7702(D)(16) intentionally omitted}

(17)   Transactional or relationship message

(A)   In general

The term "transactional or relationship message" means an electronic mail message the primary purpose of which is—

(i)   to facilitate, complete, or confirm a commercial transaction that the recipient has previously agreed to enter into with the sender;

(ii)   to provide warranty information, product recall information, or safety or security information with respect to a commercial product or service used or purchased by the recipient;

(iii)   to provide—

    (I)   notification concerning a change in the terms or features of;

    (II)   notification of a change in the recipient's standing or status with respect to; or

    (III)   at regular periodic intervals, account balance information or other type of account statement with respect to, a subscription, membership, account, loan, or comparable ongoing commercial relationship involving the ongoing purchase or use by the recipient of products or services offered by the sender;

(iv)   to provide information directly related to an employment relationship or related benefit plan in which the recipient is currently involved, participating, or enrolled; or

(v)   to deliver goods or services, including product updates or upgrades, that the recipient is entitled to receive under the terms of a transaction that the recipient has previously agreed to enter into with the sender.

 Note

{§§ 7702(D)(17)(B) to 7703 intentionally omitted}

§ 7704. Other protections for users of commercial electronic mail

(a)   Requirements for transmission of messages

(1)   Prohibition of false or misleading transmission information

It is unlawful for any person to initiate the transmission, to a protected computer, of a commercial electronic mail message, or a transactional or relationship message, that contains, or is accompanied by, header information that is materially false or materially misleading. For purposes of this paragraph—

(A)   header information that is technically accurate but includes an originating electronic mail address, domain name, or Internet Protocol address the access to which for purposes of initiating the message was obtained by means of false or fraudulent pretenses or representations shall be considered materially misleading;

(B)   a "from" line (the line identifying or purporting to identify a person initiating the message) that accurately identifies any person who initiated the message shall not be considered materially false or materially misleading; and

(C)   header information shall be considered materially misleading if it fails to identify accurately a protected computer used to initiate the message because the person initiating the message knowingly uses another protected computer to relay or retransmit the message for purposes of disguising its origin.

(2)   Prohibition of deceptive subject headings

It is unlawful for any person to initiate the transmission to a protected computer of a commercial electronic mail message if such person has actual knowledge, or knowledge fairly implied on the basis of objective circumstances, that a subject heading of the message would be likely to mislead a recipient, acting reasonably under the circumstances, about a material fact regarding the contents or subject matter of the message (consistent with the criteria used in enforcement of section 45 of this title).

(3)   Inclusion of return address or comparable mechanism in commercial electronic mail

(A)   In general

It is unlawful for any person to initiate the transmission to a protected computer of a commercial electronic mail message that does not contain a functioning return electronic mail address or other Internet-based mechanism, clearly and conspicuously displayed, that—

(i)   a recipient may use to submit, in a manner specified in the message, a reply electronic mail message or other form of Internet-based communication requesting not to receive future commercial electronic mail messages from that sender at the electronic mail address where the message was received; and

(ii)   remains capable of receiving such messages or communications for no less than 30 days after the transmission of the original message.

 Note

{§§ 7704(a)(3)(B) to 7711 intentionally omitted}

Appendix J

The Copyright Act

(17 U.S.C. §101 *et seq.*)

 Note
{§ 101 intentionally omitted}

---

§ 102. Subject matter of copyright: In general

(a)   Copyright protection subsists, in accordance with this title, in original works of authorship fixed in any tangible medium of expression, now known or later developed, from which they can be perceived, reproduced, or otherwise communicated, either directly or with the aid of a machine or device. Works of authorship include the following categories:

(1)   literary works;

(2)   musical works, including any accompanying words;

(3)   dramatic works, including any accompanying music;

(4)   pantomimes and choreographic works;

(5)   pictorial, graphic, and sculptural works;

(6)   motion pictures and other audiovisual works;

(7)   sound recordings; and

(8)   architectural works.

(b)   In no case does copyright protection for an original work of authorship extend to any idea, procedure, process, system, method of operation, concept, principle, or discovery, regardless of the form in which it is described, explained, illustrated, or embodied in such work.

 Note
{§§ 103 to 105 intentionally omitted}

§ 106. Exclusive rights in copyrighted works

Subject to sections 107 through 122, the owner of copyright under this title has the exclusive rights to do and to authorize any of the following:

(1)   to reproduce the copyrighted work in copies or phonorecords;

(2)   to prepare derivative works based upon the copyrighted work;

(3)   to distribute copies or phonorecords of the copyrighted work to the public by sale or other transfer of ownership, or by rental, lease, or lending;

(4)   in the case of literary, musical, dramatic, and choreographic works, pantomimes, and motion pictures and other audiovisual works, to perform the copyrighted work publicly;

(5)   in the case of literary, musical, dramatic, and choreographic works, pantomimes, and pictorial, graphic, or sculptural works, including the individual images of a motion picture or other audiovisual work, to display the copyrighted work publicly; and

(6)   in the case of sound recordings, to perform the copyrighted work publicly by means of a digital audio transmission.

 Note

{§ 106A intentionally omitted}

§ 107. Limitations on exclusive rights: Fair use

Notwithstanding the provisions of sections 106 and 106A, the fair use of a copyrighted work, including such use by reproduction in copies or phonorecords or by any other means specified by that section, for purposes such as criticism, comment, news reporting, teaching (including multiple copies for classroom use), scholarship, or research, is not an infringement of copyright. In determining whether the use made of a work in any particular case is a fair use the factors to be considered shall include—

(1)   the purpose and character of the use, including whether such use is of a commercial nature or is for nonprofit educational purposes;

(2)   the nature of the copyrighted work;

(3)   the amount and substantiality of the portion used in relation to the copyrighted work as a whole; and

(4)   the effect of the use upon the potential market for or value of the copyrighted work.

The fact that a work is unpublished shall not itself bar a finding of fair use if such finding is made upon consideration of all the above factors.

 Note

{§§ 108 to 122 intentionally omitted}

Appendix K

Online Copyright Infringement Liability Limitation Act (OCILLA)

(17 U.S.C. § 512)

(passed as a part of the 1998 Digital Millennium Copyright Act (DMCA)

(Pub. L. No. 105-304)

17 U.S.C. § 512: Limitations on liability relating to material

 Note
{§§ 512(a) to 512(b) intentionally omitted}

(c)	**Information Residing on Systems or Networks At Direction of Users.—**
(1)	**In general.—** A service provider shall not be liable for monetary relief, or, except as provided in subsection (j), for injunctive or other equitable relief, for infringement of copyright by reason of the storage at the direction of a user of material that resides on a system or network controlled or operated by or for the service provider, if the service provider—
(A)	
(i)	does not have actual knowledge that the material or an activity using the material on the system or network is infringing;
(ii)	in the absence of such actual knowledge, is not aware of facts or circumstances from which infringing activity is apparent; or
(iii)	upon obtaining such knowledge or awareness, acts expeditiously to remove, or disable access to, the material;
(B)	does not receive a financial benefit directly attributable to the infringing activity, in a case in which the service provider has the right and ability to control such activity; and
(C)	upon notification of claimed infringement as described in paragraph (3), responds expeditiously to remove, or disable access to, the material that is claimed to be infringing or to be the subject of infringing activity.

(2)   **Designated agent.**—The limitations on liability established in this subsection apply to a service provider only if the service provider has designated an agent to receive notifications of claimed infringement described in paragraph (3), by making available through its service, including on its website in a location accessible to the public, and by providing to the Copyright Office, substantially the following information:

(A)   the name, address, phone number, and electronic mail address of the agent.

(B)   other contact information which the Register of Copyrights may deem appropriate. The Register of Copyrights shall maintain a current directory of agents available to the public for inspection, including through the Internet, in both electronic and hard copy formats, and may require payment of a fee by service providers to cover the costs of maintaining the directory.

(3)   **Elements of notification.—**

(A)   To be effective under this subsection, a notification of claimed infringement must be a written communication provided to the designated agent of a service provider that includes substantially the following:

(i)   A physical or electronic signature of a person authorized to act on behalf of the owner of an exclusive right that is allegedly infringed.

(ii)   Identification of the copyrighted work claimed to have been infringed, or, if multiple copyrighted works at a single online site are covered by a single notification, a representative list of such works at that site.

(iii)   Identification of the material that is claimed to be infringing or to be the subject of infringing activity and that is to be removed or access to which is to be disabled, and information reasonably sufficient to permit the service provider to locate the material.

(iv)   Information reasonably sufficient to permit the service provider to contact the complaining party, such as an address, telephone number, and, if available, an electronic mail address at which the complaining party may be contacted.

(v)   A statement that the complaining party has a good faith belief that use of the material in the manner complained of is not authorized by the copyright owner, its agent, or the law.

(vi)   A statement that the information in the notification is accurate, and under penalty of perjury, that the complaining party is authorized to act on behalf of the owner of an exclusive right that is allegedly infringed.

(B)

(i)   Subject to clause (ii), a notification from a copyright owner or from a person authorized to act on behalf of the copyright owner that fails to comply substantially with the provisions of subparagraph (A) shall not be considered under paragraph (1)(A) in determining whether a service provider has actual knowledge or is aware of facts or circumstances from which infringing activity is apparent.

(ii)   In a case in which the notification that is provided to the service provider's designated agent fails to comply substantially with all the provisions of subparagraph (A) but substantially complies with clauses (ii), (iii), and (iv) of subparagraph (A), clause (i) of this subparagraph applies only if the service provider promptly attempts to contact the person making the notification or takes other reasonable steps to assist in the receipt of notification that substantially complies with all the provisions of subparagraph (A).

 Note

{§§ 512(d) to 512(e) intentionally omitted}

(f)   **Misrepresentations.**—Any person who knowingly materially misrepresents under this section — (1) that material or activity is infringing, or (2) that material or activity was removed or disabled by mistake or misidentification, shall be liable for any damages, including costs and attorneys' fees, incurred by the alleged infringer, by any copyright owner or copyright owner's authorized licensee, or by a service provider, who is injured by such misrepresentation, as the result of the service provider relying upon such misrepresentation in removing or disabling access to the material or activity claimed to be infringing, or in replacing the removed material or ceasing to disable access to it.

(g) **Replacement of Removed or Disabled Material and Limitation on Other Liability.—**

(1) **No liability for taking down generally.—** Subject to paragraph (2), a service provider shall not be liable to any person for any claim based on the service provider's good faith disabling of access to, or removal of, material or activity claimed to be infringing or based on facts or circumstances from which infringing activity is apparent, regardless of whether the material or activity is ultimately determined to be infringing.

(2) **Exception.—** Paragraph (1) shall not apply with respect to material residing at the direction of a subscriber of the service provider on a system or network controlled or operated by or for the service provider that is removed, or to which access is disabled by the service provider, pursuant to a notice provided under subsection (c)(1)(C), unless the service provider—

(A) takes reasonable steps promptly to notify the subscriber that it has removed or disabled access to the material;

(B) upon receipt of a counter notification described in paragraph (3), promptly provides the person who provided the notification under subsection (c)(1)(C) with a copy of the counter notification, and informs that person that it will replace the removed material or cease disabling access to it in 10 business days; and

(C) replaces the removed material and ceases disabling access to it not less than 10, nor more than 14, business days following receipt of the counter notice, unless its designated agent first receives notice from the person who submitted the notification under subsection (c)(1)(C) that such person has filed an action seeking a court order to restrain the subscriber from engaging in infringing activity relating to the material on the service provider's system or network.

(3) **Contents of counter notification.—** To be effective under this subsection, a counter notification must be a written communication provided to the service provider's designated agent that includes substantially the following:

(A) A physical or electronic signature of the subscriber.

(B) Identification of the material that has been removed or to which access has been disabled and the location at which the material appeared before it was removed or access to it was disabled.

(C) A statement under penalty of perjury that the subscriber has a good faith belief that the material was removed or disabled as a result of mistake or misidentification of the material to be removed or disabled.

(D) The subscriber's name, address, and telephone number, and a statement that the subscriber consents to the jurisdiction of Federal District Court for the judicial district in which the address is located, or if the subscriber's address is outside of the United States, for any judicial district in which the service provider may be found, and that the subscriber will accept service of process from the person who provided notification under subsection (c)(1)(C) or an agent of such person.

(4) **Limitation on other liability.—** A service provider's compliance with paragraph (2) shall not subject the service provider to liability for copyright infringement with respect to the material identified in the notice provided under subsection (c)(1)(C).

 Note

{§ 512(h) intentionally omitted}

(i)   **Conditions for Eligibility.—**

(1)   **Accommodation of technology.—** The limitations on liability established by this section shall apply to a service provider only if the service provider—

(A)   has adopted and reasonably implemented, and informs subscribers and account holders of the service provider's system or network of, a policy that provides for the termination in appropriate circumstances of subscribers and account holders of the service provider's system or network who are repeat infringers; and

(B)   accommodates and does not interfere with standard technical measures.

(2)   **Definition.—** As used in this subsection, the term "standard technical measures" means technical measures that are used by copyright owners to identify or protect copyrighted works and—

(A)   have been developed pursuant to a broad consensus of copyright owners and service providers in an open, fair, voluntary, multi-industry standards process;

(B)   are available to any person on reasonable and nondiscriminatory terms; and

(C)   do not impose substantial costs on service providers or substantial burdens on their systems or networks.

 Note

{§ 512(j) intentionally omitted}

(k)   **Definitions.—**

(1)   **Service provider.—**

(A)   As used in subsection (a), the term "service provider" means an entity offering the transmission, routing, or providing of connections for digital online communications, between or among points specified by a user, of material of the user's choosing, without modification to the content of the material as sent or received.

(B)   As used in this section, other than subsection (a), the term "service provider" means a provider of online services or network access, or the operator of facilities therefor, and includes an entity described in subparagraph (A).

 Note

{§§ 512(k)(2) to 512(n) intentionally omitted}

Appendix L

Computer Fraud and Abuse Act

(18 U.S.C. § 1030)

§ 1030. Fraud and related activity in connection with computers

(a)   **Whoever—**

(1)   having knowingly accessed a computer without authorization or exceeding authorized access, and by means of such conduct having obtained information that has been determined by the United States Government pursuant to an Executive order or statute to require protection against unauthorized disclosure for reasons of national defense or foreign relations, or any restricted data, as defined in paragraph y. of section 11 of the Atomic Energy Act of 1954, with reason to believe that such information so obtained could be used to the injury of the United States, or to the advantage of any foreign nation willfully communicates, delivers, transmits, or causes to be communicated, delivered, or transmitted, or attempts to communicate, deliver, transmit or cause to be communicated, delivered, or transmitted the same to any person not entitled to receive it, or willfully retains the same and fails to deliver it to the officer or employee of the United States entitled to receive it;

(2)   intentionally accesses a computer without authorization or exceeds authorized access, and thereby obtains—

(A)   information contained in a financial record of a financial institution, or of a card issuer as defined in section 1602(n) of title 15, or contained in a file of a consumer reporting agency on a consumer, as such terms are defined in the Fair Credit Reporting Act (15 U.S.C. 1681 *et seq.*);

(B)   information from any department or agency of the United States; or

(C)   information from any protected computer;

(3)   intentionally, without authorization to access any nonpublic computer of a department or agency of the United States, accesses such a computer of that department or agency that is exclusively for the use of the Government of the United States or, in the case of a computer not exclusively for such use, is used by or for the Government of the United States and such conduct affects that use by or for the Government of the United States;

(4)   knowingly and with intent to defraud, accesses a protected computer without authorization, or exceeds authorized access, and by means of such conduct furthers the intended fraud and obtains anything of value, unless the object of the fraud and the thing obtained consists only of the use of the computer and the value of such use is not more than $5,000 in any 1-year period;

Note

{§§ 1030(a)(5) to 1030(a)(7)(C) intentionally omitted}

(b)   Whoever conspires to commit or attempts to commit an offense under subsection (a) of this section shall be punished as provided in subsection (c) of this section.

(c)   The punishment for an offense under subsection (a) or (b) of this section is—

 Note

{§§ 1030(c)(1) to 1030(c)(2) intentionally omitted}

(3)

(A)   a fine under this title or imprisonment for not more than five years, or both, in the case of an offense under subsection (a)(4) or (a)(7) of this section which does not occur after a conviction for another offense under this section, or an attempt to commit an offense punishable under this subparagraph; and

(B)   a fine under this title or imprisonment for not more than ten years, or both, in the case of an offense under subsection (a)(4), or (a)(7) of this section which occurs after a conviction for another offense under this section, or an attempt to commit an offense punishable under this subparagraph;

 Note

{§§ 1030(c)(4) to 1030(d)(3) intentionally omitted}

(e)   **As used in this section—**

(1)   the term "computer" means an electronic, magnetic, optical, electrochemical, or other high speed data processing device performing logical, arithmetic, or storage functions, and includes any data storage facility or communications facility directly related to or operating in conjunction with such device, but such term does not include an automated typewriter or typesetter, a portable hand held calculator, or other similar device;

(2)   the term "protected computer" means a computer—

(A)   exclusively for the use of a financial institution or the United States Government, or, in the case of a computer not exclusively for such use, used by or for a financial institution or the United States Government and the conduct constituting the offense affects that use by or for the financial institution or the Government; or

(B)   which is used in or affecting interstate or foreign commerce or communication, including a computer located outside the United States that is used in a manner that affects interstate or foreign commerce or communication of the United States;

 Note

{§§ 1030(e)(3) to 1030(e)(5) intentionally omitted}

(6)   the term "exceeds authorized access" means to access a computer with authorization and to use such access to obtain or alter information in the computer that the accesser is not entitled so to obtain or alter;

Note

{§§ 1030(e)(7) to 1030(e)(12)(f) intentionally omitted}

(g) Any person who suffers damage or loss by reason of a violation of this section may maintain a civil action against the violator to obtain compensatory damages and injunctive relief or other equitable relief. A civil action for a violation of this section may be brought only if the conduct involves 1 of the factors set forth in subclauses (I), (II), (III), (IV), or (V) of subsection (c)(4)(A)(i). Damages for a violation involving only conduct described in subsection (c)(4)(A)(i)(I) are limited to economic damages. No action may be brought under this subsection unless such action is begun within 2 years of the date of the act complained of or the date of the discovery of the damage. No action may be brought under this subsection for the negligent design or manufacture of computer hardware, computer software, or firmware.

 Note

{§§ 1030(e)(h) to 1030(j)(2) intentionally omitted}

Appendix M

Electronic Communications Privacy Act

(18 U.S.C. § 2701 et seq.) (Including the Stored Communications Act [SCA])

§ 2701. Unlawful access to stored communications

(a)   **Offense.**— Except as provided in subsection (c) of this section whoever—

(1)   intentionally accesses without authorization a facility through which an electronic communication service is provided; or

(2)   intentionally exceeds an authorization to access that facility; and thereby obtains, alters, or prevents authorized access to a wire or electronic communication while it is in electronic storage in such system shall be punished as provided in subsection (b) of this section.

(b)   **Punishment.**— The punishment for an offense under subsection (a) of this section is—

(1)   if the offense is committed for purposes of commercial advantage, malicious destruction or damage, or private commercial gain, or in furtherance of any criminal or tortious act in violation of the Constitution or laws of the United States or any State—

(A)   a fine under this title or imprisonment for not more than 5 years, or both, in the case of a first offense under this subparagraph; and

(B)   a fine under this title or imprisonment for not more than 10 years, or both, for any subsequent offense under this subparagraph; and

(2)   in any other case—

(A)   a fine under this title or imprisonment for not more than 1 year or both, in the case of a first offense under this paragraph; and

(B)   a fine under this title or imprisonment for not more than 5 years, or both, in the case of an offense under this subparagraph that occurs after a conviction of another offense under this section.

(c)   **Exceptions.**— Subsection (a) of this section does not apply with respect to conduct authorized—

(1)   by the person or entity providing a wire or electronic communications service;

(2)   by a user of that service with respect to a communication of or intended for that user; or

(3)   in section 2703, 2704 or 2518 of this title.

§ 2702. Voluntary disclosure of customer communications or records

(a)   **Prohibitions.**— Except as provided in subsection (b) or (c)—

(1)   a person or entity providing an electronic communication service to the public shall not knowingly divulge to any person or entity the contents of a communication while in electronic storage by that service; and

(2)   a person or entity providing remote computing service to the public shall not knowingly divulge to any person or entity the contents of any communication which is carried or maintained on that service—

(A)   on behalf of, and received by means of electronic transmission from (or created by means of computer processing of communications received by means of electronic transmission from), a subscriber or customer of such service;

(B)   solely for the purpose of providing storage or computer processing services to such subscriber or customer, if the provider is not authorized to access the contents of any such communications for purposes of providing any services other than storage or computer processing; and

(3)   a provider of remote computing service or electronic communication service to the public shall not knowingly divulge a record or other information pertaining to a subscriber to or customer of such service (not including the contents of communications covered by paragraph (1) or (2)) to any governmental entity.

 Note
{§§ 2702(b) to 2702(d) intentionally omitted}

§ 2703. Required disclosure of customer communications or records

(a)   **Contents of Wire or Electronic Communications in Electronic Storage.**— A governmental entity may require the disclosure by a provider of electronic communication service of the contents of a wire or electronic communication, that is in electronic storage in an electronic communications system for one hundred and eighty days or less, only pursuant to a warrant issued using the procedures described in the Federal Rules of Criminal Procedure (or, in the case of a State court, issued using State warrant procedures) by a court of competent jurisdiction. A governmental entity may require the disclosure by a provider of electronic communications services of the contents of a wire or electronic communication that has been in electronic storage in an electronic communications system for more than one hundred and eighty days by the means available under subsection (b) of this section.

(b)   **Contents of Wire or Electronic Communications in a Remote Computing Service.**—

(1)   A governmental entity may require a provider of remote computing service to disclose the contents of any wire or electronic communication to which this paragraph is made applicable by paragraph (2) of this subsection—

(A)   without required notice to the subscriber or customer, if the governmental entity obtains a warrant issued using the procedures described in the Federal Rules of Criminal Procedure (or, in the case of a State court, issued using State warrant procedures) by a court of competent jurisdiction; or

(B)   with prior notice from the governmental entity to the subscriber or customer if the governmental entity—

(i)   uses an administrative subpoena authorized by a Federal or State statute or a Federal or State grand jury or trial subpoena; or

(ii)   obtains a court order for such disclosure under subsection (d) of this section; except that delayed notice may be given pursuant to section 2705 of this title.

(2)   Paragraph (1) is applicable with respect to any wire or electronic communication that is held or maintained on that service—

(A)   on behalf of, and received by means of electronic transmission from (or created by means of computer processing of communications received by means of electronic transmission from), a subscriber or customer of such remote computing service; and

(B)   solely for the purpose of providing storage or computer processing services to such subscriber or customer, if the provider is not authorized to access the contents of any such communications for purposes of providing any services other than storage or computer processing.

(c)   **Records Concerning Electronic Communication Service or Remote Computing Service.—**

(1)   A governmental entity may require a provider of electronic communication service or remote computing service to disclose a record or other information pertaining to a subscriber to or customer of such service (not including the contents of communications) only when the governmental entity—

(A)   obtains a warrant issued using the procedures described in the Federal Rules of Criminal Procedure (or, in the case of a State court, issued using State warrant procedures) by a court of competent jurisdiction;

(B)   obtains a court order for such disclosure under subsection (d) of this section;

(C)   has the consent of the subscriber or customer to such disclosure;

 Note
{§§ 2703(c)(1)(D) to 2703(c)(3) intentionally omitted}

(d)   **Requirements for Court Order.—** A court order for disclosure under subsection (b) or (c) may be issued by any court that is a court of competent jurisdiction and shall issue only if the governmental entity offers specific and articulable facts showing that there are reasonable grounds to believe that the contents of a wire or electronic communication, or the records or other information sought, are relevant and material to an ongoing criminal investigation. In the case of a State governmental authority, such a court order shall not issue if prohibited by the law of such State. A court issuing an order pursuant to this section, on a motion made promptly by the service provider, may quash or modify such order, if the information or records requested are unusually voluminous in nature or compliance with such order otherwise would cause an undue burden on such provider.

(e)   **No Cause of Action Against a Provider Disclosing Information Under This Chapter.—** No cause of action shall lie in any court against any provider of wire or electronic communication service, its officers, employees, agents, or other specified persons for providing information, facilities, or assistance in accordance with the terms of a court order, warrant, subpoena, statutory authorization, or certification under this chapter.

 Note
{§§ 2703(f) to 2706 intentionally omitted}

§ 2707. Civil action

(a)   **Cause of Action.—** Except as provided in section 2703(e), any provider of electronic communication service, subscriber, or other person aggrieved by any violation of this chapter in which the conduct constituting the violation is engaged in with a knowing or intentional state of mind may, in a civil action, recover from the person or entity, other than the United States, which engaged in that violation such relief as may be appropriate.

(b)   **Relief.—** In a civil action under this section, appropriate relief includes—

(1)   such preliminary and other equitable or declaratory relief as may be appropriate;

(2)   damages under subsection (c); and

(3)   a reasonable attorney's fee and other litigation costs reasonably incurred.

(c)   **Damages.**— The court may assess as damages in a civil action under this section the sum of the actual damages suffered by the plaintiff and any profits made by the violator as a result of the violation, but in no case shall a person entitled to recover receive less than the sum of $1,000. If the violation is willful or intentional, the court may assess punitive damages. In the case of a successful action to enforce liability under this section, the court may assess the costs of the action, together with reasonable attorney fees determined by the court.

(d)   **Administrative Discipline.**— If a court or appropriate department or agency determines that the United States or any of its departments or agencies has violated any provision of this chapter, and the court or appropriate department or agency finds that the circumstances surrounding the violation raise serious questions about whether or not an officer or employee of the United States acted willfully or intentionally with respect to the violation, the department or agency shall, upon receipt of a true and correct copy of the decision and findings of the court or appropriate department or agency promptly initiate a proceeding to determine whether disciplinary action against the officer or employee is warranted. If the head of the department or agency involved determines that disciplinary action is not warranted, he or she shall notify the Inspector General with jurisdiction over the department or agency concerned and shall provide the Inspector General with the reasons for such determination.

(e)   **Defense.**— A good faith reliance on—

(1)   a court warrant or order, a grand jury subpoena, a legislative authorization, or a statutory authorization (including a request of a governmental entity under section 2703(f) of this title);

(2)   a request of an investigative or law enforcement officer under section 2518(7) of this title; or

(3)   a good faith determination that section 2511(3) of this title permitted the conduct complained of;

is a complete defense to any civil or criminal action brought under this chapter or any other law.

(f)   **Limitation.**— A civil action under this section may not be commenced later than two years after the date upon which the claimant first discovered or had a reasonable opportunity to discover the violation.

(g)   **Improper Disclosure.**— Any willful disclosure of a "record", as that term is defined in section 552a(a) of title 5, United States Code, obtained by an investigative or law enforcement officer, or a governmental entity, pursuant to section 2703 of this title, or from a device installed pursuant to section 3123 or 3125 of this title, that is not a disclosure made in the proper performance of the official functions of the officer or governmental entity making the disclosure, is a violation of this chapter. This provision shall not apply to information previously lawfully disclosed (prior to the commencement of any civil or administrative proceeding under this chapter) to the public by a Federal, State, or local governmental entity or by the plaintiff in a civil action under this chapter.

 Note

{§§ 2708 to 2710 intentionally omitted}

§ 2711. Definitions for chapter

As used in this chapter—

(1)   the terms defined in section 2510 of this title have, respectively, the definitions given such terms in that section;

(2)   the term "remote computing service" means the provision to the public of computer storage or processing services by means of an electronic communications system;

 Note

{§§ 2711(3) to 2712 intentionally omitted}

Appendix N

National Labor Relations Act

(Pub.L. 74-198, 49 Stat. 449, 29 U.S.C. §§ 151–169) (*as amended*)

 Note

{§§ 151 to 156 intentionally omitted}

---

§ 157. Right of employees as to organization, collective bargaining, etc.

Employees shall have the right to self-organization, to form, join, or assist labor organizations, to bargain collectively through representatives of their own choosing, and to engage in other concerted activities for the purpose of collective bargaining or other mutual aid or protection, and shall also have the right to refrain from any or all of such activities except to the extent that such right may be affected by an agreement requiring membership in a labor organization as a condition of employment as authorized in section 158(a)(3) of this title.

§ 158. Unfair labor practices

(a)   **Unfair labor practices by employer**

It shall be an unfair labor practice for an employer—

(1)   to interfere with, restrain, or coerce employees in the exercise of the rights guaranteed in section 157 of this title;

 Note

{§§ 158(a)(2) to 169 intentionally omitted}

Appendix O

The Unlawful Internet Gambling Enforcement Act of 2006

(31 U.S.C. §§ 5361–5366)

 Note

{§ 5361 intentionally omitted}

§ 5362. Definitions

In this subchapter:

(1) **Bet or wager.— The term "bet or wager"—**

(A) means the staking or risking by any person of something of value upon the outcome of a contest of others, a sporting event, or a game subject to chance, upon an agreement or understanding that the person or another person will receive something of value in the event of a certain outcome;

(B) includes the purchase of a chance or opportunity to win a lottery or other prize (which opportunity to win is predominantly subject to chance);

 Note

{§§ 5362(1)(C) to 5362(1)(D) intentionally omitted}

(E) does not include—

 Note

{§§ 5362(1)(E)(i) to 5362(1)(E)(vii) intentionally omitted}

(viii)   participation in any game or contest in which participants do not stake or risk anything of value other than—

(I)   personal efforts of the participants in playing the game or contest or obtaining access to the Internet; or

(II)   points or credits that the sponsor of the game or contest provides to participants free of charge and that can be used or redeemed only for participation in games or contests offered by the sponsor; or

Note
{§ 5362(1)(E)(ix) intentionally omitted}

(2)   **Business of betting or wagering.—** The term "business of betting or wagering" does not include the activities of a financial transaction provider, or any interactive computer service or telecommunications service.

Note
{§§ 5362(3) to 5362(9) intentionally omitted}

(10)   **Unlawful internet gambling.—**

(A)   In general.— The term "unlawful Internet gambling" means to place, receive, or otherwise knowingly transmit a bet or wager by any means which involves the use, at least in part, of the Internet where such bet or wager is unlawful under any applicable Federal or State law in the State or Tribal lands in which the bet or wager is initiated, received, or otherwise made.

Note
{§§ 5362(10)(B) to 5362(11)(E) intentionally omitted}

§ 5363. Prohibition on acceptance of any financial instrument for unlawful Internet gambling

No person engaged in the business of betting or wagering may knowingly accept, in connection with the participation of another person in unlawful Internet gambling—

(1)   credit, or the proceeds of credit, extended to or on behalf of such other person (including credit extended through the use of a credit card);

(2)   an electronic fund transfer, or funds transmitted by or through a money transmitting business, or the proceeds of an electronic fund transfer or money transmitting service, from or on behalf of such other person;

(3)   any check, draft, or similar instrument which is drawn by or on behalf of such other person and is drawn on or payable at or through any financial institution; or

(4)   the proceeds of any other form of financial transaction, as the Secretary and the Board of Governors of the Federal Reserve System may jointly prescribe by regulation, which involves a financial institution as a payor or financial intermediary on behalf of or for the benefit of such other person.

Note
{§ 5364 intentionally omitted}

§ 5365. Civil remedies

(a)   Jurisdiction.— In addition to any other remedy under current law, the district courts of the United States shall have original and exclusive jurisdiction to prevent and restrain restricted transactions by issuing appropriate orders in accordance with this section, regardless of whether a prosecution has been initiated under this subchapter.

(b)   Proceedings.—

(1)   Institution by federal government.—

(A)   In general.— The United States, acting through the Attorney General, may institute proceedings under this section to prevent or restrain a restricted transaction.

(B)   Relief.— Upon application of the United States under this paragraph, the district court may enter a temporary restraining order, a preliminary injunction, or an injunction against any person to prevent or restrain a restricted transaction, in accordance with rule 65 of the Federal Rules of Civil Procedure.

(2)   Institution by state attorney general.—

(A)   In general.— The attorney general (or other appropriate State official) of a State in which a restricted transaction allegedly has been or will be initiated, received, or otherwise made may institute proceedings under this section to prevent or restrain the violation or threatened violation.

(B)   Relief.— Upon application of the attorney general (or other appropriate State official) of an affected State under this paragraph, the district court may enter a temporary restraining order, a preliminary injunction, or an injunction against any person to prevent or restrain a restricted transaction, in accordance with rule 65 of the Federal Rules of Civil Procedure.

 Note

{§ 5365(b)(3) to 5365(d) intentionally omitted}

§ 5366. Criminal penalties

(a)   In General.— Any person who violates section 5363 shall be fined under title 18, imprisoned for not more than 5 years, or both.

(b)   Permanent Injunction.— Upon conviction of a person under this section, the court may enter a permanent injunction enjoining such person from placing, receiving, or otherwise making bets or wagers or sending, receiving, or inviting information assisting in the placing of bets or wagers.

Appendix P

Communications Decency Act (CDA) of 1996

(47 U.S.C. § 230)

 Note

{§§ 230(a) to 230(b) intentionally omitted}

(c) **Protection for "Good Samaritan" blocking and screening of offensive material**

(1) Treatment of publisher or speaker

No provider or user of an interactive computer service shall be treated as the publisher or speaker of any information provided by another information content provider.

(2) Civil liability

No provider or user of an interactive computer service shall be held liable on account of—

(A) any action voluntarily taken in good faith to restrict access to or availability of material that the provider or user considers to be obscene, lewd, lascivious, filthy, excessively violent, harassing, or otherwise objectionable, whether or not such material is constitutionally protected; or

(B) any action taken to enable or make available to information content providers or others the technical means to restrict access to material described in paragraph (1).

 Note

{§§ 230(d) to 230(e)(4) intentionally omitted}

(f) **Definitions**

As used in this section:

(1) Internet

The term "Internet" means the international computer network of both Federal and non-Federal interoperable packet switched data networks.

(2)   Interactive computer service

The term "interactive computer service" means any information service, system, or access software provider that provides or enables computer access by multiple users to a computer server, including specifically a service or system that provides access to the Internet and such systems operated or services offered by libraries or educational institutions.

(3)   Information content provider

The term "information content provider" means any person or entity that is responsible, in whole or in part, for the creation or development of information provided through the Internet or any other interactive computer service.

(4)   Access software provider

The term "access software provider" means a provider of software (including client or server software), or enabling tools that do any one or more of the following:

(A)   filter, screen, allow, or disallow content;

(B)   pick, choose, analyze, or digest content; or

(C)   transmit, receive, display, forward, cache, search, subset, organize, reorganize, or translate content.

Index

B

D

M

N

O

T

U

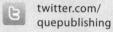
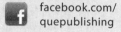

Safari Books Online

FREE Online Edition

Your purchase of *Navigating Social Media Legal Risks* includes access to a free online edition for 45 days through the **Safari Books Online** subscription service. Nearly every Que book is available online through **Safari Books Online**, along with thousands of books and videos from publishers such as Addison-Wesley Professional, Cisco Press, Exam Cram, IBM Press, O'Reilly Media, Prentice Hall, Sams, and VMware Press.

Safari Books Online is a digital library providing searchable, on-demand access to thousands of technology, digital media, and professional development books and videos from leading publishers. With one monthly or yearly subscription price, you get unlimited access to learning tools and information on topics including mobile app and software development, tips and tricks on using your favorite gadgets, networking, project management, graphic design, and much more.

Activate your FREE Online Edition at
informit.com/safarifree

STEP 1:   Enter the coupon code: PEFXNGA.

STEP 2:   New Safari users, complete the brief registration form.
Safari subscribers, just log in.

If you have difficulty registering on Safari or accessing the online edition,
please e-mail customer-service@safaribooksonline.com